"We can scarcely account for the varied spelling."

John W. Spaight, Editor
The Fishkill Standard
May 18, 1876

Marriages and Deaths Reported in
The Fishkill Standard
Fishkill Landing, New York,
1874–1877

Extracted by

Katharine M. Chamberlain

HERITAGE BOOKS
2013

HERITAGE BOOKS
AN IMPRINT OF HERITAGE BOOKS, INC.

Books, CDs, and more—Worldwide

For our listing of thousands of titles see our website
at
www.HeritageBooks.com

Published 2013 by
HERITAGE BOOKS, INC.
Publishing Division
5810 Ruatan Street
Berwyn Heights, Md. 20740

International Standard Book Numbers
Paperbound: 978-0-7884-1652-1
Clothbound: 978-0-7884-6930-5

INTRODUCTION

These are abstracts of a microfilm of clippings from *The FISHKILL STANDARD*, a four-page weekly newspaper published in Fishkill Landing, Dutchess County, New York. The Landing later merged with the village of Matteawan to become the village of Beacon, New York.

The microfilm consists of a series of scrapbooks, into which an unknown archivist clipped and saved articles including the Local Record column, the Married and Died columns, and articles of local interest.

This volume contains marriages, deaths and other genealogical data from January 3, 1874 to December 29, 1877.

Because this time period included the Centennial of the United States, a series of articles, entitled, "Fishkill in the Revolution," were included. From these I have extracted only a few, which might be of interest to people seeking information about their ancestors during the Revolution. These articles are in the Appendices.

Long newspaper items have been either condensed or broken into several items for this volume. I have tried to keep the style of the writing.

In the index the honorific "Miss" or "Mrs." is used if the sex of the person is defined in the item, but would be unclear in the index. I have also indexed women's names by what might be the middle or maiden name, if it were not clear which was given.

I am indebted to my daughter, Katharine Gillican Chamberlain Jaunet, for her assistance in editing, and to my husband, Donald L. Chamberlain, for his continued encouragement and support

Table of Contents

0001   THE FISHKILL STANDARD
is published
Every Saturday Morning at Fishkill Landing, New York
James E. MEMBER, Proprietor
John W. SPAIGHT, Editor

SATURDAY, JANUARY 3, 1874

0002   Mrs. Susannah Ager, wife of Mr. John Ager, died
very suddenly at her residence in Matteawan, on New
Year morning, supposed to be of heart disease.

0003   Lewis Coe, the well-known merchant of Poughkeepsie, died on Friday night of last week, from the
effects of an overdose of morphine, taken to relieve distress in
the head. He was formerly a minister of the gospel and
prominent in the temperance reform.

0004   Married in Matteawan, December 24th, by the Rev.
Jabez Marshall, Mr. Nelson Tompkins to Miss Laney
Griffin, both of Matteawan.

0005   Married on Christmas Day, at the home of the bride's
parents in Glenham, Harry Smith to Mary Ann Fields,
all of Glenham.

0006   From Fishkill-on-the-Hudson, Sabbath evening, Dec.
28th, 1873, Hiram R., son of William H. and Hettie M.
Ashworth, aged 1 month and 13 days, passed through the gates
which angels left ajar, to tread the flower-gemmed fields of the
spirit land.

0007   Died in Matteawan, December 24th, an infant son of
Theodore and Julia Hadden, aged five months.

0008   Died in Matteawan, December 28th, Henry E.

Hamlin, aged 38 years.

0009   Died at Matteawan, January 1st, Mrs. Susannah,
           wife of Mr. John Ager, aged 44 years.

0010   Died at Matteawan, December 27th, Maggie, infant
           daughter of Shadrack H. and Jennie Crindland, aged 5
weeks.

SATURDAY, JANUARY 10, 1874

0011   A sad accident occurred here on Saturday last.
           Although the ice on the creek had been considerably
weakened by the rain and thaw, three boys, Jacob Moseman,
Hasbrouck B. Van Nostrand, and Philip Cassidy, 11, 10, and 9
years of age respectively, made the dangerous attempt to try it
once more, before it should go away entirely. The result was
that the two latter went through. Cassidy, however, by his own
strength and assisted by Moseman, got up again, but Van
Nostrand was drawn by the current under the ice. The body
was thrown over the dam, and disappeared in the violent
current, until taken up dead some hundred yards below. The
funeral service was performed on Monday last at the Episcopal
Church, by Rev. J.R. Livingston, in the midst of the deep
sorrow of parents, brothers, sisters, friends and playmates of
the deceased.

0012   Henry Haight, a farmer and butcher, living at Dover
           Plains, died on Friday, 2d inst., at noon, after an
illness of a few days. He buried his wife on Christmas day.

0013   Married at the M.E. Parsonage, Fishkill Landing,
           Sunday, January 4th, by Rev. W.G. Browning, Philip B.
Daniell, of New York city, to Ella A. Denike, of Matteawan.

0014 Married January 6th, at the residence of the bride's
   parents, by the Rev. D.I. Putnam, P.H. Dorland and
Miss J. Morey, all of Stanford.

0015 Died at Fishkill Landing, Friday evening, January 2d,
   Willie W. Merritt, only son of John D. and Sarah
Merritt, aged 13 years, 7 months and 11 days.

0016 Died at Moore's Mills, Dutchess county, on the sixth
   day, first month 2d, Fanny, widow of Benjamin Merritt,
in the 91st year of her age.

0017 Died at Glenham, December 27th, Miss Jane Cooper,
   aged 75 years.

0018 Died at Glenham, January 3d, Hasbrook [sic] B. Van
   Nostrand, aged 10 years.

0019 Died near Fishkill Village, January 6th, Abram, son of
   James H. and Josephine Morse, aged 8 years.

0020 Died in Matteawan, January 2d, Willie, son of
   Edward L. and Ophelia G. Hookey, aged 9 years, 8
months, and 2 days.

0021 Died at East Fishkill, January 5th, Abraham
   Brinckerhoff, in the 76th year of his age.

SATURDAY, JANUARY 17, 1874

0022 Jacob Hembt, the little, lame German, who attended the
   door of the gentlemen's room, at the Poughkeepsie
depot, a character well known to all who had occasion to visit
that city by way of the Hudson River Railroad, died quite

suddenly on Wednesday, from long difficulties. He was 62 years of age, and is said to have had no relatives in this country. He was a member of the Masonic Order, and was buried with all the honors, by the Knights Templar.

0023   Died in Fishkill Landing, January 9th, Ezekial Scofield, aged 38 years and 6 months.

0024   Died on Sabbath morning, January 11, 1874, at the residence of her grandson, Benson Van Vliet, Rachel, wife of the late Peter Brett of Fishkill Landing, in the 81st year of her age.

0025   Died at New Hamburgh, on Wednesday, January 7th, Mrs. Sincerbaugh, aged 87 years.

0026   Died in Fishkill Village, January 14th, Mary, widow of the late Norris Baxter, in the 71st year of her age.

0027   Died at Stormville, January 1st, Euphana [sic] T. Phillips, aged 39 years, 10 months and 27 days.

0028   Died at Patterson, N.J., Monday, January 5, William DeHart, aged 29 years.

SATURDAY, JANUARY 24, 1874

0029   Married at the parsonage of the Reformed Church, Glenham, N.Y., by the Rev. Dr. Scudder, Jan. 19th, 1874, William S. Norris to Clara Virginia Vail, both of Hughsonville.

0030   Married at Ellenville, Jan. 21st, at the residence of the bride's sister, by Rev. E.W. Bently, Mr. Samuel C.

Stebbins to Miss Fannie L. Ostrander, both of this village.

0031 Married in East Fishkill, at the residence of the bride's
parents, by Rev. D.W. Sherwood, Mr. George W.
Baxter, of Fishkill, to Miss Laurie P. Tompkins, of East
Fishkill.

0032 Married at Millbrook, by Rev. R. Kay, Jan. 17, John
Welling, of Millbrook, to Mrs. Harriet Devine, of
Verbank.

0033 Died at Fishkill Landing, January 21st, James H.
Gilgan, aged 3 years and 5 months, son of James and
Margaret Gilgan.

0034 Died at Fishkill Landing, January 21st, Ann Pollard,
aged 16 months, daughter of John and Julia Pollard.

0035 Died at Fishkill Landing, January 21st, Eugene
Anderson, aged 3 months, son of Joseph and Siggins
Anderson.

0036 Died at Matteawan, January 15th, Thomas A.
Edmonds, aged 37 years.

0037 Died in Fishkill, Jan. 19, Willie W., aged 31 days, only
child of C. Wesley and Mary E. Turrell.

0038 Died at Glenham, Jan. 20, Miss Jane Pine, in the 77th
year of her age.

0039 Died at LaGrange, Jan. 19, David VerValis, in the 78th
year of his age.

SATURDAY, JANUARY 31, 1874

0040   Married at Freedom Plains Manse, Jan. 23, by Rev.
O.H. Hazard, Joshua B. Kelley, of Pawling, and
Angeline Hyser, of Beekman.

0041   Died at Matteawan, Jan. 28th, Mary Ann Klanka, aged
7 years and 8 months.

0042   Died at Matteawan, Jan. 29th, Catharine, wife of
Charles W. Bogardus, aged 21 years and 9 months.
Taken to Fishkill for interment.

0043   Died at Millbrook, Dec. 20th, Mrs. Eliza Todd, aged
76 years.

0044   Died at Prattsville, N.Y., Jan. 16th, Adaline Mase, aged
25 years.

SATURDAY, FEBRUARY 7, 1874

0045   Silas Haight, a well-known hotel keeper of Elmira, is
dead. He commenced hotel keeping in Elmira, in 1839.
He was born in Dutchess county in 1812.

0046   On the 22d of January, the twenty-fifth anniversary of
the wedding of Mr. and Mrs. Daniel M. Daly, of
LaGrange, was celebrated as a silver wedding occasion. There
was a large attendance, and the parties were the recipients of
many valuable presents.

0047   Diana Sales, who was, we believe, the oldest colored
woman in the neighborhood, died about two weeks
ago, at her residence in this village. How old she was is not

6

known, but she was very aged. She was well-known to our citizens generally, having managed to feebly get about the streets up to a few months previous to her death. Her funeral was largely attended, and her remains were deposited in the colored burying ground in this village.

0048   Died in Matteawan, February 3d, Mrs. Mary F. Kinnan, daughter of the late Wilbur Heroy, aged 25 years.

0049   Died in Matteawan, February 2d, Thomas Kernan, aged 65 years.

SATURDAY, FEBRUARY 14, 1874

0050   On Tuesday evening, Capt. Daniel McMillin, a Scotchman, engaged in sailing a boat from the freighting of brick from Aldridge's yard, was accidentally killed at Dutchess Junction. The manner of his death is a matter of conjecture, but is supposed he was run over by a train on the Hudson River Railroad, and then by a Dutchess and Columbia train, about twenty minutes later. The remains were taken to the freight house, when an inquest was held next morning by Coroner Schouten.

0051   Death of Daniel McMillin, cont.
Mr. McMillin resided a short distance below the Junction, was in the habit of going up to the depot evenings after tea, and it is supposed that he was on his way up as usual when he met his sudden death. He is from Newburgh, a member of the Masonic order, and about 32 years of age. He was a steady, sober and industrious man. He leaves a wife and four small children. His remains were taken to Newburgh for interment.

7

0052   The Congressional Directory gives the following
           biographical sketch of the Member of Congress from
this District: "John O. Whitehouse, of Poughkeepsie, was born
at Rochester, New Hampshire, July 19, 1817; received a
common school education; graduated a farmer boy, at eighteen
years of age; left his New England home in 1835; went to the
State of New York, and has since resided at Brooklyn and
Poughkeepsie; is a merchant and manufacturer; never held
public office until elected to the Forty-third Congress as a
Liberal, receiving 14,800 votes against 13,932 votes for J.H.
Ketcham, Republican."

0053   The death of Samuel Bogardus, Jr., is peculiarly sad
           and touching. It removes the youngest member of the
household, and one to whom long life seemed to be a certainty.
But a few days' sickness brought him to the portals of the
grave. He was taken sick on Tuesday, and died on Thursday
evening. He was engaged to be married soon to a young lady
residing at Poughkeepsie, and the last interview between them
is said to have been very sad and heart-rending.

0054   Mrs. Ellen Shove, widow of the late Seth Shove, died
           at Albany, on Sunday last, of rupture of the heart, and
her remains were brought to
this village for interment on Tuesday. She is a sister of Mr.
John Cherry. She leaves about $13,000 to go to her relatives.

0055   Mrs. Maria Cooper, wife of the late Tunis Cooper, of
           this town, died at Poughkeepsie on Monday of this
week, aged 69 years.

0056   Married February 4th, by Rev. O.H. Hazzard [sic], Mr.
           Wellington Vail, of Union Vale, to Miss Alice A. Van
Voorhis, of LaGrange.

8

0057 Married at the residence of the bride's parents, February 4th, by Rev. E.H.W. Barden, Egbert Traver, of Pleasant Valley, to Mary R. Cae, of North Clove, daughter of R.L. Cae.

0058 Died at the residence of Sidney Scofield, Fishkill-on-Hudson, February 12th, Mary C. Annin, in the 61st year of her age. The relatives and friends of the family are invited to attend the funeral on Monday, 16th inst., at 11 o'clock, a.m., from the residence of Mr. Sidney Scofield.

0059 Died at Fishkill Landing, February 12th, Samuel Bogardus, Jr., in the 25th year of his age. The relatives and friends of the family are invited to attend the funeral on Sunday, 15th inst., at 3 o'clock, from the residence of his father.

0060 Died at Poughkeepsie, February 12th, Lavinia, wife of H.D. Bogardus, in the 31st year of her age. Friends and acquaintances are invited to attend her funeral from her late residence, No. 82 Market street, Poughkeepsie, on Monday, February 16th, at 2½ o'clock, p.m.

0061 Died at Fishkill Landing, February 8th, Nettie, infant daughter of George and Augusta Van Sicklin, aged 2 years and 8 months.

0062 Died at Matteawan, February 11th, George McGawley, infant son of William and Rebecca Lee, aged 4 weeks.

0063 Died in Fishkill Village, February 9th, Charles Oliver, son of Nathan and Ann Adkins, aged 14 years, 9 months, and 26 days.

9

0064 Died at Courtlandville, February 9th, Phebe, wife of
Nelson Lounsberry, aged 72 years.

0065 Died in Poughkeepsie, February 9th, Mrs. Maria
Cooper, formerly of Fishkill, aged 69 years.

0066 Died at Albany, February 8th, Mrs. Ellen Shove, aged
35 years.

SATURDAY, FEBRUARY 21, 1874

0067 Coroner Schouten held an inquest on Tuesday morning,
over the body of Mrs. Sigenia M. Anderson, the wife of
Joseph Anderson, of this village. She had for some months
been in a very weak, physical condition. On Sunday evening
last, being in great bodily pain, she requested that she might
have something to relieve her. Her husband and little girl went
to a near neighbor and the little girl went in and asked for some
laudanum. They found something which they said was
laudanum, but it was poured from a bottle labeled "paregoric,"
and the little girl thought it was therefore paregoric, and told
her father so, who was waiting for her on the outside.
   Mr. Anderson, at his wife's request, administered about half
a teaspoonful. This failing to quiet her restlessness, she asked
for and received about a half a teaspoonful more. After a time
she seemed to quiet, and fell asleep. Her little girl kept watch in
the same room through the night. She said she herself fell
asleep, and woke up about 11 o'clock, and that she heard her
mother breathing, as if sleeping naturally. Her husband woke,
he thinks, about 3 a.m., and found her cheeks and hands were
cold, and then came the terrible revelation that she was dead.
The daughter, who had fallen asleep, was awakened, and Dr.
Adams summoned. Drs. Adam and Schenck were summoned
before the Coroner as experts, and their opinion was that the

quantity of laudanum that had by mistake been administered, was sufficient in the state of her great physical weakness, to have caused her death.

0068 Married at St. Joachim's Church, Matteawan, February 17th, by Rev. P. McCourt, Mr. Edward Rogers, Jr., and Miss Kate Higgins, all of Matteawan.

0069 Married at the residence of the bride's parents, February 11th, by E.H.W. Barden, William F. Phillips to Miss Ida E. Duncan, both of LaGrange.

0070 Married at St. Denis Church, Beekman, February 17th, by Rev. Denis [sic] Sheehan, Mr. Daniel Delaney, of Sylvan Lake, to Miss Lizzie P. Jackson, of East Fishkill.

0071 Died at Fishkill Landing, February 16th, Sigenia M. Anderson, aged 43 years and 5 months.

0072 Died at Fishkill Landing, February 15th, Francis Johnson, colored, aged 20 years, son of Louisa and the late Harvey Johnson.

0073 Died at Matteawan, February 16, Cora May, infant daughter of John and Anna Hoard, aged 2 months.

0074 Died at Matteawan, February 15, Louisa Strong, daughter of John and Rebecca Mullen, aged 14 years and 9 months.

0075 Died in LaGrange, February 16th, Ann Maria, wife of Garrett Shearman, in the 60th year of her age.

0076 Died at East Orange, N. J., February 16th, of whooping

cough, George A. Boyce, Jr., only son of George A. and Kate
Rankin Boyce, aged 3 months and 19 days.

SATURDAY, FEBRUARY 28, 1874

0077   Married in Matteawan, on Wednesday, February 11th,
          by the Rev. Jabez Marshall, Mr. Walter Harrison to
Miss Hattie A. Smith.

0078   Married in Fishkill Village, at the M.E. Parsonage,
          February 10th, by Rev. T. Elliott, Mr. John Cornelius
Losee to Miss Laurie Ida Higgs, both of Fishkill.

0079   Married at East Fishkill, February 23d, by Rev. Mr.
          Ashton, Mr. William F. Phillips and Miss Harriet Ann
Peterson, all of East Fishkill.

0080   Died at Fishkill Landing, February 25th, Alson Rozell,
          son of William H. and Helena Rozell, aged 11 months
and 29 days.

0081   Died at Glenham, February 25th, Maria, wife of W.
          Anson Wood, in the 50th year of her age.

SATURDAY, MARCH 7, 1874

0082   For many years Mr. William N. Vanderwerker and his
wife Rebecca   have resided in Fishkill Landing, Dutchess
county. They are both over fifty years of age, and have several
grandchildren. Mr. Vanderwerker was a prominent Republican
politician and Justice of the Peace. In the spring of 1872, this
model judge deserted his wife and family and went to Indiana.
He was away for nearly a year, his wife and family never
hearing of him or from him in the interval. In January, 1873, he

12

returned to Fishkill Landing with a young woman, known as Minnie Lane, on his arm, and opened a shoe shop within two doors of his wife's residence.

Mrs. Vanderwerker wanted to know what such behavior meant. Mr. V. informed her that she was no longer his wife, as he had been divorced from her in Indiana, and introduced Minnie Lane as the real Mrs. Vanderwerker, to whom he had been married in Buffalo two days before his return to Fishkill Landing.

0083   William N. Vanderwerker Bigamy, cont.

Mrs. Vanderwerker, No. 1, claimed that the divorce was invalid as she had received no notice, and preferred against her husband a charge of bigamy. He was duly indicted, and his trial was set down for next week. Mrs. Vanderwerker has commenced an action for an absolute divorce, and the matter was up in the Supreme Court, Special Term, this morning on a motion for alimony. The defendant did not appear, and Justice Pratt granted Mrs. Vanderwerker $25 a week, and gave $100 counsel fees.

Justice Vanderwerker has, it is said, jumped his bail, and left for parts unknown. He is said to be worth over $5,000. Mr. C.F. Brown, of Newburgh, is Mrs. Vanderwerker's counsel. -*Brooklyn Daily Eagle,* March 2.

0084   Died at Fishkill Landing, on Saturday, Feb. 28th, of scarlet fever, Frances H., aged four years, and on Tuesday, March 3d, Helen M., aged twelve years, daughters of Dr. H. and Frances M. Slack.

0085   Died at Fishkill Landing, February 28th, Charles E. Mead, aged 27 years.

0086   Died at Fishkill Landing, March 3d, Frank Mead, aged

20 years.

0087   Died in Newburgh, March 3d, Phebe Adaline, wife of
Jas. J. M. Nally, aged 48 years.

0088   Died at Fishkill Landing, February 25th, Alson Rozell,
son of William H. and Helena Rozell, aged 2 years, 11
months and 29 days. This notice was erroneous last week, the
words "2 years" having been omitted.

SATURDAY, MARCH 14, 1874

0089   On Thursday of last week, Major Dennis, of the 21st
Regiment, held a Court Martial at Meyers' [sic] Hotel,
in this village, to try various members of the Denning Guard
for certain acts or delinquencies. There were nineteen under
court martial, twelve of whom were found guilty and fined in
sums varying from $2 to $10 each, viz: Andrew Eagan,
Jeremiah Stevenson, W.J. Pralatowski, Charles Ackerman,
Charles Blight, William Coleman, Willet Dates, Rudolph Fuller,
John B. Heroy, George Kaine, Albert Lounsberry, Robert
McFarlane.

0090   On the 17th of January, we chronicled the death, at
Stormville, in this county, of Mrs. Euphemia [sic] T.
Phillips, who expired at her residence on the 11th [sic] of that
month, in the 40th year of her age. She was the wife of James
D. Phillips, and they occupied a fine farm about a mile above
the village of Stormville. Ever since that time there have been
whisperings among the neighbors, and it was openly stated by
some as their candid belief, that Mrs. Phillips' death was the
result of poison administered to her by her husband. On the 2d
inst., Dr. Clark A. Nicholson, of Beekman, and Dr. G.S.
Sutton, of East Fishkill, both of whom had visited Mrs. Phillips

during her late illness, wrote to Coroner Hicks, of
Poughkeepsie, stating their suspicions and requesting an
examination of the remains. The Coroner had the remains
disinterred, and on Tuesday, had Drs. R.K. Tuthill and E.H.
Parker, of that city, hold a post mortem examination.

The reporter of the *Poughkeepsie Eagle* gives the following
[abridged] particulars of the case." The deceased and her
husband have been married about fifteen years, and have a son
fourteen years of age. The neighbors say they did not live
happily, and it is alleged that Phillips has a paramour in New
York city. Last fall, he forged a note and being detected, his
wife consented to mortgage the farm to save him from State
Prison. The money on the mortgage was due in January last,
and Mrs. Phillips was taken ill the last part of December. She
remained ill until the 11th day of January, when she died. It is
alleged that towards the first of January, Phillips was in the
town of Pawling, where he called upon Dr. Fox and wife, and
asked for arsenic, which he obtained, and it is believed that
from that time he administered poison to his wife daily, till she
died."

0091   Death of Mrs. Euphemia T. Phillips, cont.

At the inquest, Dr. Tuthill testified that he found that
the stomach indicated inflammation which could have been
caused by arsenic. Dr. Parker corroborated this. Dr. G.L. [sic]
Sutton, of East Fishkill, testified that Mrs. Phillips' symptoms
indicated arsenic poison. Susan Griffin testified that she was in
attendance upon Mrs. Phillips during her illness, but was not
present when she had hard attacks of vomiting. Witness never
gave her medicine; Mr. Phillips always did that.

In the afternoon, Robert Milliken, a blacksmith and his wife,
of Pawling, testified that Phillips came to their house and asked
for arsenic, while partially under the influence of liquor. He
left, saying he could get it down by the depot, and when he

returned, he had some packages.

James D. Phillips, husband of the deceased, was called to the witness stand, but he refused to testify until he could obtain his witnesses and consult counsel. His examination was postponed, and the inquest adjourned until Monday next. The jury agreed with the Coroner that Phillips should be held in the Poughkeepsie jail till Monday.

The stomach and part of the liver have been taken for analyzation.

Mr. Phillips has retained B. Platt Carpenter as counsel.

0092   Died in Fishkill Village, March 9th, Mary E. Hamer, aged 16 years and 10 months.

0093   Died at Matteawan, March 11th, Lyman Robinson, Jr., aged 9 years, 6 months and 12 days.

0094   Died at Matteawan, March 7, Henry Webb, aged 80 years.

0095   Died at Fishkill Village, March 9th, Stephen H. Sherwood, aged 68 years.

0096   Died in the town of Fishkill, March 2d, Amelia Wanzer, only child of William H. and Caroline Height, aged five weeks and four days.

0097   Died in Newburgh, March 7th, Aletta, widow of the late Theodore Brett, in the 84th year of her age.

0098   Died at Matteawan, N.Y., Saturday morning, March 7th, Mrs. Mary J. Manning, aged 22 years. Lackawanna and Scranton, Pa., papers please copy.

SATURDAY, MARCH 21, 1874

0099   Wednesday, Hon. Jacob Sisson died at his residence in
        Lithgow, Dutchess county, aged eighty-three years.
The *Poughkeepsie Eagle* says Mr. Sisson, in times gone by,
was a very prominent citizen of this county. He was candidate
for election to the Constitutional Convention of 1846, but was
defeated; was sent to the Legislature once or twice when the
county was represented by three members chosen at large, and
he also represented his town once or twice in the Board of
Supervisors. In the time of Henry Clay he was an
uncompromising Whig, and when the Republican party started
he became an ardent Republican. He was always known as an
honest, upright man, a kind neighbor and a true hearted friend.

0100   Mrs. Sarah Parker Holden, mother of J.G.P. Holden,
        editor of the Yonkers *Gazette*, died at her son's
residence, in that city, on Wednesday of this week, aged 72
years. Mrs. Holden was one of those rare domestic women
who always looked well to the ways of her household, and
whose pride was to see her sons and daughters grow up into
useful members of society.

0101   Mr. John Osborn, residing near Otisville, Orange
        county, and a well-to-do farmer, is now in his
eighty-second year. He was born and has always lived in the
house he now owns and occupies.

0102   James D. Phillips is still in jail at Poughkeepsie, upon
        the Coroner's commitment. Mr. B. Platt Carpenter has
been retained as his counsel, and forbids his conversing upon
the subject of his wife's death. The stomach and liver of Mrs.
Phillips have been placed in the hands of Dr. Guy Bayley
and Mr. D.B. Ward, of Poughkeepsie, who will make the

17

chemical analysis, and will be engaged upon it about three weeks.

The Coroner resumed the inquest at Beekmanville on Monday. The most important testimony taken was that of Jane A. Peck, of East Fishkill, who attended Mrs. Phillips during her illness. She is a cousin of James D. Phillips.

0103 Married at the house of the bride's father, E.R. Hatch, March 18, by the Rev. W.E. Clarke, Henry Clarkson and Emma T. Hatch, both of Matteawan. No cards.

0104 Married in Matteawan, March 18th, by Joseph L. Hubbell, Justice of the Peace, Timothy Lawler and Mary E. Gerow, both of New York city.

0105 Married at Hughsonville, Feb. 26th, at the house of the bride's parents, by Rev. Van Ness Traver, Mr. Robert H. Traver to Miss Julia C. Vail, daughter of Mr. Benjamin Vail, of Hughsonville.

0106 Died at Matteawan, March 16th, Benjamin Ireland, aged 15 years and 7 months.

0107 Died at Fishkill Landing, March 16th, Forrest Darroch, aged 8 years and 6 months.

0108 Died at New Hamburgh, March 12th, Peter A. Mesier, in the 62d year of his age.

0109 Died at Wappingers Falls, on Friday, March 13th, Mary, wife of Mr. Bartley Doyle, aged 24 years.

0110 Died at North Highlands, Putnam county, March 14th, Mrs. Esther Dykeman, in the 68th year of her age.

0111   Died in Brooklyn, suddenly, at the residence of her
son-in-law, I.D. Fletcher, Wednesday, March 18th,
Adeline, wife of the late Wm. L. Pickering, of New York, aged
69 years. The friends of the family are invited to attend the
funeral services at the Reformed Dutch Church, Fishkill
Landing, on Saturday, the 21st inst., at 2 p.m.

0112   Died at Yonkers, on Wednesday night, March 18th,
Mrs. Sarah Parker Holden, mother of the editor of the
Yonkers Gazette, in the 72d year of her age. Relatives and
friends of the family are invited to attend the funeral, from the
residence of her son, North Broadway, Yonkers, on Saturday
morning, March 21st, at 11 o'clock. Interment at Yonkers.

0113   Died at Sowerby Bridge, England, February 28th,
William Bates, father-in-law of Benj. M. Talbot, of this
village, aged 61 years.

SATURDAY, MARCH 28, 1874

0114   Rev. A.A. Marshall, who was for some years pastor of
the Protestant Methodist Church, Matteawan, but who
has for a year or so past been residing at Manorville, Long
Island, was taken sick, while attending Conference in New
York city, and on Monday, last, 23d inst., died at his father's
residence, in that city. His disease was congestion of the lungs,
assuming the form of pneumonia. He was sick nine days. Upon
learning of his serious illness, his wife repaired to the city, and
was present with him for several days before he died. He was
46 years of age. His remains were brought to Matteawan on
Wednesday, and the funeral services held in the Presbyterian
Church. The remains were interred in the Presbyterian
Cemetery.

19

0115   We received by mail, a few days ago, a neat card:
        "Amesville, N.Y., March 20, 1874, 2 o'clock a.m. Mr.
and Mrs. A.O. Bunnell have the pleasure of announcing the
advent of a son and heir as per the above date."

0116   The wife of Augustus A. Brush, of East Fishkill, died
        on Sunday evening of pneumonia. She had been ill but a
week. She was widely known and respected, and her sudden
demise has caused profound sorrow in the vicinity. She leaves
five children.

0117   The funeral services of Mr. George Callan, who died in
        New York city on Saturday last, were held at the Castle
Hall of Hudson River Lodge, No. 57, Knights of Pythias, at
Matteawan, on Tuesday afternoon.

0118   On Friday of last week, Stephen A. Guernsey, of
        Stanford, an old and highly respected citizen of that
town, died.

0119   A Mrs. Waldron, of East Fishkill, died at Matteawan on
        Thursday.

0120   Died, March 19th, 1874, Adeline Pickering, in the
        sixty-ninth year of her age. This estimable lady was a
native of our county. She was the daughter of the Honorable
Abraham H. Schenck, of Matteawan, the proprietor and
founder of the extensive manufacturing establishments on the
Matteawan creek. Mr. Schenck held many important public
stations, having represented our county in the State
Legislature, and the State as one of its representatives in
Congress. Miss Schenck was married in early life to Wilco
Peter Wilkens, a native of Amsterdam, Holland, and son of
Hendrick Wilkens, who was Governor of Surinam, Dutch

20

Guiana. His father and grandfather had proceeded him as Governors of that rich and important colony.

0121   Obituary of Adeline (Schenck) Wilkens Pickering, cont.
While traveling in this country for recreation and improvement, [Wilco Peter] Wilkens met and married Miss Adeline, at the family residence. Their marriage was blessed with two children, the first being a daughter, Annette, who married Henry W. Hicks, son of Samuel Hicks, one of the oldest merchants of New York City. The second child was a son, who died in his early youth. Mr. Wilkens, on his marriage, took up his residence at Fishkill-on-the-Hudson. After his death, about the year 1840, his widow married William Langdon Pickering, grandson of Timothy Pickering, a name so eminent in the early history of our nation. This marriage resulted in one child, a daughter, who married Mr. Fletcher, of Boston. It was at their residence at Brooklyn, Long Island, that the subject of this notice died. After several years of declining health, she finally died, suddenly, of heart disease. Her remains were interred, on Saturday last, in the cemetery of the Schenck family, adjoining the old Dutch Church of our village, attended by a large concourse of all our old and respected families.

0122   Married in Newburgh, March 12th, by Rev. Wendell Prime, George H. Brownell to Miss Fannie T. Sherman, both of Verbank.

0123   Died in Brooklyn, N.Y., suddenly, at the residence of her son-in-law, I.D. Fletcher, on Wednesday, March 18th, Adeline, wife of the late William L. Pickering, of New York city, aged 69 years.

0124   Died on Monday morning, March 23d, after a short illness, of Typhoid Pneumonia, at the residence of his father, New York city, Rev. Albert A. Marshall, of Matteawan.

0125   Died at Fishkill Landing, March 25th, Thomas
Flanegan, aged 4 years and 8 months.

0126   Died at Tioronda, March 26th, Mrs. Dora Fedden, aged
73 years.

0127   Died in Fishkill Village, March 23d, Betsey, wife of
Erastus Beecher, aged 70 years.

0128   Died at Fishkill Plains, March 22d, Susan E., wife of
Augustus A. Brush, aged 42 years.

0129   Died in New York city, March 21st, 1874, George
Callan, aged 30 years.

SATURDAY, APRIL 4, 1874

0130   Married by Rev. Chas. W. Fritts, March 25th, Sylvester
Van Wagner to Grace Stephenson, both of LaGrange,
N.Y.

0131   Married by Rev. T. Elliott, March 16th, Robert Jackson
to Mary Ella McVey, both of Matteawan.

0132   Died at Matteawan, N.Y., on Wednesday, April 1st, of
Typhoid Pneumonia, Aminda C. Grant, wife of Wm.
Miller, aged 42 years. Greene Co. papers please copy.

0133   Died at North New York, April 2d, Charles Leach,
brother of Daniel Leach, of this village, aged 63 years.

0134   Died at Matteawan, April 2d, Mrs. Sarah Bloomer,

22

wife of John Bloomer, aged 75 years.

0135   Died at Matteawan, April 3d, Lavinia Burnett, aged 58
years and 9 months.

SATURDAY, APRIL 11, 1874

0136   The inquest in the Phillips case was resumed last
Monday at Beekman. It was stated that the chemist was
not through with his examination of the contents of Mrs.
Phillips' stomach, two weeks being required to finish it. The
jury however, returned the following verdict: "We, the jury,
after hearing all the evidence against James D. Phillips, charged
with poisoning his lawful wife, Euphemia D. Phillips, do agree
that Euphemia D. Phillips came to her death by the hands of
her lawful husband, by administering poison."

0137   Married April 8, at the house of the bride's mother,
Fishkill Landing, David Davis, of Matteawan, to Sarah
M., daughter of the late William Brett, of Fishkill-on-the-
Hudson.

0138   Married on the 23d of March, at the residence of Levi
Whitney, in Beekman, by Gabriel D. Coutant, Esq., Mr.
John J. Eastwood to Amelia Angsman, all of Beekman.

0139   Died at Fishkill Landing, on Wednesday, April 8th,
Charlotte, only child of Willis and Virginia Van Buren,
aged 2 years, 6 months and 23 days.

0140   Died in Fishkill Village, April 1st, Teressa, wife of Levi
Ireland, aged 32 years.

0141   Died in LaGrangeville, April 3d, Oscar F. Bacon,

23

Formerly of New York, in the 41st year of his age.

0142   Died in Phillipstown, April 6th, Isaac B. Davenport, aged 50 years.

0143   Died in Beekman, April 5th, Stephen Buck, aged 82 years.

0144   Died at Stanford, March 28th, Samuel C. Pugsley, in the 35th year of his age.

0145   Died at Bedford, New Hampshire, April 1st, of brain fever, Eddie R. Tyson, eldest son of Rev. Ira C. Tyson, formerly of Hughsonville, Dutchess county, aged 10 years, 5 months and 18 days.

SATURDAY, APRIL 18, 1874

0146   Married at Fishkill-on-Hudson, April 5th, by Rev. Wm. E. Clarke, Richard J. Horton and Katie L. Jackson, both of Fishkill Landing.

0147   Married at Matteawan, on Thursday, April 15th, by Rev. J.L. Scott, Mr. Ermon R. Weed and Miss Elizabeth Pendleton, all of Matteawan.

0148   Married at St. Joachim's Church, Matteawan, at High Mass, on Wednesday, April 15th, by Rev. Peter McCourt, Mr. William A. Toohey and Miss Maggie T. Smith, daughter of Mr. Philip Smith, all of this village.

0149   Married in Poughkeepsie, April 16th, at the residence of Jas. H. Weeks, Esq., by Rev. Mr. Van Gieson, Mr. Maurice Bradley to Miss Cynthia Pinkney, all of Poughkeepsie.

0150   Died in Matteawan, April 14th, Mary Ann Ellis, wife of William H. Miller, aged 46 years and 4 months.

SATURDAY, APRIL 25, 1874

0151   Married at the residence of the bride's parents, at Amityville, Long Island, on Tuesday, April 21st, by the Rev. Mr. Graham, Mr. Robert Pearsall, of New York, to Miss Mary Elizabeth, only daughter of William A. Baldwin, of the former place.

0152   Died at Fishkill Landing, April 18th, Susan Cunningham, wife of Matthew Cunningham, aged 58 years.

0153   Died in Matteawan, April 17th, Oliver Ladue, aged 55 years and 9 months.

0154   Died in the town of LaGrange, April 22, Elizabeth A., wife of Simon Frear, aged 58 years, 10 months and 17 days.

0155   Died at Fort Montgomery, April 18th, Mrs. Eliza Cooper, daughter of John Day, aged 21 years, 1 month and 8 days.

SATURDAY, MAY 2, 1874

0156   Drs. Bayley, Lansing and Ward have completed their analysis of the stomach and liver of the wife of James D. Phillips, deceased, and have found no trace of arsenic poison in them. They will communicate this fact in an official report to Coroner Hicks to-day, or to-morrow. Acting upon the above information, we understand that the counsel for James D. Phillips will make application for the prisoner's discharge on nominal bail. -*Poughkeepsie Eagle,* 30th.

0157   S.L. Walker, one of the first in this country to make
       pictures by the daguerrean process, died in
Poughkeepsie, on Saturday evening last, aged 72 year.

0158   From a book of biographical sketches of members of
       the legislature of this state, we take the following:
James Mackin is a lineal descendant of genuine Irish stock,
though his parents were natives of this country, his father
having been born in New York, and his mother in Newburgh.
They both died, however, within three years of each other,
before young Mackin had reached his eighth year. He was born
in Newburgh, Orange county, on the 25th of December, 1823;
he was educated in the common schools of Newburgh and
Fishkill, and has spent the greater portion of his life in the latter
town.
   He was married, July 1858, to Miss Sarah E. Wiltsie, a very
intelligent and accomplished young lady, and a daughter of
James Wiltsie, an old and respected citizen of Fishkill. She was
a devout member of the Reformed Church, where Mr. Mackin
also worshipped. Her death took place in 1862, and her place
in the family circle has never been filled.

0159   Married at the residence of the bride's parents, in
       Fishkill, April 27th, by the Rev. E.S. Bishop, of New
York city, Oscar H. Newton, of Sutter county, Cal., to Emily
Scofield, of Fishkill.

0160   Married in Fishkill Village, at the residence of the bride,
       by Rev. I.R. Vandewater, April 23d, Mr. Evans R.
Tomlinson, of Mount Holly, N.J., to Miss Susie Wilde.

0161   Died in the town of Fishkill, near Breakneck, April

27th, Nellie, daughter of Platt and Mary Mosher, aged 15 years, 7 months and 8 days.

0162   Died in Poughkeepsie, April 29th, at the residence of her aunt, Jennie Pells, wife of Ebenezer Platt, aged 33 years.

SATURDAY, MAY 9, 1874

0163   The Shawangunk boiler explosion appears to have been particularly severe upon those who resided or had relatives in this neighborhood. Robert J. Owen, the dead fireman, lived in Mr. Henry Mosher's house, in Newburgh avenue, and was all ready to move to his new location. William B. Hill, the dead boiler tender, was a brother of Abraham Hill, who works for the Sewells and lives in Mr. Haver's house. Eliza Conklin, also killed, was a sister of Egbert Conklin, of the firm of Green & Conklin, Matteawan.

0164   Mr. Samuel Addington died at his residence in this village on Monday of this week, aged 67 years. He was a brother of Mr. William R. Addington, the founder and for eighteen years editor and proprietor of this paper. Mr. Addington was in the cabinet repairing business, and followed his calling until confined to the house by sickness. He had led a varied life, having at one time been proprietor of the Eagle Hotel, in this village, and then of a hotel in Harlem, and later a policeman in the city of New York, under the Mayorality [sic] of the noted Fernando Wood.

0165   Mr. John Bloomer, one of the oldest residents of this neighborhood, died at Wiccopee on Saturday last, aged 79 years. We believe Mr. Bloomer was a native of this town, and has resided in this village and vicinity for a great number of years, and was engaged as a teamster until the infirmities of age compelled him to relinquish such an arduous business. The recent decease of his wife, who had traveled through life with him for scores of years, affected the old man deeply, and no doubt hastened his own death. Although walking in the humblest paths of life, "Uncle John" will be missed by many.

0166   Mr. Oliver S. Strong, father of Mr. Benjamin Strong, of this village, died at the residence of his son-in-law at Yonkers, on Friday of last week. Mr. S. was a frequent visitor to his relatives here. The N.Y. *Observer* says he was for many years the able and efficient President of the House of Refuge, and that institution owes its present high condition to his indefatigable energy and devotion. As a director of the New York Institution for the Deaf and Dumb, he was equally active and interested.

0167   Died in Matteawan, on Saturday, May 2d, John Bloomer, aged 79 years.

0168   Died at Fishkill Landing, on Monday, May 4th, Samuel Addington, aged 67 years.

0169   Died in Matteawan, at the residence of her son, Benjamin Sullivan, May 6th, Mrs. Mary Sullivan, aged 67 years. Relatives and friends of the family are invited to attend the funeral on Saturday, 9th inst., at 2 ½ o'clock, from the M.E. Church, Matteawan.

SATURDAY, MAY 16, 1874

0170   Mr. William Richards, for many years connected with the press of Peekskill, died at his residence in that village on Thursday of last week.

0171   Col. [David S.] Cowles, whose death is mentioned at
        length in the history of the 128th Regiment, died in the
arms of Private George Deacon, formerly of this place, now of
California, as we are informed by a comrade of his who was in
the same regiment.

0172   Died at Fishkill-on-the-Hudson, May 10th, Lulu,
        daughter of the late William C. and Louise Oakley,
aged 6 years and 23 days.

0173   Died in Matteawan, May 13th, Eddie, son of William
        and Mary A. Montfort, aged 10 years and 6 months.

SATURDAY, MAY 23, 1874

0174   James Collingwood, an extensive lumber merchant and
        proprietor of the Opera House, Poughkeepsie, died at
this residence in that city on Saturday morning of last week,
aged 61 years. His trouble was neuralgia of the heart.

0175   Edgar Vincent, ex-County Clerk, died at his residence
        in Union Vale on Thursday afternoon of last week,
aged 60 years. He had been Supervisor, Member of Assembly,
and County Clerk. He was engaged in farming at the time of
his death.

0176   Rev. Dr. Thomas DeWitt, in his younger years pastor
        of the Reformed Dutch Church at Hopewell, but for a
great number of years senior pastor of the Collegiate Reformed
Church of New York city, died at his residence, in that city, on
Monday last, aged 83 years.

0177   Just as we were going to press this Friday afternoon,
        we learned that Mr. Richard Omrad committed suicide

at his residence near the Mill Bridge, Matteawan, by cutting his throat with a razor. The deed was done a little before 3 o'clock, and he expired in about half an hour.

It is said his brain had been affected lately, impelling him to do the rash deed. He had been in the employ of the Seamless Clothing Manufacturing Company until recently.

0178   Married by Rev. Philip Germond, at Fishkill-on-the-Hudson, May 21, Charles Torrey and Emma Frast, both of Cornwall, N.Y.

0179   Died in Matteawan, May 19th, Henry Smith, aged 69 years.

0180   Died in New York, May 18th, Rev. Thomas DeWitt, in the 83d year of his age.

0181   Died in East Fishkill, May 18th, George Waldron, aged 21 years.

0182   Died at Glenham, May 14th, Mary, wife of Abram W. Green, in the 54th year of her age.

SATURDAY, MAY 30, 1874

0183   We mentioned briefly last week, the sudden and severe illness of Rev. Dr. [Francis R.] Masters, of Matteawan. While at the Howland Library last week, he was suddenly taken with an apoplectic spasm, which resulted in his death the following Tuesday night. He was unable to bear the effort of removal to his home, but remained at the Library until his death, the family of the Librarian, Mr. J.N. Badeau, doing everything in their power to minister unto him. When first attacked, Drs. Wilson and Doughty were at once summoned

30

and his wife and daughters notified of his illness. They at once repaired to his assistance. He remained unconscious from the time he was taken until death released him from his sufferings.

0184   Sketch of Rev. Dr. [Francis R.] Masters.

Dr. Masters was born in New York city on the 27th of July, 1819. His father was Mr. Thomas Masters, of the mercantile firm of Masters & Markoe. He was educated at Yale College. His health failing him while at study, he did not immediately enter upon his profession, but spent some thirteen years farming at Goshen, Orange county, N.Y., where he was an Elder in the Presbyterian Church and also Superintendent of the Sabbath School. When his health improved, he entered the Theological Seminary at Princeton, N.J., and after graduating was licensed to preach by the Presbytery of Hudson, in April, 1855. He was ordained and installed in the First Presbyterian Church, Matteawan, on the 17th of July, 1855. He remained Pastor of this church until about two years ago, when he was attacked with a partial paralysis. He leaves a wife, two sons, and three daughters. His eldest son, William H., is a civil engineer in Texas, in government employ.

0185   The funeral of Rev. Dr.[Francis R.] Masters took place from the Presbyterian Church, at 11 o'clock on Friday morning, there being a very large attendance of people, not only from this vicinity, but many from abroad, among whom were many clergymen of different denominations and members of the North River Presbytery.

0186   William F. Stearns, brother-in-law of Dr. C.M. Kittredge, of this village, died at Orange, N.J., on Thursday of last week, aged 39 years. He was a son of President Stearns, of Amherst College. He had been a merchant at Bombay, India, for several years, but returned to

31

Orange, where he again entered into business. He was a
zealous supporter of missionary enterprises, and corresponded
for years with David Livingstone [sic], the African explorer.

0187 Our readers will hear with regret of the severe and
        sudden illness which recently overtook Rev. Dr.
Kimball, formerly pastor of the Reformed Church of this
village, on Sunday morning last. The *Tribune* of last
Tuesday states that the pastor, Joseph Kimball, was preaching
the anniversary sermon of the First Reformed Dutch Church of
Brooklyn, when he suddenly stumbled in his speech, swayed
from side to side, and fell forward over the reading desk. He
recovered sufficiently to be able to walk with assistance to his
house, having two more fainting fits, but was somewhat
improved on Monday. His trouble is apoplexy.

0188 Married at New Hamburgh, May 24th, by the Rev. J.H.
        Hawxhurst, Isaac Horton, of Fishkill Landing, to Miss
Mary E. Wood, of Glenham.

0189 Married at Hopewell, May 24th, by Rev. James
        Gregory, Mr. John Beecher to Miss Mary L. Sedore,
both of Fishkill.

0190 Married at Claverack, May 20th, at the residence of the
        bride's parents, by Rev. G.W. Knapp, Mr. Oscar
Shann, of Brooklyn, L.I., to Miss Ella L. Fowler, sister of
Milton A. Fowler, of Poughkeepsie.

0191 Married at Glenham, by Rev. John R. Livingston,
        Thursday, May 28th, James Dunnican to Hannah
Townsend, of Glenham, at the residence of the bride.

0192 Died at Fishkill Landing, May 25th, Hannora, wife of

Nicholas Mara, aged 42 years.

0193 Died at Matteawan, May 25th, Rev. F.R. Masters,
        D.D., in the 55th year of his age.

0194 Died at Fishkill Landing, May 24th, Ellen Jane,
        daughter of Caleb and Anna Hawks, aged 5 years and 5
months.

0195 Died in Fishkill Village, May 22d, Mrs. Helena DuBois,
        in the 91st year of her age.

0196 Died at Glenham, May 23d, Miss Josephine Lelever,
        aged 28 years.

0197 Died May 11th, John Briggs, of Stanford, aged 64
        years.

0198 Died at Bridgeport, Conn., May 15th, Maud E.,
        daughter of James and Jane E. Myatt, and grand-
daughter of Mr. John M. Goring, Sr., of Wappingers Falls,
aged 4 years and 7 months.

SATURDAY, JUNE 6, 1874

0199 James H. Miller, a farmer of Lagrange, committed
        suicide on Saturday last, by hanging himself in his barn.

0200 Among the many ceremonies on Decoration Day, an
        elegant wreath of white flowers was placed on the
monument of Lieut. Col. C.E. Davies, son of Judge Henry E.
Davies, in the Episcopal cemetery, Matteawan.

0201 Died at Matteawan, May 23d, Emma, daughter of

Frederick and Hattie Reick, aged 2 years and 9 months.

0202 Died at Fishkill Landing, June 5th, Mary Frances,
   daughter of F.R.M. and Harriet F. Green, aged 2 years
and 7 months.

0203 Died in Brooklyn, May 30th, Mary Sherwood, daughter
   of Augustus and Jane E. Bartow, in the 7th year of her
age.

0204 Died at Johnsville, March 25th, Wesley, son of Bennett
   Chatterton, aged 21 years.

0205 Died at Fishkill Landing, on Friday, June 5th, George
   Godfrey, youngest son of H.E. and M.A. Traver, aged
six years and four months.

SATURDAY, JUNE 13, 1874

0206 Married at the residence of the bride's parents, June
   10th, by Rev. O. Ward, Mr. Frank St. John, of
Lagrange, to Miss Allie M. Sheldon, youngest daughter of
Wilson B. Sheldon, of Beekman.

0207 Died in Matteawan, Sunday, June 7th, Carrie, wife of
   N.W. Earl, aged 27 years and 6 months.

0208 Died at Brinckerhoffville, June 3d, George M., only son
   of George and Kate Foley, aged 3 years, 11 months and
10 days.

SATURDAY, JUNE 20, 1874

0209 Married at the M.E. Parsonage, Matteawan, June 6th,

by the Rev. C.W. Millard, George Taggart, to Nellie, daughter of David Stitt, both of Newburgh.

0210   Married at Wappingers Falls, June 15th, at the bride's father's, by Rev. J.H. Hawxhurst, Daniel S. Dougherty, editor of the *Wappingers Chronicle*, to Miss Annie Sanders, all of Wappingers Falls.

0211   Died at Wappingers Falls, June 14th, John Laforge, aged 88 years.

0212   Died at New Hamburgh, June 17th, Samuel M. Wilsey.

FISHKILL LANDING, JUNE 27, 1874

0213   Married at Fishkill Landing, June 21st, by Rev. Philip Germond, Harvey A. Jaycocks, of the above place, to Mary C. Lamox, of Fishkill.

0214   Married at the residence of Mr. Monfort, Matteawan, June 24th, by Rev. Philip A. Germond, Mr. Elijah A. Briggs, of Fishkill Landing, and Miss Lizzie H. Monfort, of the former place.

0215   Died in Matteawan, June 24th, Horace M. Riggs, aged 33 years.

FISHKILL LANDING, JULY 4, 1874

0216   Bunnell has named his boy baby, Mark Holden Bunnell. We would suggest that a comma be put after the word Holden.

0217   Married at Fishkill Landing, by Rev. Philip Germond,

July 2d, James Benedict, of New Hackensack, N.Y., and Mrs. Mary Phillips of the former place.

0218 Married by Rev. P.E. Kipp, June 29th, Milton H. Thomas, of Glenham, to Sarah F. DePew, of Washingtonville, N.Y.

0219 Married June 17th, by Rev. D.W. Sherwood, of Ludingtonville, Mr. Abijah Hagar and Miss Esther Robinson, both of East Fishkill.

0220 Married at the parsonage of the M.E. Church, in Saugerties, by the Rev. William E. Clarke, June 27th, William H. Shoonmaker, of Dutchess Junction, and Miss Margaret A. Valk, of Malden, Ulster county.

0221 Married at the M.E. Parsonage, Bullville, June 25th, by the Rev. R.L. Shurter, James McCord to Sarah A. Shurter, both of Newburgh.

0222 Died at Matteawan, June 23d, Annie, infant daughter of Robert and Theressa Gordon, aged 11 months and 15 days.

0223 Died at Fishkill Landing, July 2d, Miss Evelina Montross, aged 76 years. Funeral Sunday at 2 o'clock p.m. from the residence of Miss Deborah Tillott.

0224 Died at Poughkeepsie on Tuesday, June 30th, of Cerebro Spinal Meningitis, Miss Sarah A. Holden, sister of Mr. J.G. P. Holden, editor of the *Yonkers Gazette*.

SATURDAY, JULY 11, 1874

0225   Prof. Charlouis, formerly of Matteawan, who married
          in Poughkeepsie and subsequently obtained a divorce
from his wife, was again married in Albany last week.

0226   Another of our citizens, Mr. Joseph W. Owen, has
          passed away, as will be seen by turning to our obituary
column. His health has been poor for a number of years, so that
he could not give full attention to his business, that of saddler
and harness maker. He came to this village from Fishkill, some
five or six years ago. He leaves a wife and two children to
mourn his loss. His wife was the daughter of D.T. Valentine,
one of the old Knickerbockers, so long a clerk of the Common
Council, in New York city, and honorably known as the city
historian.

0227   Married at Matteawan, on Thursday, July 2d, by the
          Rev. Jabez Marshall, Mr. George F. Gollow to Miss
Julia A. Hoard, both of
Matteawan.

0228   Married in Albany, June 30th, by Right Rev. Bishop
          Doane, Prof. John L. Charlouis and Miss Lizzie
Lathrap, of Albany.

0229   Died in Fishkill Landing, July 9th, J.W. Owen, aged 50
          years. Relatives and friends of the family are invited to
attend the funeral on Saturday, at 11 o'clock, from his late
residence.

SATURDAY, JULY 18, 1874

0230   Rev. Dr. Hibbard, of Brooklyn, occupied the pulpit of
          the M.E. Church, of this village, last Sunday morning.

37

The Doctor is Rev. Mr. Germond's father-in-law.

0231   Married at the Brewster House, Brewsters, N.Y., July
        9th, by Rev. Philip Germond, Stanley Fairchild, of
Danbury, Conn., and Jennie Williamson, of New York city.

0232   Married at the M.E. Parsonage, Fishkill Landing, July
        14th, by Rev. Philip Germond, William E. Bell, of
Rondout, and Minnie Houghtaling, of Port Ewan.

0233   Died in Fishkill Village, July 13th, Hattie E., wife of
        Thomas Andrews, aged 33 years.

0234   Died in New York, July 14th, Peter F. Day, for
        forty-eight years the attached and faithful friend of and
servant of H.W. Sargent, of this village.

0235   Died at Matteawan, July 12th, Hannah Smith, aged 18
        years.

0236   Died at Wiccapee [sic], July 16th, Angie, infant
        daughter of Joseph and Julia Conklin, aged 2 months
and 14 days. Funeral on Saturday 18th inst., at 2 ½ o'clock,
from the residence of its parents.

SATURDAY, JULY 26, 1874

0237   Married at Fishkill Landing, July 22d, by Rev. Philip
        Germond, Mr. Charles Bell and Miss Emily Talbot, all
of the above place.

0238   Died in Matteawan, July 21st, Julia B., wife of Charles
        B. Knapp, aged 30 years.

0239   Died at Glenham, July 20th, John McGregor, aged 50 years.

0240   Died at Wappingers Falls, July 11th, Mr. Jeptha Bridge, aged 31 years and 6 days.

0241   Died at Wappingers Falls, July 10th, Mrs. Patrick Dewyre, aged 40 years.

SATURDAY, AUGUST 1, 1874

0242   Rev. Henry Boehm, the patriarch of American Methodism, was 100 years old on June 28th. He had been a preacher 73 years.

0243   Wales A. Candee, over forty years ago a resident of this town, died at Poughkeepsie on Sunday last, in the 71st year of his age.

0244   Horatio Potter, Jr., son of Bishop Potter, of the Episcopal Church, and a native, we believe, of this county, died of consumption contracted by exposure as a soldier, at New York city, on Saturday last, aged thirty-three years.

0245   Died at Fishkill Landing, July 29th, Eddie W. Kittredge, son of Dr. C.M. Kittredge, aged 9 months and 27 days.

0246   Died in Matteawan, July 25th, Carrie, daughter of William H. Van Voorhis, aged 22 years.

0247   Died in Matteawan, July 29th, Eliza J. Streeter, aged 46 years. Relatives and friends of the family are invited to attend the funeral on Saturday, August 1st, at two o'clock, from St. Luke's Church.

0248   Died on Monday, July 20th, at Warsaw, Minn., William
         J. Wall, formerly of Matteawan.

SATURDAY, AUGUST 8, 1874

0249   Married at Grace Church, Millbrook, July 29th, by the
         Rev. P.K. Cady, D.D., Thomas T. Haviland, of
Newburgh, to Miss Lillie S. Merritt, daughter of Alfred T.
Merritt, of the former place.

0250   Died at the residence of her son-in-law, William O.
         Jaycox, in Breakneck Hollow, July 17th, Mrs. Susan
Laforge.

0251   Died at Matteawan, August 1st, Benjamin V. Smith,
aged 46 years, 2 months, and 21 days.

0252   Died at Union, New Jersey, Miss Augusta L.
         McCloskey, formerly teacher of the Parish School of
St. Luke's Church, Matteawan. [No date given.]

0253   Died in Fishkill Village, August 1st, Baron Van Slike,
         aged 58 years.

SATURDAY, AUGUST 15, 1874

0254   On Monday afternoon, a lad about seven years of age,
         named Walter Brown, son of the late Charles Brown,
teamster, was drowned in the reservoir of the Dutchess Hat
Works, in this village, the water at the time being about six feet
deep. He was playing near the edge of the reservoir, putting
sticks into the water, in company with a lad about his own age,

son of Mr. Darius Glover, engineer of the Hat Works, when he accidentally fell in. His companion was too young to help him, but ran home and told his mother and the drowned boy's mother, who was visiting Mrs. Glover, that Walter was in the water. Another lad, Tommy Corcoran, went in and raised the body. An attempt was made to resuscitate him, but without success. His funeral took place on Tuesday afternoon.

0255 Hon. John Stanton Gould, of Hudson, well known as President of the Agricultural Society of this state for a number of years, and also as a profound thinker, industrious student, and popular essayist and lecturer on scientific subjects, died of congestion of the lungs, at Hudson, on Saturday night last, aged 63 years.

0256 Died at his residence, near Fishkill Village, August 12th, William S. Dudley, aged 55 years, 1 month and 20 days. Funeral from his late residence, on Saturday, at 11 a.m., and from the Reformed Church at 11½ o'clock.

0257 Died in Poughkeepsie, August 9th, Lilie Martin, infant child of Rev. A.L. and Josie R. Culver.

SATURDAY, AUGUST 22, 1874

0258 Died in Matteawan, August 15th, Eva, infant daughter of Charles W. and Sarah E. Van Vort, aged 1 year, 6 months, and 17 days.

0259 Died at Glenham, August 17th, John Jackson, aged 87 years.

0260 Died at Union, Broome county, August 4th, Samuel Colwell, aged 92 years and 6 months; formerly of East

Fishkill.

0261 Died at Belvit, Wisconsin, on the 11th of August, at the
residence of her son, Mrs. Cordelia, wife of the late
Jacob Washburn, formerly a resident of this village.

SATURDAY, AUGUST 29, 1874

0262 On Monday last Rev. C.W. Millard, of the M.E.
Church, Matteawan, in company with his
brother-in-law, Rev. Mr. Baldwin, a Baptist minister of Albany,
and the latter's daughter, about ten years of age, had a
runaway. All were thrown out of the buggy, and sustained
minor injuries, but Mr. Millard will be unable to occupy his
pulpit on Sunday.

0263 Thomas Smith, editor of the Yonkers Herald, died at
his residence, on Friday afternoon of last week.

0264 The wife of ex-Judge George G. Barnard, died last
week, and was buried in Greenwood Cemetery.

0265 Holden, J.G.P., of the *Yonkers Gazette*, was 40 years
old on Saturday last. He requests us not to say anything
about it, so, out of respect to his feelings, we won't mention it.

0266 Married at home, Newburgh, Tuesday evening, August
25th, by Rev. Andrew Longacre, Henry E. Sharp, to
Ada C. Green, both of Newburgh.

SATURDAY, SEPTEMBER 5, 1874

0267 We are pleased to learn that Rev. Mr. Millard is around
as usual, his runaway accident not resulting at all

seriously.

0268   Mrs. Mary Brundage, wife of Capt. C.W. Brundage, of
the firm of Brundage & Place, died on Thursday
evening, aged 45 years.

0269   But faint hopes are entertained of the recovery of Mr.
J.B. Hall, editor of the *Catskill Recorder*, one of the
best weekly papers published.

0270   The remains of Captain William Weller were brought
from New York city on Thursday, and interred in the
Fishkill Rural Cemetery. Captain W. was known to a large
circle of friends and acquaintances in this neighborhood. He
was for many years captain and engineer on board the
ferryboat here, and afterward engineer at Lomas' brickyard.
Some years ago he moved to New York city, where he died on
Monday last, in the 68th year of his age. His disease was
consumption.

0271   Mr. Robert Wilson, whose death is announced in
another column, was well-known in this neighborhood.
He was for a good many years a dyer in the old cotton factory
at Matteawan; afterwards kept a grocery in this village, in the
store now occupied by S.G. & J.T. Smith; was in the army a
couple of years; and since the war has been engaged in the
dyeing business at Newburgh. His death was quite sudden. His
funeral was attended by the Free Masons, who conducted the
ceremonies at his grave, in the Reformed Cemetery of this
village.

0272   Martin Fuller, nephew of Josiah Fuller, of Matteawan,
was one of the unfortunates at the Pittsburgh flood. He
sustained severe injuries about the head. He is still weak and

43

feeble. He is a boiler-maker by trade, and formerly worked for Alex Cauldwell, Newburgh. He is presently stopping with his aunt, Mrs. Jaycox, at Matteawan. He is in quite destitute circumstances.

0273   Married in the M.E. Church, Brewster, August 31st, by Rev. Philip Germond, George Moore, Esq., and Addie M. Vansony, both of Brewster.

0274   Married at the residence of the bride, at Millbrook, Monday, August 31st, by the Rev. Mr. Grant, W. Wallace Smith to E. Anna Weston, formerly of Newburgh.

0275   Died September 3d, Mary, wife of Captain C.W. Brundage, aged 45 years. Funeral on Sunday, the 6th inst., at 2 o'clock, from the Reformed Church. Relatives and friends of the family are invited to attend.

0276   Died September 3d, at Wiccapee, Margaret Farley, aged 24 years.

0277   Died in Newburgh, August 30th, Robert Wilson, aged 60 years. His remains were brought to Fishkill Landing for interment.

0278   Died at Arthursburgh, N.Y., 8th month, 28th, Moses Alley, in the 79th year of his age.

0279   Died at Millbrook, 8th month, 31st, Alfred Treadway, youngest son of Barclay and Susan T. Haviland, in the 20th year of his age.

44

SATURDAY, SEPTEMBER 12, 1874

0280   The relatives and friends of Mr. and Mrs. Nelson F.
Hyatt, of Matteawan, celebrated the crystal wedding of
this pair, on Monday evening.

0281   Married at the parsonage, Matteawan, Sept. 2, by the
Rev. C.W. Millard, Mr. M. Frank Miller, of Vineland,
N.J., to Miss Celia M. Wellman, of Matteawan.

0282   Died in Matteawan, Sept. 11th, Mrs. Harriet White,
aged 51 years. Funeral on Saturday, at 2 o'clock, from
the M.E. Church, Matteawan.

0283   Died at Wappingers Falls, September 3d, Mrs. Mary
Johnson, widow of the late David Johnson, aged 80
years.

SATURDAY, SEPTEMBER 19, 1874

0284   Edmund Morris, of Poughkeepsie, celebrated his
eighty-eighth birthday on Saturday night last.

0285   J.B. Hall, editor of the *Catskill Recorder*, and late
member of the Constitutional Commission, died at
Catskill on Monday morning.

0286   Abram T. Van Steenburgh, Kingston, father of "Boots"
Van Steenburgh, is dead. He was over 89 years old,
and was born and always lived in the same house he occupied
when he died.

0287   On Saturday night last, four men who were out of
funds, and were on their way from Springfield, Mass.,

to New York city, traveling precariously by stealing rides on freight trains, got on board the down milk train at Poughkeepsie and came as far as this place. One of them, whose name is Mulcahey, given name unknown, jumped off as the train was approaching the station, when he made a misstep and fell under the train, the wheels of the following car passing over his body, killing him instantly. The remains were interred in the free ground of the M.E. Cemetery, on Sunday. Deceased was about 25 years of age, single, and formerly resided in New York city. He was a laborer, American, of Irish descent.

0288   Mrs. Charlotte H. Taylor, wife of James Taylor, of this village, died very suddenly on Sunday night last, in the 67th year of her age. Heart disease is supposed to have been the cause. Her maiden name was Telford, and her father was one of the first three settlers in New Windsor, Orange county. Her funeral took place on Thursday morning, from her late residence, and her remains were interred in the Episcopal Cemetery, Matteawan.

0289   Died in Fishkill Landing, September 13th, Charlotte H., wife of James Taylor, aged 67 years.

0290   Died in Fishkill Landing, September 18th, Terrence J. Sullivan, aged 24 years. Relatives and friends of the family are invited to attend the funeral on Sunday, at 2 o'clock, from the residence of his father, Bernard Sullivan.

SATURDAY, SEPTEMBER 26, 1874

0291   Mr. John A. deWint, eldest son of the late John P. deWint, was accidentally killed on the railroad at Hartford on Thursday. We have not learned particulars.

0292 Died in Fishkill Landing, September 23d, Elizabeth, widow of the late William Tomlins, aged 73 years.

0293 Died in Matteawan, September 22d, Lizzie Organ, aged 33 years.

0294 Died suddenly, at Hartford, on Thursday, September 24th, John A., eldest son of the late J.P. DeWint.

SATURDAY, OCTOBER 3, 1874

0295 We announced briefly last week the death of Mr. John A. DeWint, eldest son of the late John P. DeWint. For some years he had been an inmate of the Retreat for the Insane at Hartford, Conn. One day last week he came down a ladder placed close to his window by workmen, and fled. He was gone two days, when he was discovered in the person of a man who was killed upon a railroad thirty miles from Hartford. It seems he was walking upon the track early in the morning, during a heavy fog, and the engineer did not discover him until it was too late to stop the locomotive, which struck him and threw him off the track. He died from his injuries in a short time. The funeral services took place on Sunday, and his remains were interred in the family vault.

0296 Isaac C. Buckhout, chief engineer of the Harlem Railroad, died one day this week. He was a man of extraordinary talents in his profession.

0297 Married at Hopewell, September 27th, by the Rev. Graham Taylor, Lafayette G. Smith, of German, N.Y., to Emma A. Mead, of Gayhead, N.Y.

0298 Died in Fishkill Village, September 17th, Charles W., son of Walter and Elizabeth Ladue, aged 3 years.

0299   Died at Hughsonville, on Wednesday, September 23d,
             Ada, wife of William Serrine, aged 69 years, 5 months
and 21 days.

SATURDAY, OCTOBER 10, 1874

0300   A child of Mr. Weeks, farmer on the Merritt place,
             Carthage Landing, died on Thursday morning from the
effects of lockjaw. Two weeks ago, while playing about the
premises barefooted, it ran a nail in its foot. Ten days afterward
the child was taken with lockjaw, every muscle of its body
becoming rigid, and it passing from one convulsion to another,
at short intervals, dying in terrible agony.

0301   Married September 30th, at the house of the bride's
             parents, by Rev. E.H.W. Barden, Ellathan G. Doughty,
of Salt Point, to Mary S. Knapp, of LaGrange.

0302   Married October 6th, at the house of Henry Nobles, in
             Beekman, by Rev. E.H.W. Barden, Edgar J. Banks, of
Pawling, to Ella F. Colliar [sic], of Beekman.

0303   Married October 1st, at Liberty, Sullivan county, N.Y.,
             at the residence of the bride's mother, by Rev. Thomas
Mack, H.B. Clements to Miss Hattie S. Mead.

0304   Died at Wappingers Falls, October 2d, Mrs. Almira
             Shrader, aged 53 years.

0305   Died at Hughsonville, October 2d, Miss Aurelia
             Vandewater, aged 27 years; of consumption.

0306   Died at Fishkill Landing, October 8th, Michael Martin, aged 7 years and 4 months.

SATURDAY, OCTOBER 17, 1874

0307   Married October 7th, by the Rev. Thomas T. Everett, David H. Vosburg, of Stanford, Dutchess county, and Ella J. Fowler, of Elizaville, Columbia county.

0308   Married on Thursday, October 15th, at the residence of the bride's parents, Glenham, by Rev. John R. Livingston, James E. Milner, Jr., of Norwalk, Conn., to Mary E. Northrop, of Glenham.

0309   Died in Fishkill Landing, on the 15th inst., Abby, wife of Morris Collins, aged 29 years.

0310   Died in Fishkill Landing, on the 16th inst., Stephen D. Youmans, aged 33 years.

0311   Died near Carthage Landing, October 8th, Hattie, daughter of G. Washington and Electa Jane Weeks, aged 4 years, 11 months and 12 days.

0312   Died in Fishkill Village, October 10th, Sarah Polick, aged 94 years.

FISHKILL LANDING, OCTOBER 24, 1874

0313   Mr. Chauncey B. Black, well known in this neighborhood, having been a bookkeeper in the First National Bank for a considerable period, died in Newburgh, of consumption, on Wednesday, aged 28 years. His funeral took place on Friday afternoon.

0314   Married in Brooklyn, at the residence of the bride's
        parents, on Wednesday, October 21st, by her father,
Rev. W.G. Browning, former pastor of the M.E. Church of this
village, assisted by Rev. A.S. Hunt, D.D., and Rev. C.M.
Griffin, Samuel G. Collins, Esq., of Denver, Colorado, and
Miss Emilie Browning.

0315   Married on Wednesday, October 21st, at the residence
        of Mr. W.A. Fosdick, Fishkill Village, by Rev. Charles
W. Fritts, Silas F. Riley, of Hadley, Mich., to Miss Elsie M.
Wiltsie, of Fishkill Village.

0316   Married October 15th, at the residence of the bride's
        parents, by Rev. Graham Taylor, assisted by Rev. O.E.
Cobb, Walter N. Hart, of Manchester, N.Y., to Cornelia,
daughter of J.T. Storm, of Hopewell, N.Y.

0317   Married at Low Point, October 14th, by Rev. E.P.
        Ackerman, James Rhone to Lillie A. Trow.

0318   Married in New York, October 8th, at St. Ann's
        Church, by the Rev. Dr. Gallaudet, assisted by the Rev.
William G. Andrews, of New Haven, James Watson Andrews,
of Fishkill, and Laura Hoppock, daughter of Henry L. Cotheal,
of New York.

0319   Died at Shenandoah, October 14th, Elizabeth, wife of
        James Horton, aged 60 years.

0320   Died at Newburgh, October 21st, Chauncey B. Black,
        aged 28 years.

SATURDAY, OCTOBER 31, 1874

0321   Married in New York, on Thursday, October 22d, at
        the residence of the bride's parents, by Rev. James M.
Ludlow, D.D., assisted by Rev. Dr. Hurst, President of Drew
Theological Seminary, James Moore, Jr., to Clare Mead,
daughter of Nathan J. Bailey, Esq.

SATURDAY, NOVEMBER 7, 1874

0322   Married at the residence of Mr. Madison Smith, in East
        Fishkill, November 1st, by Rev. S. Prague, Theodore
Barrett to Sarah M. Purdy; both of the above place.

0323   Died at Matteawan, October 24th, Gracie A., aged 5
        years and 1 month; October 31st, Cynthia, aged 11
months; November 4th, Watson T., aged 2 years and 9 months;
children of George H. and Augusta Pollock.

0324   Died at New York city, October 29th, Eva, infant
        daughter of Charlotte and Edward Adams.

SATURDAY, NOVEMBER 14, 1874

0325   Mr. Aaron Fielding, engaged in the business of buying
        and selling old paper, rags, etc., in Newburgh, and
well-known on this side of the river, died very suddenly of
heart disease on Monday morning of this week. The *Newburgh
Journal* says deceased was forty-eight years of age and leaves
a wife and several children. Mrs. Fielding has been in Europe
for two or three months past, on a visit to old country friends,
and was expected to reach New York on Monday on her
return.

51

0326   Married at the residence of the bride's father, in
          Poughkeepsie, October 26th, by Rev. Mr. Coxe, Mr.
Albert Rothery, of Poughkeepsie, to Miss Allie Cook, of
Burlington.

0327   Died at Fishkill Landing, on Sunday, November 8th,
          Walter L., son of Gilbert D. and Sarah Theal [sic], aged
2 years and 7 months.

0338   Died at Matteawan, November 7th, at 7½ o'clock p.m.,
          Patience Spooner, widow of the late Isaac Spooner,
aged 88 years, 5 months and 29 days.

0329   Died in New York city, November 10th, of diphtheria,
          Una Felicia Howland, aged 13 years, daughter of Rev.
Dr. Howland, and niece of Mrs. Joseph Howland, of this place.

0330   Died at Fishkill Plains, November 5th, Sarah Jane, wife
          of Alonzo Townsend, aged 30 years.

SATURDAY, NOVEMBER 21, 1874

0331   Mr. Isaac Tice, one of the oldest residents of
          Poughkeepsie, died in that city on Saturday of last
week, aged about 90 years.

0332   Zebedee Shaw, of Putnam Valley, is the oldest man in
          Putnam county. He is now in his 98th year, and is hale
and hearty.

0333   Mr. Nicholas Hopper has met with a very sad affliction
          in the loss of his wife, who died quite suddenly, after a
brief and severe illness of but a few days, on Wednesday
evening of this week, in the 53d year of her age. She leaves a

52

numerous family, who feel deeply this great loss.

0334   In Fishkill Landing, November 18th, Harriet, wife of
       Nicholas Hopper, aged 52 years and 6 months, of
inflammation of the lungs. Relatives and friends of the family
are invited to attend the funeral on Saturday, 21st inst., at 10½
o'clock, from the M.E. Church

0335   Died November 17th, William Eno, of Pine Plains, aged
       74 years.

SATURDAY, NOVEMBER 28, 1874

0336   The wife of Rev. William P. Abbott, formerly pastor of
       the Trinity M.E. Church, Newburgh, died in New York
city on Sunday last, aged 32 years.

0337   Isaac Butts, one of the editors and proprietors of the
       Rochester Union, died in that city on the 21st inst. Mr.
Butts was formerly an apprentice in the *Poughkeepsie
Telegraph* office, which has graduated a great number of
editors. Mr. Butts was 58 years of age. He leaves a wife and
five children.

0338   Married in St. Joachim's Church, Matteawan,
       November 26th, by Rev. P. McCourt, Mr. Thomas
McCaffery, of New York, to Miss Mary Ann, daughter of
Philip Grady, Esq., of Matteawan.

0339   Married at the house of Albert Eighmie, in
       LaGrangeville, November 18th, by Rev. E.H.W.
Barden, Leonard J. Vincent, and Sarah A. Brownell, both of
Union Vale.

0340   Married November 12th, at Hopewell by Rev. Graham
        Taylor, Delancey L. Meyers, of Hughsonville, to Jennie
E. Haight, of Gayhead.

0341   Married November 17th, at Hopewell by Rev. Graham
        Taylor, William Calkin, of Sylvan Lake, to Mary L.
Bennett, of the former place.

0342   Married in Beekman, November 21st, by Gabriel D.
        Coutant, Esq., Mr. John W. Baker, of Beekman, to
Miss Ophelia Penny, of the same place.

0343   Died in New York city, November 20th, Ellen P., wife
        of James C. Gulich, formerly of Matteawan.

0344   Died at Matteawan, November 23d, John Hoard, aged
        42 years.

0345   Died in Fishkill Village, November 24th, Gertrude
        Brinckerhoff, aged 78 years.

SATURDAY, DECEMBER 5, 1874

0346   Capt. Henry Ogden, aged 74 years, and for nearly 60
        years a boatman on the Hudson river, died suddenly of
heart disease, at Poughkeepsie, Thursday night.

0347   Mr. Chauncey M. Leonard, Mayor of Newburgh, died
        on Thursday morning. Disease [was] abscess of the
bowels. Mr. L. was 49 years of age, and was one of the most
prominent and worthy citizens of that city. He will be buried
with Masonic honors, this afternoon. Beacon Lodge, of this
place, will attend the funeral in a body.

0348 Married at the house of Mr. Thos. Duff, in Matteawan, on Nov. 25th, by Rev. J.L. Scott, Mr. M.W. Burns and Miss Martha Adams.

0349 Married at Matteawan, Nov. 26th, by the Rev. Charles W. Millard, Mr. Dewitt Bogardus, of Glenham, to Miss Rose L. Harp, of Matteawan.

0350 Married in Poughkeepsie, Nov. 29th, by the Rev. P.R. Hawxhurst, Mr. Henry Gallagher to Miss Katie Van Dyne, both of Fishkill Plains.

0351 Died in Phillipstown, Putnam County, Nov. 24th, Isaac Knapp, aged 86 years.

0352 Died in the village of Fishkill, December 2d, Phebe E., daughter of Mary E. and David Kniffin [sic], aged 4 years, 9 months and 3 days. Friends and acquaintances are invited to attend her funeral on Saturday, at the M.E. Church, in the above place, at 11 o'clock a.m.

SATURDAY, DECEMBER 12, 1874

0353 George Ham, of Salt Point, Duchess county, has celebrated his golden wedding day.

0354 Colonel Peter I. Feller, an old resident of Red Hook, died very suddenly on Thursday of last week.

0355 Captain Henry Ogden died at Poughkeepsie on the 3d inst., in the 74th year of his age. He was born at Peekskill, but most of his life as a boatman had been passed in Poughkeepsie as captain of sailing vessels and the ferryboat. For twenty years he was a resident here, and sailed the sloop

Linnet for the Matteawan factories. He is well remembered by many of our old citizens.

0356 Rev. Dr. Joseph Kimball, formerly pastor of the Reformed Church of this village, died at Newburgh on Sunday last, and was buried on Thursday. He was in the fifty-fifth year of his age. Dr. Kimball was born in Newburgh on the 10th of August, 1820. He [attended] Union College and the old Associate Reformed Seminary of Newburgh. He served in the town of Hamptonburgh, Orange county, nine years; Brockport, N.Y., eight and a half years; and from thence came to the Reformed Church at Fishkill Landing, two and a half years. He then accepted a call to the First Reformed Church, Brooklyn, where he has remained. He received his Doctorate from Rutger's College in 1866.

It was while preaching in the Brooklyn Church, some six months ago, after the exhaustive labors of preparing an anniversary sermon, that he was attacked with the brain malady which finally terminated his existence. Dr. Kimball was buried in Cedar Hill Cemetery.

0357 Married at the M.E. Church in Matteawan, November 25th, by the Rev. C.W. Millard, Mr. R.M. Woodin, of Po'quag, to Mary A. Barlow, of Matteawan.

0358 Died in Matteawan, December 2d, William W. Van Vort, aged 67 years.

0359 Died in Matteawan, December 10th, Maggie, daughter of William H. and Kate Drew, aged 5 years and 7 months.

0360 Died in Fishkill Village, December 3d, George, son of Mary E. and David Kniffen [sic], aged 2 years, 11 months and 20 days.

56

0361   Died in Fishkill Village, December 4th, Ann, wife of Jas. T. Way, aged 69 years.

0362   Died at Glenham, December 6th, Mrs. Louisa Fawcett, aged 42 years.

0363   Died in East Fishkill, December 6th, Isaac Purdy, aged 35 years.

0364   Died at Wethersfield, Conn., December 2d, Susan Van Wyck, eldest daughter of Rev. W.W. Andrews, of Wethersfield, and grand-daughter of the late James Given, of Fishkill.

SATURDAY, DECEMBER 19, 1874

0365   The late Mayor Leonard, of Newburgh, had his life insured for $10,000, and that sum was paid his widow within a week after his death.

0366   Mr. Henry H. Hazzard, the groom mentioned in the following from the *Austin (Texas) Statesman*, is the son of the late Capt. Hazzard: Thursday evening, November 26th, at the residence of the bride's parents, was the marriage of Miss Molly Sisson and Harry Hazzard, Esq., both well known and highly esteemed in the social circles of Austin. The ceremony was performed by Rev. Mr. Rogers, after the forms of the Episcopal service. The bride was tastefully and elegantly attired. After the ceremony and greeting of the friends, the company sat down to a sumptuous repast.

0367   Married by Rev. Philip Germond, November 15th, Mr. James W. Way and Alveretta Haver, both of Fishkill Landing.

0368   Married at Austin, Texas, November 26th, at eight
o'clock, p.m., by the Rev. B.A. Rogers, of the
Episcopal Church, at the residence of the bride's father, Mr.
H.H. Hazzard and Miss Mary A. Sisson, all of that city.

0369   Married at the M.E. Parsonage, Fishkill Landing, by
Rev. Philip Germond, December 15th, D. Secor Bolson
and Mary Conklin, both of Blooming Grove, N.Y.

0370   Married at New Hamburgh, December 9th, by Rev. C.
Sturges, Abram M. Dumond, of Kingston, to Mary
DuBois, daughter of the late John H. Ross, of Fishkill Village.

0371   Married in Fishkill Village, December 14th, by H.F.
Walcott, Esq., Jesse Heady, of East Fishkill, to
Elizabeth Morison [sic], of New York city.

0372   Married on Saturday, December 12th, by J.M.
Tompkins, Justice of the Peace, Alexander Heady and
Susan Harris, both of East Fishkill.

0373   Died in Fishkill Landing, December 12th, Letitia, wife
of Robert McCord, aged 52 years.

0374   Died in Brooklyn, December 6th, of small pox, William
McDougall, in the 23d year of his age, son of Maria
McDougall, formerly of Fishkill Village.

SATURDAY, DECEMBER 26, 1874

0375   Married in Newburgh, December 15th, at the residence
of the bride's parents, by Rev. T.T. Farrington, John
Tracy, of Fishkill Landing, and Miss Elizabeth Moore, of
Newburgh.

58

0376 Died in Matteawan, Wednesday, December 23d, Harry, son of Crawford C. and Jennie Mac Neil, aged 5 years and 4 months.

0377 Died at Plainfield, N.J., Dec. 23d, Martha Remsen, wife of John W. Anthony.

SATURDAY, JANUARY 2, 1875

0378 Married at the residence of the Misses Laforge, Fishkill Landing, on Wednesday morning, December 30th, by Rev. O.V. Amerman, Mr. John T. Foshay, of the firm of Foshay Brothers, editors and proprietors of the *Peekskill Democrat*, and Miss Marietta Bowne, of Matteawan.

0379 Married at Carthage Landing, December 17th, by Rev. M. D'C. Crawford, Mr. George Hunt and Miss Teressa J. Aldridge.

0380 Married at Fishkill Landing, December 30th, by Rev. Philip Germond, Allen W. Gordon, of New Haven, Conn., to Elizabeth Pfister, of Glenham.

0381 Married at the M.E. Parsonage, in LaGrangeville, Dec. 23d, by Rev. E.W. [sic] Barden, Godfrey Wolven, of LaGrangeville, to Libbie Buck, of Beekman.

0382 Married at Johnsville M.E. Parsonage, Nov. 26th, by Rev. George Daniel, Mr. Henry Bowman to Miss Justina Atkins, both of Fishkill.

0383 Married at the bride's residence, Dec. 9th, by Rev. George Daniel, Mr. Robert L. Knapp to Miss Melissa B. Gilbert, both of East Fishkill.

0384 Married at the bride's residence, Dec. 16th, by Rev.
George Daniel, Mr. DeWitt Clinton Conover, of
Wappingers Falls, to Miss Hettie Pierce, of East Fishkill.

0385 Married at the M.E. Parsonage, Johnsville, Dec. 24th,
by Rev. George Daniel, Mr. Charles I. Way to Miss
Mary Ellen Light, both of East Fishkill.

0386 Died at Hopewell, December 26th, Elsey D., wife of
Abram E. Stockholm, in the 75th year of her age.

0387 Died at Farmer's Mills, Dec. 25th, Fanny, wife of
Joseph Sprague, aged 83 years.

0388 Died at Hopewell, Dec. 26th, Elsey D., wife of Abram
B. [sic] Stockholm, aged 75 years.

0389 Died in Fishkill Village, Dec. 27th, Ada F., wife of
Lucius N. Hayt, aged 21 years.

SATURDAY, JANUARY 9, 1875

0390 Mr. Willard H. Mase's family, Matteawan, have been
deeply afflicted by the death of two of their little ones,
both daughters, Jennie, a little over three years of age, and
Kittie, almost seven years old. We learn that the other children,
several in number, are also sick. Every one will join in
sympathy with the family in this affliction, and pray that the
other children may be spared to their parents.

0391 Married by Rev. Philip Germond, at Fishkill Landing,
December 31st, Edward Smith and Annie Harris, both
of Newburgh.

0392   Married on Monday, January 4th, at the home of the
          bride's parents, by the Rev. John R. Livingston, Rector
of Trinity church, Fishkill, Anton Frederick Hellerich, of
Matteawan, to Gertrude Frost, of Stormville.

0393   Married January 6th, at the residence of Laban Rogers,
          Fishkill Village, by Rev. S.L. Holman, of Millerton, Mr.
G. Clark, of Millerton, to Miss Emily Harrington, of Fishkill
Village.

0394   Died in Matteawan, January 3d, Jennie, daughter of
          W.H. and J.E. Mase, aged 3 years, and 3 months.

0395   Died in Matteawan, January 7th, Kittie, daughter of
          W.H. and J.E. Mase, aged 6 years and 11 months.

0396   Died at Fishkill Plains, December 29th, Mrs. Mary Ann
          Higgins, aged 81 years, 7 months and 25 days.

0397   Died in the town of LaGrange, January 2d, Nanthiel
          [sic] Powell, in the 89th year of his age.

0398   Died at Morrisania, Westchester county, N.Y., October
29th, Mrs.
          M'Kinley, wife of S.A. M'Kinley, aged 51 years.

SATURDAY, JANUARY 16, 1875

0399   Married by Rev. C.W. Millard, at the M.E. Parsonage
          of Matteawan, January 3d, Edgar D. Jewell, of Fishkill
Landing, and Annie M. Streeter, of Matteawan.

0400   Married on Wednesday, Jan. 26 [sic], at the residence
          of D.D. Willsea, Tarrytown, N.Y., by Rev. John A.

Todd, D.D., Charles W. Bartrum, of Sing Sing, to Hannah E. Willsea, of the former place.

0401   Died in New York, January 9th, after a protracted illness, Henry H. Christie, eldest son of William H. and Christina Christie.

0402   Died in Matteawan, January 10th, Reuben H., son of Edward and Anna Kelly, aged 8 years and 10 months.

0403   Died at Hughsonville, Thursday, Jan. 5, Emma, wife of James Foster, aged 24 years.

0404   Died at Bangall, Jan. 6, Eleanor Guernsey, widow of the late Stephen G. Guernsey, in the 62d year of her age.

SATURDAY, JANUARY 23, 1875

0405   Died in Matteawan, January 19th, Samuel Henry, aged 55 years and 7 months.

0406   Died in New York city, January 4th, Augustus, son of the late Theodorus Brett, in the 62d year of his age. His remains were brought hither and interred in the family burying ground, attached to the Reformed Dutch Church of this village.

0407   Died at New Hackensack, January 14th, Henry D. Needham, aged 76 years.

0408   Died on Monday, January 18th, at East Fishkill, of pneumonia, Louisa, wife of Rev. Samuel Van Vechten, and daughter of the late General Abraham Van Wyck, in the 72d year of her age. Sweetly, and without a struggle, and with but few hours warning, she ceased to be with us. More than fifty years the idol of a home, she was the household delight to husband, and children.

SATURDAY, JANUARY 30, 1875

0409 Mr. Lasher, 87 years of age, living with Peter Marquart, Glenham, died of old age on Saturday last.

0410 William H. Williams, proprietor of the Olympic Hotel, on the Matteawan road, died very suddenly on Thursday morning. His funeral took place at 2 o'clock on Friday afternoon, and was attended by the firemen of this village in a body.

0411 Married at St. Mark's Church, Carthage Landing, January 27th, [by] Rev. F.W. Shelton, Mr. Julius Jenks, of Sing Sing, and Miss Lottie, daughter of Captain John L. Collyer, of Carthage Landing.

0412 Died in Matteawan, January 23d, Charlotte Emily Louisa, wife of J. Miller, M.D., aged 22 years.

0413 Died in Matteawan, January 27th, William H. Williams, aged 34 years and 6 months.

0414 Died at Poughkeepsie, January 25th, Thomas S., only son of Julia A. and Thomas S. Martin, aged 1 month and 26 days.

0415 Died in Newburgh, January 26th, Selah T. McCollum, aged 60 years, 8 months and 18 days.

0416 Died at Glenham, January 21st, Melissa A., wife of

William H. Weeks, aged 39 years.

0417   Died on Saturday, January 23d, at the residence of her
            brother, Theodorus Van Wyck, Martha Van Wyck,
widow of General Abr'm Van Wyck, aged 89 years, 11 months
and 25 days.

0418   Died in Fishkill Hook, Miss Susan Purdy, aged about
            55 years.

SATURDAY, FEBRUARY 6, 1875

0419   On Tuesday, Hopewell and Wappingers Falls Masonic
            Lodges united in the services of the order at the funeral
of Mr. W.H. Van Voorhis, a well-known New Hamburgher, at
Fishkill Rural Cemetery.

0420   The many friends of Henry Davids, at Fishkill Landing,
            will be glad to learn that that gentleman is pleasantly
located in the position of Chief Engineer of Mare Island Navy
Yard, on the Sacramento river, California. He as been in the
employ of the U.S. Government for seventeen years. He spent
four years on the Sandwich Islands, and enjoyed the friendship
of King Kalakana during that time. He married Miss Adeline
Browne, daughter of Calvin Browne, and old and popular Civil
Engineer of the U.S. Government, with whom the happy
couple now reside. - *Poughkeepsie Eagle.*

0421   The death of Mrs. Theall, wife of Mr. Gilbert D. Theall,
            was not only a sudden one, but is also a heavy blow to
a happy family and large circle of relatives and friends. She was
one of the converts at the recent revival of the Methodist
Episcopal Church of this village, and was a prominent member
of the Sunday School, being the head teacher of the infant

64

class. She leaves a husband and several small children. The funeral took place from the Church on Wednesday morning, and the body was interred in the Methodist Cemetery.

0422   Married at the residence of the bride's mother, January 27th, by the Rev. W.G. Hillman, of Wappingers Falls, Mr. Thomas W. Jaycox, Jr., of Washington, D.C., to Miss Mary A., daughter of the late Mr. Peter Dates, of Poughkeepsie Township, N.Y.

0423   Died in Fishkill Landing, February 1st, Sarah Jane, wife of Gilbert D. Theall, aged 35 years and 5 months.

0424   Died at Middlebush, January 24th, Mrs. Mary A. Roe, aged 74 years.

0425   Died January 24th, 1875, at the residence of Truman B. Brown, in Auburn, N.Y., Guernsey Smith, aged eighty-two years. He has resided most of the time for the last fourteen years with the family of his kindred, where he died. He was the uncle of Mrs. T.B. Brown, and Rev. E. Smith, and was himself the last of a family of ten children, born and reared in Durham, Connecticut. While in his youth, he went to Fishkill, Dutchess county, in this State, and engaged in teaching, where he resided for more than forty years. He has been a professed follower of the Savior for some sixty years; a part of the time a member of the Reformed Church of Fishkill Landing, and later a member of the Second Presbyterian Church in Auburn (Dr. Boardman's). His funeral was attended at the place of his late residence, No. 19 Grover street, at 10 o'clock, Tuesday morning, 26th, after which his remains were taken to Moravia for interment in the cemetery where reposes the dust of many of his kindred. -*Auburn Journal*.

0426   Died at Sprout Creek, January 27th, Mrs. Elizabeth
      Van Voorhis, aged 79 years.

0427   Died near Fishkill Village, January 30th, Sarah, wife of
      Joseph Wood, aged 74 years.

SATURDAY, FEBRUARY 13, 1875

0428   The eighty-eighth birthday of the Hon. Gouv. Kemble,
      of Cold Spring, occurred on the twenty-eighth ult., and
was celebrated at his residence.

0429   Mrs. James E. Seamans, mother-in-law of Mr. S.R.
      Vines, Newburgh, died at the residence of the latter, on
Wednesday, at the extreme old age of one hundred years and
six months. She was born near Albany in 1774, and was
remarkably active, having attended a Sunday School picnic last
summer.

0430   Married on Tuesday, February 2d, by Rev. J.L. Scott,
      Mr. Silas Terwilliger, of Matteawan, and Miss Sarah E.
Sutherlin, of Newburgh.

0431   Died in Fishkill Landing, February 11th, Ellen, widow
      of the late Alfred Gerow, aged 62 years. Relatives and
friends of the family are invited to the funeral on Saturday,
February 13th, at 3 o'clock, from the Reformed Church.

0432   Died near Fishkill Landing, February 5th, John B., son
      of James A. and Elizabeth Hall, aged 21 years.

0433   Died near Stormville, February 2d, George Wright,
      aged 70 years.

SATURDAY, FEBRUARY 20, 1875

0434   Married at the house of the bride's father, February
        18th, by Rev. J.L. Scott, Mr. Charles Dickinson, of
Saint Andrews, Orange county, N.Y., to Miss Maggie A. Van
Houten, of Matteawan.

0435   Died at Fishkill Landing, February 17th, the infant son
        of Dr. C.K. and Jennie Barlow, aged 5 weeks.

SATURDAY, FEBRUARY 27, 1875

0436   Ezra Farrington, postmaster of Newburgh, died of
        apoplexy, on Thursday night.

0437   Captain Valentine C. Nye, an old North River captain,
        died at Hudson on Monday, aged 67 years.

0438   Rev. Stephen D. Brown, last Presiding Elder of the
        New York District of the New York Conference of the
Methodist Episcopal Church, and one of the most eminent
divines of that denomination, died on Friday of last week, aged
59 years, at his residence in New York. He had been suffering
for some time past with a severe cold, which finally assumed
the more dangerous form of pneumonia.

0439   The startling intelligence of the sudden death of Mr.
        James Wade, at Ogdensburgh, on Sunday evening, fell
like a flash from a clear sky, on our community. He had so
lately been among us, in perfect health, and was so robust. His
remains were brought here for interment, the funeral services
taking place at St. Luke's Church on Friday noon.
    Mr. Wade came to Ogdensburgh from Burlington in April,
1851, and engaged in the flour, grain and western products

67

trade. A few years after coming here, he also engaged in the vessel trade, and was whole or part owner of the fine schooners *Adirondack, Dashing Wave* and *James Wade*. To know him was to respect him.

Last Wednesday he complained of a bad cold; Friday he was confined to his room, and Saturday he took to his bed. Mrs. Wade was notified of his serious illness on Saturday and expected to return Sunday night, about the time Mr. W. expired. His son Ralph, who had only just recovered from a similar attack, was present at the time of his death.

0440   On Sunday night last, Frederick Terry, 23 years of age, who lived just below Dutchess Junction, stabbed himself with a penknife, making a mortal wound. He had been ill for some weeks with inflammation of the bowels, but was supposed to be in a fair way to recover. Sunday night, however, being made partially delirious with his pain, he took his penknife, thrust the blade into his left side just below the heart, and pushed it in until the entire knife disappeared from view. His attempt was not discovered until the next morning, but the knife could not be reached. He was conscious, and explained how and why he did it. Terry was unmarried and has been employed in the brickyard of Budd & Terry, the latter being a brother. He died on Tuesday, and was buried on Thursday.

0441   Married at Johnsville, February 4th, at the residence of the officiating Justice, by John M. Tompkins, Esq., Mr. William R. Heady to Mrs. Emalinda Williams, all of the above place.

0442   Married at Bellvale, Orange county, N.Y., February 22d, by the Rev. Mr. E. Rude, Mr. George A. Member, of Kingston, N.Y., to Mrs. Sarah J. Flagler, of Bellvale.

0443   Married at the residence of the bride's parents,
          Haverstraw, February 24th, by the Rev. O.V.
Amerman, Mr. W.H. Aldridge, of Fishkill Landing, to Miss
Lizzie Blair, of the former place.

0444   Married at Hopewell, N.Y., February 23d, by the Rev.
          Graham Taylor, James H. Ashby to Maria S. Rogers,
both of Poughquag, N.Y.

0445   Died at Ogdensburgh, N.Y., Sunday evening, February
          21st, of pneumonia, Mr. James Wade, of this village,
aged 57 years.

0446   Died at Fishkill Plains, February 15th, Edgar Wygant,
          aged 30 years.

0447   Died in Newburgh, February 24th, Cicero A. Gardiner,
          aged 66 years, 8 months and 12 days.

SATURDAY, MARCH 6, 1875

0448   The oldest man ever in the town of Fishkill, has had his
          memory kept green by a record on a silver communion
pitcher, as follows: Presented by Samuel Ver Planck, Esq., in
the town of Fishkill, to commemorate Mr. Eglebert Huff, by
birth a Norwegian, in his lifetime attached to the Life Guards
of the Prince of Orange, (afterward King William III of
England). He resided for a number of years in this county and
died with unblemished reputation at Fishkill, 21 March 1765,
aged ONE HUNDRED AND TWENTY-EIGHT YEARS.
—Fishkill, January, 1820

0449   On Friday afternoon of last week, conductor John A.
          Noble, of the Dutchess and Columbia Railroad, met

with his death in a sudden and fearful manner. He was in charge of a special freight train between Dutchess Junction and Glenham. Mr. Noble was on top of a boxcar, walking toward the rear of the train, which was going north. Just as he was about to let himself down to the platform of the car, his head came in contact with the Walcott bridge, and he was knocked off to the platform, and fell thence to the road-bed, between the cars. Mr. Noble had been connected with the road for about a year and a half, and resided at Matteawan. His funeral took place in the M.E. Church of that village, on Sunday afternoon. His remains were taken to Bordentown, N.J., for interment. He leaves a wife and three small children.

0450 Henry A. Green has been appointed by Congressman James O. Whitehouse, to fill a vacancy at the Military Academy at West Point. He is the young man who has been assistant at the Howland Library. His father is Edgar Green, a machinist employed, we believe, in Schenck's shop.

0451 Died at Fishkill Landing, March 1st, Mrs. Rose Ann McCormick, mother of Mrs. George Peattie, aged 95 years.

0452 Died at Fishkill Landing, February 27th, Griffin N. Snook, aged 52 years.

0453 Died at Matteawan, February 26th, John A. Noble, aged 37 years and 8 months.

SATURDAY, MARCH 13, 1875

0454 Mr. John Boyce has passed away. He was a native of this county. For a time he was a teacher and had charge of public schools. Then he went to the great metropolis, and became a successful merchant; and was elected an Alderman. He returned to his community more than twenty years ago, retiring from business; for some years he was a member of the Board of Education in Matteawan. His funeral took place on Tuesday, at 1:30 p.m., at his late residence. His remains were placed in the family vault in the Reformed Church yard in this village.

0455   A few weeks since, Dr. John Kenworthy, formerly of Poughkeepsie, and brother of ex-Sheriff Kenworthy, was married to Mrs. Mary L. Paxton, Matron of the Oregon Insane Asylum, of which institution the bridegroom is Superintendent.

0456   The death of Gilbert T. Bush removes another of our old and respected citizens. Mr. Bush was born in Fishkill, and came to this city, which was then a small village, in 1812, and learned the trade of shoemaker with Mr. Edmund Morris. In 1840 he was Under Sheriff under Josiah Burritt, and also under Mr. Thomas N. Perry. Two years since he was partially prostrated by a stroke of paralysis, and has gradually declined from that time until last evening, when he died. He was the father of John H. Bush. -*Poughkeepsie News.*

0457   Married Wednesday, March 3d, by Rev. Henry Ward, Austin T. Fink, M.D., of LaGrange, to Libbie E., daughter of the late John C. Pudney, of Poughkeepsie town.

0458   Married at Binghamton, N.Y., February 25th, by the Rev. Dr. Paddock, Mr. John A. Rider to Miss Ella M., Ingraham, all of Binghamton.

0459   Died in Matteawan, March 11th, Edith, infant daughter of Edward and Emma Hyson, aged 1 year and 2 months. Relatives and friends of the family are invited to attend the funeral on Saturday, March 13th, at 3 o'clock, from the residence of her parents.

0460   Died at Matteawan, March 5th, George E. Darling, aged 85 years.

0461   Died at Matteawan, March 6th, John Boyce, aged 75 years and 10   months.

0462   Died at Fishkill Landing, March 6th, Patrick Costello, aged 55 years.

0463   Died at Centropolis, Franklin county, Kansas, February 20th, in the 55th year of her age, Mary Ann, wife of the Hon. George T. Pierce, and daughter of the late Judge Jackson, of Fishkill.

0464   Died in Fishkill Landing, March 9th, Helen, widow of the late Henry Churchill, aged 76 years.

0465   Died in Fishkill Village, March 6th, Caroline, wife of James A. Van Nostrand, in the 64th year of her age.

0466   Died at Hampton, Orange county, March 6th, Helen J., wife of DeWitt H. Van Nostrand, aged 37 years.

SATURDAY, MARCH 20, 1875

0467   Rev. H.E. Duncan's youngest daughter died early on Thursday morning, at Newburgh. The interment took place at Matteawan, on Friday afternoon.

0468   Theodore Davies died in this city yesterday at the

residence of his father, ex-Judge Henry E. Davies. He was in
the twenty-eighth year only, and death cut short a career whose
promise was great and whose work thus far indicated a future
growth and development not at all common. He was just
beginning to be known by reputation to popular readers. -*New
York World*, Tuesday, March 16.

0469   Married in Newburgh, March 10th, by the Rev. W.
            Prime, Mr. L.E. Aldridge, of Fishkill on the Hudson, to
Mrs. Jeannette Gould, of Newburgh.

0470   Married at the house of Mr. Joseph Metcalf, in
            Matteawan, March 16th, by Rev. J.L. Scott, Mr.
William H. Surrine, of Carthage Landing, to Mrs. Martha
Aberoyed [sic], of the same place.

0471   Died in East Fishkill, near Hoyt's Mill, March 11th,
            Sarah, wife of Redmond Ashby, aged 57 years.

0472   Died at Matteawan, March 13th, Deborah Ann, widow
            of George Waldron, aged 23 years.

0473   Died at Arthursburgh, March 14th, Mary F., child of
            William H. Gifford, aged 7 months and 3 days.

0474   Died at Glenham, March 15th, Jane A., child of George
            Mann, aged 2 months and 16 days.

0475   Died in Newburgh, March 14th, Willie F. Cameron, Jr.,
            son of William F. and Hannah C. Cameron, aged 9
years and 6 months.

0476   Died in Matteawan, March 17th, Almira, wife of
            George McCreary, aged 29 years and 6 months.

0477   Died in New York city, March 15th, Theodore Davies,
     son of Henry E. and Rebecca W. Davies, in the 28th
year of his age. His remains were brought to this village and
placed in a vault on Wednesday.

0478   Died at Hyde Park, March 17th, Susan E. Dorland,
     youngest daughter of Adrian and Pauline Dorland, aged
27 years, 10 months and 14 days.

0479   Died in Newburgh, Thursday, March 18th, at 1
     o'clock, a.m., Edith, youngest daughter of Rev. Henry
E. and Catharine B. Duncan.

SATURDAY, MARCH 27, 1875

0480   Dr. Richard A. Varick, late of Poughkeepsie, was a
     shareholder in the Tontine Association.

0481   Mr. G.H. Carswell, formerly principal of a select school
     in this village, but of late years residing at Highland
Falls, died in Jersey City on Sunday last, aged 47 years. The
funeral and interment took place at Highland Falls on
Wednesday. Mr. Carswell was a good teacher and an excellent
citizen, and his death will be sincerely regretted by many.

0482   Died in Matteawan, March 20th, Edwin I., son of the
     late Joseph H. and Sarah I. Northrop, aged 5 years and
6 months.

0483   Died in Jersey City, N.J., on Sunday, March 21st, G.H.
     Carswell, of Cornwall, N.Y., aged 47 years.

0484   Died in Fishkill Village, March 23d, Mrs. Elias Sutton,
     aged 71 years.

0485 Died at Arthursburgh, February 21st, Daniel W. Odell, aged 54 years.

0486 Died in Matteawan, March 24th, Addie Knapp, aged 20 years and 4 months. Relatives and friends of the family are invited to attend the funeral on Saturday, at 4 o'clock, from St. Luke's Church.

0487 Died at Dover Plains, January 29th, of scarlet fever and congestion of the brain, after an illness of only 17 hours, Norris E., youngest child of Lafayette and Mary E. McFarlin, aged 5 years, 2 months and 29 days.

SATURDAY, APRIL 3, 1875

0488 Married on Wednesday, March 24th, at the residence of Mr. William Barber, New York city, by the Rev. F.B. Van Kleeck, Rector of Grace Church, White Plains, N.Y., James C. Teller to Clara E. Losee, both of Ulster county.

0489 Died at Matteawan, March 27th, Isabella R. Burnett, wife of Walter Forbes, aged 30 years and 3 months.

0490 Died at Brooklyn, on Thursday, April 1st, Mrs. Jane A., widow of Robert Lawrence, and daughter of the late Abraham H. Schenck, in the 76th year of her age. Her remains will be interred here, on Saturday afternoon, April 3d, at 4 ½ o'clock.

SATURDAY, APRIL 10, 1875

0491 Fishkill Village was greatly excited on Saturday evening by the suicide of John Erwin, a lad about 18 years of age, drug clerk in the store of William B. Hayt. The boy had been accused by Mr. Hayt of purloining some dry goods, which were discovered in his trunk. Mr. James Erwin, the boy's father, came from Newburgh to settle the matter. The boy was later discovered to have taken opium or morphine, and he could not be revived. The body was taken to Newburgh and interred on Sunday afternoon.

0492   Married at the M.E. Church, Matteawan, N.Y., Wednesday, March 24th, by Rev. C.W. Millard, George H. Bontecon, to Miss Emma Mase.

0493   Married on Wednesday, March 31st, at the M.E. Church, Cold Spring, by the Rev. Mr. Brown, Thomas Whitsour of Newark N.J., to Susie A. Pearce, of Glenham.

0494   Married at Arthursburgh, November 19th, 1874, by Rev. Graham Taylor, George W. Emans, of Lagrangeville, to Miss Libbie, eldest daughter of Jonathan Dorland.

0495   Married at Arthursburgh, February 24th, according to Friends Ceremony, Elias Eighmie, of Beekmanville, to Miss Annie, youngest daughter of Jonathan Dorland.

0496   Married at Beekmanville, March 17th, by Rev. E.H.W. Barden, Francis Emans, of LaGrangeville, to Miss Libbie, youngest daughter of Harvey Eighmie.

0497   Died in Matteawan, April 6th, James Bogardus.

0498   Died in Wiccopee, April 5th, William McNealan, aged 15 years.

0499   Died in Fishkill Landing, April 5th, John Chapman, aged 38 years, 11 months and 5 days.

0500   Died at Glenham, April 1st, Anna A. Richards, in the 32d year of her age.

0501   Died in East Fishkill, March 30th, Catharine, wife of Enoch Shaw, aged 71 years.

0502   Died at Billings, April 5th, Rachel E. Montfort, in the 30th year of her age.

0503   Died in Poughkeepsie, April 3d, Lily, only child of Conrad and Alvira Gutgesell, aged 11 years, 11 months and 14 days.

SATURDAY, APRIL 17, 1875

0504   Married at the Rectory, Glenham, April 10th, by Rev. John R. Livingston, John Cavanaugh to Lucinda Potter, both of Matteawan.

0505   Married at the residence of the bride's father, April 7th, by the Rev. D.L. [sic] Putnam, Mr. Seth K. Winans, of Washington, and Miss Nettie B. Robinson, of Stanford.

SATURDAY, APRIL 24, 1875

0506   Dr. T.B. Smith, a prominent physician and President of Nyack village, died suddenly on Wednesday morning of hemorrhage of the lungs.

0507   Mrs. Catharine Mearns, mother-in-law of the late G.H. Carswell, died at Highland Falls on the 8th inst., in the 91st year of her age. Her husband is still living.

0508 The father of Miss Warner, author of this "Wide, Wide
World", died recently at their home on Constitution
Island, on the Hudson, near West Point. She sent for two
clergymen to conduct the funeral services, but they failed to
come. She therefore knelt down by the coffin and led the
mourners in prayer.

0509 Miss Antoinette Sterling was married in London on
March 28th, to Mr. John McKinley, of New York. The
ceremony was performed in the Chapel Royal. The service was
read by the Rev. Henry White, Chaplain in ordinary to the
Queen, and the bride was given away by Mr. George
Macdonald, at whose house the wedding party was
subsequently received.

Mr. McKinley is a well known resident of Wappingers Falls,
and was formerly organist of Trinity Church, Newburgh. *-N.Y.
Tribune.*

0510 Died in Matteawan, April 19th, Winnie, son of Charles
F. and Lucy Brett, aged 8 months and 15 days.

0511 Died in Fishkill Landing, April 16th, Charles Westlake,
aged 53 years and 8 months.

SATURDAY, MAY 1, 1875

0512 Mr. P.R. Brinckerhoff died at his residence in
Matteawan on Thursday, in the 38th year of his age. He
had been sick all winter.

0513 Charles B. Nash, proprietor of the Columbia Springs
Hotel, Columbia county, committed suicide on
Thursday morning, 23d ult., by cutting one of the veins of his
throat with a pen knife. He had been ill for some time. Mr.

Nash was in his sixty-second year, and had been proprietor of the Columbia White Sulphur Springs for twenty years.

0514   Our Methodist friends particularly will regret to hear of the death of Rev. J.B. Wakeley, the veteran itinerant, who died of pneumonia in New York city, on Tuesday morning. He had been complaining about two weeks. He was sixty-six years of age, and leaves a wife and one daughter. Mr. Wakeley's first appointment was at Salisbury, Conn., in 1833. In 1859-'60 he was pastor of the Hedding Church, Poughkeepsie; in 1866-'68, Presiding Elder of this district; and in 1869-'72, Presiding Elder of the Newburgh district. Last year he was stationed at the Lexington avenue church, New York city, and this year was appointed to the Cold Spring Church.

Rev. Wakeley's reputation as a writer of religious works was quite extended. His funeral took place in New York on Thursday, and he was buried at Sing Sing on Friday.

0515   Died at Matteawan, April 29th, P. Remson Brinckerhoff, son of the late Peter R. Brinckerhoff, of New York city, in his 38th year. Relatives and friends of the family are invited to attend the funeral on Monday, May 3d, at 12 o'clock noon, at St. Luke's Church.

0516   Died in Fishkill Landing, April 29th, Eliza, daughter of William Henry, aged 27 years. Relatives and friends of the family are invited to attend the funeral on Sunday, May 2d, at 3 o'clock, from the Reformed Church.

0517   Died in Matteawan, April 29th, Miss Martha Budd. Relatives and friends of the family are invited to attend the funeral on Sunday, May 2d, at 3 o'clock, from her late residence.

SATURDAY, MAY 8, 1875

0518   P.R. Brinckerhoff was born in Florence, Italy, in 1837, and while yet a child took a severe cold which resulted in the rheumatism that clung to him from his boyhood. Immediately after his marriage in 1867, he came to Fishkill, where the mountain air greatly overcame his disease. Last summer he suffered a partial sun-stroke; then soon after being called to the bedside of his dying father, his constitution appeared to have broken down. — He leaves a wife and three young boys.

0519   Charles Bullock, for over twelve years station agent at Cold Spring, for the Hudson River Railroad, died on Wednesday. Mr. Owen Grady has been appointed agent to fill the vacancy.

0520   It is generally believed that Mr. E. Ball, of Fishkill Village, absconded to get rid of paying his debts. The *Journal* says he disappeared on the 26th of April. He has been ordered by the Court to appear for examination, to show what he has done with the insurance money he received since he was burned out. He is a man about seventy years old, a native of England, and it is believed that he has sailed for that country. Mrs. Ball remained in the village. About ten o'clock on Friday evening last, she went to Fishkill Landing, where she took the cars.

0521   Married on Saturday, May 1st, at the residence of the bride's parents, by Rev. D.C. Hughes, John H. Cunningham and Ella J. Abrams, all of Brooklyn.

0522   Married at the house of the bride, May 6th, by Rev. J.L. Scott, assisted by Rev. A.N. Wyckoff, Mr. George

E. Cross, of Brooklyn, N.Y., to Miss Flora Reynolds, of
Matteawan, N.Y.

SATURDAY, MAY 15, 1875

0523   Mr. William Stotesbury and wife propose to leave for
        California on Monday, 24th inst., to visit a daughter,
Mrs. William Deacon, who resides in San Francisco.

0524   George W. Halliwell, a well-known Poughkeepsie
        jeweler, died on Sunday.

0525   Married by Rev. George Daniels [sic], of Johnsville,
        May 9th, at the residence of the bride's parents,
Gayhead, Mr. Frank M. Robinson to Miss Henrietta Dodge,
both of Fishkill Landing.

0526   Died in New York, May 12th, Mr. Jerome Briggs, aged
        31 years.

0527   Died at Hughsonville, May 12th, Eliza Vermilyea,
        widow of the late Gideon T. Vermilyea, aged 69 years,
9 months and 3 days.

0528   Died at Hopewell, May 10th, John Rapelje, aged 83
        years.

0529   Died at Bangall, May 8th, Peter G. Bullis, in the 50th
        year of his age.

SATURDAY, MAY 22, 1875

0530   Queen Victoria presented Antoinette Sterling, the
        prima donna, with a silver service on the occasion of

81

her marriage in London, recently, to Mr. McKinley, of
Wappingers Falls, this county.

0531　It is stated that Mr. E. Ball, the absconding merchant of
　　　　Fishkill Village, was one of the passengers by the
ill-fated *Schiller*, and was drowned. Letters to this effect have
been received from the old country, by friends at the above
place.

0532　William Chamberlain, of Red Hook, died at his
　　　　residence in that place, on Wednesday, 12th inst., in the
seventy-sixth year of his age. He was a man widely known and
appreciated for his many sterling qualities, and has advanced
the welfare of both the town and county where for the last
quarter of a century his lot has been cast.

0533　Married on Thursday noon, May 20th, at the residence
　　　　of the bride's father, in Matteawan, by the Rev. C.W.
Millard, Miss Mary E. Woolhiser, of Matteawan, N.Y., to Mr.
Edward A. Hulbert, of Chatham.

0534　Married in Newburgh, May 19th, by Rev. W.K. Hall,
　　　　H. Berrien Shaw to H. Isabel, daughter of Daniel
Smith, all of that city.

0535　Married on Wednesday, May 12th, at the residence of
　　　　the bride's parents, at Red Bank, N.J., by the ceremony
of the Society of Friends, Justus E. Ralph to Hannah Virginia
Conover.

0536　Married in the Washington street M.E. Church,
　　　　Poughkeepsie, May 19th, by Rev. J.F. McClelland,
John Fuller, of Matteawan, and Miss Dora Butler [sic], of
Tioronda.

SATURDAY, MAY 29, 1875

0537   Married on Thursday, 27th inst., at the residence of the bride's parents, Fishkill, by Rev. P.M. Kip, William J. Conklin, M.D., to Etta B. Walcott, all of Fishkill. No cards.

0538   Married in the Washington street M.E. Church, Poughkeepsie, May 19th, by Rev. J.F. McClelland, John Fuller, of Matteawan, and Miss Dora Baker [sic], of Tioronda.

0539   Died at Fishkill Landing, May 28th, Jennie Maud, daughter of Sarah M. and Joseph Quick, aged 3 years and 7 months.

0540   Died in Fishkill Landing, May 25th, Charles L. Halstead, aged 22 years.

0541   Died at East Fishkill, May 26th, Daniel Bull, in the 77th year of his age. Funeral from his late residence on Saturday, 29th inst., at 2 o'clock p.m.

0542   Died in Poughkeepsie, May 24th, Richard D.C. Stoutenburgh, in the 78th year of his age.

SATURDAY, JUNE 5, 1875

0543   Thomas D. Sherwood, brother of Isaac Sherwood, of Fishkill Village, and a Police Justice of New York city, died on the 25th ult.

0544   Married on Thursday, June 3d, at the residence of the bride's parents, by the Rev. Charles W. Fritts, Cyrus Patton, of Newburgh, to Mrs. Kate Mosher, daughter of M.D.

Lonsberry, of Fishkill Landing.

0545 Married on Thursday, June 3d, at the residence of the
bride's parents, at Carthage Landing, by the Rev.
Charles W. Fritts, Thomas Aldridge, Jr., to Mary A. Van Cott,
daughter of W.H. Van Cott.

0546 Married at Matteawan, March 30th, by the Rev. C.W.
Millard, Mr. Willard I. Barton to Miss Mary E.
Birdsall, all of Nelsonville.

0547 Died in Matteawan, May 30th, Emmet, son of Ebenezer
and Tamer Ticehurst, aged 6 years and 4 months.

SATURDAY, JUNE 12, 1875

0548 Louis M. Fouquet, brother of J.D. Fouquet, of Fishkill
Village, died at Plattsburgh, on the 26th ult.

0549 Hon. Stephen Baker, of Hyde Park, Member of
Congress from this district in 1861, died on the Pacific
Railroad, near Odgen, on Wednesday, while on his way to visit
a son in California.

0550 Moses George, of Dansville, in this state, a veteran of
the war of 1812, over eighty years of age, recently
extracted from his groin a bullet which was buried there by the
rifle of an Indian, at the battle of Chippewa, on the 5th day of
July, 1815. He now carries it in his vest pocket, which he
considers a more comfortable way than the other.

0551 The Rev. Thomas T. Farrington, pastor of the
Associate Reformed Church, of Newburgh, dropped
dead at his residence last Saturday afternoon, of heart disease.

He was a brother of Postmaster Ezra Farrington, who died as suddenly, about three months ago. Mr. Farrington was fifty-four year old, and had filled pastorates in Geneva, Salem, and Oxbow, and has been pastor of the Newburgh church eleven years.

0552   An interesting family gathering met at the house of Mr. John Rothery, Matteawan, on Saturday evening of last week, to celebrate the 75th birthday of Mrs. Rothery, widow of the late John Rothery, and mother of John and William Rothery, present owners of the Matteawan File Works.

0553   Married on Monday, May 31st, at Newburgh, Amos Jones, of Fishkill Landing, to Ida Robinson, daughter of Mrs. Mary E. Robinson, of Matteawan.

0554   Died, Mrs. Catharine Corwin, widow of David Wells Corwin, aged 87 years. The funeral will take place from the residence of Mr. W.H. Mase, June 12th, at three o'clock, p.m. The friends of the family are invited to attend without further notice. Orange county papers please copy. -Matteawan, June 10th, 1875.

0555   Died in Fishkill Landing, June 5th, Frank Wood, youngest child of Dr. J. and Mary J. Young, aged 14 months.

0556   Died in Matteawan, June 7th, Freddie, infant son of Cornelius and Nancy Ireland, aged 2 years and 8 months.

85

SATURDAY, JUNE 19, 1875

0557 William Graham, for forty years one of the constables
of this county, died at Poughkeepsie, on Sunday last,
aged seventy-eight years.

0558 Rev. Dr. Van Cleef, of Poughkeepsie, a prominent
clergyman of the Reformed Church, formerly pastor of
the church at New Hackensack, died on Sunday last, aged
seventy-six years.

0559 Joseph Albertson, a veteran of the war of 1812, died at
the residence of his daughter, in Newark, N.J., on the
8th instant, in the eighty-third year of his age. He was born in
Newburgh, and was for many years a prominent citizen of that
place, but for the last thirty-five years he had resided in the city
of New York.

0560 The *Amenia Times* says that Mrs. Fitzgerald, of that
town, is one hundred and two years of age. She
possesses all her faculties in a remarkable degree. She lives
about half a mile from Wassaic, on the mountain. On
Wednesday we met her on the train, on her way to Dover, to
visit the grave of her son, having walked from her mountain
home to the
depot at Wassaic.

0561 Married at Matteawan, June 9th, by the Rev. J.L. Scott,
Mr. Samuel J. Barrett, of Peekskill, and Miss Hattie D.
Denike, of Matteawan.

0562 Married April 30th, at the residence of the bride's
brother-in-law, William H. Odell, by Nathaniel
Ormsbee, Justice of the Peace, Benjamin I. Cole, of

86

Wappingers Falls, to Lydia J. Higgs, of Fishkill.

0563   Married June 10th, by Rev. O.H. Hazard, Orren T. Van
       Tine to Rachel A. Burnett, both of Freedom Plains.

0564   Married in the First Reformed Church, Poughkeepsie,
       June 16th, by Rev. Dr. Van Giesen, Prof. Nathan
Barrows and Etta Knapp, daughter of Chauncey Knapp, all of
that city.

0565   Died in Matteawan, June 18th, Harry, son of Salethiel
       and Harriet Hyatt, aged 3 years and 5 months. Relatives
and friends of the family are invited to attend the funeral on
Saturday, June 19th, at 3 o'clock, from the M.E. Church,
Matteawan.

0566   Died in Worcester, Massachusetts, June 14th, Ellen,
       wife of William Smith, aged 36 years, a native of
England.

0567   Died in East Fishkill, June 14th, Lemuel Wixon, aged
69 years.

0568   Died in East Fishkill, June 16th, George Bowne.

0569   Died at Baltimore, June 13th, Charlie, only child of
       Charles S. and Hannah E. Read, aged 11 months and
13 days.

SATURDAY, JUNE 26, 1875

0570   Mr. I.C. [sic] Wood, of the firm of Burrows & Wood,
       nurserymen, Fishkill Village, has took unto himself a
better half, from over the Canadian border. Much joy.

87

0571   Mr. and Mrs. Sherwood, of Morristown, N.J., have
        been summoned to the bedside of their daughter, who
has been lying very sick for some days at their brother-in-law's,
Dr. Mapes, in this village.

0572   Married on Wednesday, June 16th, at the residence of
        the bride's uncle, Thomas Nugent, London, Ontario, by
the Rev. D. Camelon, of St. James, Isaac Secor Wood, of
Fishkill, N.Y., to Emma A., daughter of John Morgan, Esq., of
Monticello, Iowa.

0573   Died in Matteawan, June 24th, Hannah Ireland, aged 18
        years and 6 months. Relatives and friends of the family
are invited to attend the funeral on Saturday, June 26th, at 3
o'clock, from the M.E. Church, Matteawan.

0574   Died in Newburgh, June 23d, William I. Allen, formerly
        of Fishkill, in the 70th year of his age.

0575   Died at Hopewell, June 22d, Abraham Adriance, aged
        64 years.

SATURDAY, JULY 3, 1875

0576   Married at Fishkill Landing, by Rev. Philip Germond,
        June 17th, Millard Ackert, of Rhinebeck, N.Y., and
Miss Carrie W. Snook, of the former place.

0577   Married June 30th, at the M.E. Parsonage, Matteawan,
        by Rev. C.W. Millard, Miss Anna W. Dorr to Mr.
Frederick Ives, both of Matteawan.

0578   Married on Sunday, May 9th, in Glenham, at the
        rectory of the Free Church of St. John Baptist, by the

Rev. J.R. Livingston, A.H. Yates to Miss C.E. Phesay, both of Matteawan.

0579 Married at East Fishkill, May 31st, at the residence of J.M. Tompkins, Justice of the Peace, Thomas Soden to Lavina Ferris, both of Fishkill.

0580 Married June 5th, at the Church of the American College, Rome, Italy, by the Very. Rev. F.S. Chatard, D.D., M. Henri Mathias Vincent, of Paris, France, Member of the Cabinet at Versailles, to Elizabeth, daughter of Dennis Crimmins, of LaGrange, Dutchess county, N.Y.

0581 Died at Pawling, Dutchess county, N.Y., June 22d, Jonathan Akin, in the 84th year of his age.

0582 Died in Poughkeepsie, June 29th, Maggie E. Velie, aged 27 years, wife of George A. Velie.

0583 Died at Union Vale, June 20th, Hubert Emigh, aged 30 years.

0584 Died at Phillipstown, June 25th, Mary Hester, daughter of James and Emeline F. Knapp, aged 18 years.

0585 Died near Hughsonville, June 25th, Olivia A., widow of Ezekiel Scofield, aged 33 years.

0586 Died at Phillipstown, June 28th, Philena, wife of William Knapp, aged 41 years.

0587 Died at Middlebush, on Friday, June 18th, Mary C. Livingston, youngest daughter of A.M. Livingston, aged 8 years.

0588   Died at Wappingers Falls, June 23d, Joanna, wife of Charles Norris, aged 20 years.

SATURDAY, JULY 10, 1875

0589   Married at St. Luke's Church, Matteawan, on Wednesday, June 30th, by Rev. Edward T. Bartlett, Mr. Peyton F. Miller, of Albany, N.Y., to Miss Catharine H., daughter of Mr. S.T. Van Buren, of Fishkill Landing.

0590   Married at Matteawan, July 3d, by Justice Ormsbee, Marcus Mackey, of Croton Valley, Putnam county, N.Y., to Susie Lovett, of Poughkeepsie.

0591   Died in Matteawan, July 2d, Lillian, infant daughter of Eugene and Melissa Smith, aged 2 years, 4 months and 17 days.

0592   Died at Corning, N.Y., on the 6th inst., Daniel D. Rogers, formerly of Matteawan, aged 47 years.

0593   Died at his residence, near Wappingers Falls, July 3d, Dr. William Baxter, aged 70 years.

0594   Died near Myers Corners, June 26, Edward Scofield, aged 69 years.

0595   Died in New York city, June 27, Henry Hughson, aged 84 years.

SATURDAY, JULY 17, 1875

0596   The wife of Leon Pralatowski was arrested, charged with assault and battery on her husband, and threatening his life. After an examination by competent physicians, she was adjudged insane and sent to the Hudson River Hospital at Poughkeepsie.

0597   On Wednesday, Frank Van Voorhis, a youth rising
            thirteen years of age, an adopted son of William Henry
Van Voorhis - his father, Henry S. Lester, brother of Thomas
S. Lester, of this village, having died in St. Louis some eight
years ago - was arrested for stealing a double-barreled shot
gun, game bag, etc., worth seventy-five dollars, and sent to the
House of Refuge on Randall's Island, where he will have to
stay for an indefinite time.

0598   Died in Fishkill Hook, July 1st, Rachel Jerls, in the 90th
            year of her age.

0599   Died at New Hamburgh, on Saturday, July 3d, Henry
            T. Smith, aged 54 years, of pneumonia.

SATURDAY, JULY 24, 1875

0600   Mrs. Harriet Bayard Van Rensselaer, widow of General
            Stephen Van Rensselaer, died at the manor house,
Albany, N.Y., on the 19th inst., aged seventy-six years.

0601   David Rider, formerly of Matteawan, died at the
            residence of his father, in Amenia, last Saturday. His
remains were taken to Bangall for interment, and the funeral
was attended by a delegation of Hudson River Lodge, No. 57,
Knights of Pythias, of Matteawan, of which lodge he was a
member, and according to the rites of which order he was
buried.

0602   We have in our own village, a colored woman, Aunt

91

Katy Reynolds, as she is generally called, who is 106 years of age, having been born in the West Indies in the year 1760. Mr. Van Buren, census enumerator, assures us her age is well established by documentary evidence.

0603   Died at Fishkill Landing, July 16th, James Edward, infant son of Edward J. and Mary F. Member, aged 1 year and 8 days.

0604   Died at Matteawan, July 17th, Ida Slidders, aged 18 years.

0605   Died at Matteawan, July 19th, Mary, wife of John Druhan, aged 34 years.

0606   Died at Millbrook, July 19th, Lillian F., infant daughter of Frank and Mary Welling, aged 4 months and 2 days.

0607   Died at Brooklyn, N.Y., July 3d, 1975, after a long illness, Margaretta, wife of Edgar F. Peck, M.D., and daughter of the late Rev. John F. Jackson, of Harlem, N.Y., aged 66 years.

SATURDAY, JULY 31, 1875

0608   Mr. James Higgins went to Port Jervis on Wednesday, and died there on Friday, at 1 a.m. His funeral will take place at Port Jervis on Monday, at 1 p.m., at the residence of his father-in-law, Mr. Darragh, which relatives and friends are invited to attend.

0609   Married at the M.E. Parsonage, Fishkill Village, July 17th, by Rev. W.F. Brush, Jacob Ireland to Mary L. Warren, both of Phillipstown.

0610   Married at the house of the bride, in East Fishkill, July
       4th, by John M. Tompkins, Justice of the Peace, Mr.
John Lockwood to Miss Theda Smith.

0611   Died in Newburgh, July 23d, Ellen A., wife of Rev.
       William H. Gleason, in the 38th year of her age.

0612   Died at Stanfordville, July 23d, Philip G. Dorland, in
       the 54th year of his age.

0613   Died at Johnsville, July 27th, Nettie [sic], wife of
       Dewitt C. Connover [sic], aged 24 years.

0614   Died at Middletown, July 27th, of cholera infantum,
       Virginia A., infant daughter of M.A. and Virginia Brett.

SATURDAY, AUGUST 7, 1875

0615   We announced last week the sudden death of Mr.
       James Higgins, of this village, which took place at Port
Jervis, Orange county, on Friday of last week. Mr. Higgins had
been sick for a long time, but had remained at his business until
some two or three months ago. Since that time he has remained
at home most of the time. On Wednesday he started for Port
Jervis against the remonstrance of his friends, and upon
arriving at the house of his relatives, complained of being very
tired. Shortly afterward he went to bed, and gradually sank
until death closed his mortal career. He was a member of
Beacon Lodge, F. & A.M., and a committee from the same
attended the funeral. Mr. Higgins was about 42 years of age, a
cabinet maker by trade. He leaves a wife and several children.

0616   Married July 25th, in the town of Warwick, by Rev.
       Mr. Spears, Ephriam Cherry, of Fishkill, N.Y., to Mrs.

93

Mary Ann Wood, of Vernon, N.J.

0617   Died at Fishkill Landing, August 4th, Wilber, son of
James A. and Alida Hopper, aged 11 months and 12
days.

0618   Died at Matteawan, N.Y., July 25th, of cholera
infantum, Effie, infant daughter of John W. and Sarah
M. Donald, aged 4 months and 22 days. Orange county papers
please copy.

0619   Died in Matteawan, July 31st, George McCreary, aged
40 years.

0620   Died at his residence, in Newburgh, July 31st, John
Robinson, formerly of Matteawan, aged 63 years.

0621   Died at Glenham, August 1st, Sarah, wife of James
Morse, aged 51 years.

0622   Died at Poughkeepsie, August 3d, Charles Odell, aged
55 years.

0623   Died in Albany, N.Y., August 2d, of diphtheria, Mary
Louisa, daughter
of E. Augustus and Mary C. Brett, aged 7 years and 3
months.

0624   Died in Beekman, July 31st, Miss Pamelia [sic],
daughter of Nicholas and Hannah German.

0625   Died in Louisville, Ky., August 1st, at the residence of
his son-in-law, W.H. Wiltsie, Abraham Tomlinson,
formerly of Dutchess county, aged 69 years.

SATURDAY, AUGUST 14, 1875

0626   Another of our old residents has passed away, Mr.
Felix Shurter. He passed quietly away on Friday
evening of last week, at the advanced age of ninety years, at
the residence of his son, Mr. James E. Shurter. His
funeral took place on Monday. For over fifty years he was a
worthy and consistent member of the Methodist Episcopal
Church. For the last fifteen years, Mr. Shurter has resided with
his son in this village. He was born in Orange county, but in
early life came to Low Point, where he was married and
resided nearly all his life. He had several sons and daughters,
two of the sons having become ministers of the Gospel. He has
a younger brother still living in Poughkeepsie, Mr. Isaac
Shurter, who attended the funeral.

0627   Married at the Free Church of St. John Baptist,
Glenham, by Rev. John R. Livingston, on August 11th,
Robert Lowery to Jane Livingstone [sic], both of Glenham.

0628   Died at Fishkill Landing, August 6th, at the residence
of his son, Mr. Felix Shurter, aged 90 years.

0629   Died in Matteawan, August 9th, Eugene McArdle,
aged 19 years, 1 month and 19 days.

0630   Died at Fishkill, August 8th, Adrianna, daughter of
Harvey and Jane A. Rozell, aged 24 years.

0631   Died at Peekskill, August 8th, Mrs. Dorothea
Furguson, aged 66 years, daughter of Levi Owen,
deceased.

0632   Died in LaGrange, August 10th, of diphtheria, Katie

95

Ethel, youngest child of Andrew J. and Abigal [sic] A. Van Kleeck, aged 5 years, 9 months and 2 days.

0633   Died at Spencerport, Monroe county, N.Y., August
6th, Wilkens, Jr., son of Wilkens and Annie Schenck, aged 6 months.

0634   Died at Galveston, Texas, on Sunday, August 8th, Albert Ball, President of the Galveston Insurance Company, aged 64 years.

0635   Died on Saturday, July 10th, on board [a] boat between New Orleans and Cincinnati, Ella Louise, youngest child of W.H. Lyon and Clara M. Sullivan, aged 3 years and 5 months. Remains interred at Cincinnati, Ohio.

SATURDAY, AUGUST 21, 1875

0636   Captain John F. Tallman, a well-known Hudson river steamboat captain, died at Harlem last Saturday morning. He was born at Nyack, and was fifty-nine years of age. He was captain of the *Henry Clay* at the time she was burned near Yonkers, about twenty years ago.

0637   On Wednesday morning, 4th inst., at the old farm house on the Van Vechten place, Jefferson, Greene county, a flagstaff was raised on the cemetery hill. It was the birthday of Rev. Samuel Van Vechten, of East Fishkill, N.Y., who is now in his eightieth year.

0638   Died at Fishkill Landing, August 19th, Ulysses S. G. Sampson, aged 9 years.

0639   Died at Fishkill Landing, August 20th, Albert, son of

George Jones, aged 2 years.

0640   Died in Matteawan, August 18th, Ernest, infant son of
S.H. and H.A. Tillman, aged 1 year and 2 months.

0641   Died at Fishkill, August 15th, of typhoid pneumonia,
Miss Caroline Van Wyck, in the 71st year of her age.

SATURDAY, AUGUST 28, 1875

0642   And now there is another Member of the family.

0643   James B. Hulse, President of the Middletown National
Bank, was thrown from a wagon on Tuesday evening,
and fatally injured.

0644   Married at Fishkill-on-the-Hudson, August 25th, at the
residence of the bride's parents, by the Rev. Edward T.
Bartlett, Charles Leed, of New York, to Susie B. Furman.

0645   Married at Walden, July 27th, by Rev. Mr. Snoden, Mr.
Almond H. Garrison and Mrs. Katie Nunnick, both of
Fishkill Landing.

0646   Died at his residence near New Hamburgh, Rev.
George B. Andrews, D.D., Rector of Eton Church,
Wappingers Falls, aged 90 years.

0647   Died at Johnsville, August 24th, Louisa, infant daughter
of Richard T. and Sarah E. Van Wyck, aged 4 months
and 22 days.

0648   Died in the Town of Washington, Dutchess county,
N.Y., August 18th, Jessie Davis, in the 76th year of his

age.

SATURDAY, SEPTEMBER 4, 1875

0649   The notice of the death of Mrs. J. Hervey Cook, which
we publish this week, will call forth the sympathy of all
who were acquainted with the family. She had not been in
robust health for a long time, and a couple of weeks ago, her
husband and only child accompanied her to her parents' home,
in Waterloo, N.J., where she gradually sank until death
released her, on Thursday of this week.

0650   Married August 21st, at the residence of the bride's
parents, by the Rev. Edward T. Bartlett, Mr. Edmund
G. Taylor to Miss Alice Hughes, both of Fishkill Landing.

0651   Died at Waterloo, N.J., September 2d, 1875, Mrs.
Carrie Smith Cook, wife of James Hervey Cook, of this
village, and daughter of Hon. Peter Smith, of Waterloo, aged
32 years, 5 months and 28 days. Funeral services will be held
today (Saturday), to meet at her father's residence, at 2 ½
p.m., and at the village church at 3 p.m. Friends are invited to
attend without further notice.

0652   Died in Fishkill Landing, September 1st, Lewis, infant
son of Edgar C. and Sarah E. Bloomer, aged 2 years,
11 months and 12 days.

0653   Died at Williston, Vt., August 6th, Oscar A. Ormsbee,
aged 48 years and 7 months.

SATURDAY, SEPTEMBER 11, 1875

0654   Samuel Newcomb, who died at Glenham last week,

98

aged 82 years, was one of the oldest engineers in the United States, and had been in Commodore Vanderbilt's employ for over fifty years.

0655   Hon. John W. Brown, of Newburgh, died at his residence in that city, on Monday morning. He was a Scotchman, having been born at Dundee, October 11th, 1796. His father came to this country five years later, and finally settled in Newburgh. The son studied law, and was admitted to the bar in 1818. In 1824, and for three years, he was Colonel of the Nineteenth Regiment. In 1832 he was first elected to Congress. He was a member of the Constitutional Convention of this State in 1846. In 1849 he was elected Justice of the Supreme Court, and occupied that position for sixteen years in all.

0656   Married by C.W. Millard, on the evening of September 4th, at the parsonage of the Matteawan M.E. Church, Dewitt Clinton Smith, and Mary Eliza Smith [sic], both of Fishkill-on-the-Hudson.

0657   Died at Fishkill Landing, on Sunday, September 5th, Miss Charlotte A. Rumsey, daughter of the late Dr. J.S. Rumsey.

0658   Died in Matteawan, September 6th, Charlotte, daughter of William H. and Mary A. Miller, aged 15 years, 4 months and 12 days.

0659   Died at Montclair, N.J., on Sunday, September 5th, Christiner [sic], wife of John W. Sandford, aged 63 years, formerly of Matteawan.

0660   Died at Glenham, September 2d, at the residence of

R.P. Newcomb, Samuel Newcomb, aged 82 years.

0661 Died near Fishkill Village, September 2d, Hubert C.,
child of James H. and Jane Knapp, aged 1 month and
14 days.

SATURDAY, SEPTEMBER 18, 1875

0662 Married on Tuesday, September 14th, by the Rev. F.
Kratz, at Matteawan, Mr. John O. Ladue to Miss
Josephine Williams, both of Matteawan.

0663 Married by C.W. Millard, on the evening of September
4th, at the parsonage of the Matteawan M.E. Church,
Dewitt Clinton Smith and Mary Eliza Lucas, both of
Fishkill-on-the-Hudson.

0664 Married September 12th, in the Free Church of St. John
Baptist, Glenham, by Rev. J.R. Livingston, Francis
Edward Williamson to Mary Wilson; both of Wappingers Falls.

0665 Married in Fishkill Village, August 26th, by Rev. W.F.
Brush Fillmore Hawks to Mary J. Ireland; both of Cold
Spring.

0666 Died on Thursday, September 9th, in the Town of
LaGrange, Susan A., daughter of John and Phebe
Fraleigh, aged 32 years, 11 months and 25 days.

0667 Died at Hopewell, September 12th, Catharine, wife of
Patrick Burns, aged 36 years.

SATURDAY, SEPTEMBER 25, 1875

0668   Rev. Philip Germond and wife, the former Miss Emma
        Croft, have gone on a tour of Niagara, Canada, and
some of the Eastern States.

0669   Hon. Gouverneur Kemble died at this residence in Cold
        Spring, on Thursday morning of last week, in the
ninetieth year of his age. The *Cold Spring Recorder* says: "Mr.
Kemble was born in the city of New York, January 25th, 1786.
He was the son of Peter Kemble, of the mercantile firm of
Gouverneur and Kemble. His graduation from Columbia
College took place in 1803, after which he traveled in Europe,
spending much time in Spain. About fifty years ago, he was
foremost in instituting the West Point Foundry." He was the
representative in congress for two terms, 1837-41, and a
member of the constitutional convention of 1846.

0670   Married at Washingtonville, N.Y., on Thursday,
        September 23d, by Rev. Joel Croft, at the residence of
the bride's parents, Rev. Philip
Germond, of this village, to Miss Emma Place Croft, daughter
of the officiating clergyman.

0671   Married in Fishkill Village, September 20th, by Rev.
        W.F. Brush, Edwin Howe, of Hughsonville, to
Francena Van Nosdall, of Wappingers Falls.

0672   Married on Thursday, September 16th, at the residence
        of Joseph A. Slauson, at Dwight, Ill., by Rev. M.M.
Longley, William R. Clark, of Piqua, O., to Julia A., daughter
of the late Seely Slauson, of Fishkill, N.Y.

0673   Died at Matteawan, September 18th, Chloe, wife of

101

Samuel H. Bryant, aged 63 years.

SATURDAY, OCTOBER 2, 1875

0674   Mr. Henry B. Alden, son of Mr. Henry A. Alden,
President of the N.Y. Rubber Company, was
accidentally shot in the leg while out gunning, on Thursday
morning. Amputation was necessary to save his life, but about
half-past five in the afternoon, the young man was dead. He
had been hunting with Mr. George B. [sic] Kittredge, brother
of Dr. C.M. Kittredge.

Mr. Alden's mother, uncle and other relatives were present
during his final hour. His wife had also arrived, but was not
admitted to the room. Mr. Alden's father was in New York
city. His brother in law, Mr. George C. Smith, met him at the
six o'clock train, and drove him rapidly to Fishkill Village.

0675   The Verplanck family are one of the oldest and most
honorable of the New York families of Holland origin.
Judge Daniel Crommelin Verplanck was, for many years a
member of congress. He married the daughter of Dr. Johnson,
the first president of Columbia college. His father was Samuel
Verplanck, who was betrothed to his cousin, Judith
Crommelin, when seven years of age. Their grandson, Gulian,
so well known to New York political and social life, entered
Columbia college at age eleven. He served in the state
legislature and was sent to congress. In 1855 he was made
vice-chancellor of the board of regents for the State of New
York.

0676   Married on Wednesday, September 29th, by Rev.
Asher Anderson, at the residence of the bride's father,
Charles D. Cooper to Sarah, daughter of Harvey Rozell; all of
Fishkill.

0677   Married at Rondout, Ulster county, N.Y., September
27th, by Rev. John Steiner (the bride's father), Mr.
Eugene Haight, of Fishkill, to Miss Millie R. Steiner, of
Rondout.

0678   Married at the residence of the bride's parents,
Kingsbury, N.Y., September 21st, by Rev. Edward
Toser, A.M. Uhl, of North Clove, N.Y., to Lottie E., only
daughter of A.R. Crouse.

0679   Married by Friends' Ceremony, at the residence of the
bride's father, Reuben S. Haight, of Millbrook, N.Y.,
Albert F. Swift to Gertrude L. Haight.

0680   Married on September 22d, by Rev. O.H. Hazard, at
Freedom Plains Parsonage, Mr. Hamilton Pray, of
Beekman, to Miss Libbie Gregory, of Union Vale.

0681   Married September 28th, at the residence of the bride's
parents, by Judge Taylor, of Poughkeepsie, Townsend
M. Cole, of LaGrange, N.Y., and Josie E. Bates, of
Mabbettsville, N.Y.

0682   Married in the Town of LaGrange, September 29th, by
the Rev. W.N. Sayre, Samuel D. Hewlett, of Pleasant
Valley, and Augusta Marshall, of LaGrange.

0683   Died suddenly, September 30th, Henry B. Alden, aged
25 years, 7 months and 13 days. Relatives and friends
of the family are invited to attend the funeral on Sunday,
October 3d, at two o'clock, from the residence of his father,
Mr. H.A. Alden.

0684   Died at Byrnesville, September 28th, Mrs. Esther Paye,

aged 73 years.

0685 Died in Poughkeepsie, September 28th, at the residence
of his son, Stephen H. Merritt, Andrew Merritt, of
Washington, Dutchess county, N.Y., in the 59th year of his
age.

0686 Died in Matteawan, September 26th, Lena, daughter of
L.W. Reid, of Hudson.

0687 Died at Stanfordville, July 24th, Philip G. Dorland,
aged 54 years.

0688 Died at Arthursburgh, August 11th, Samuel P.
Dorland, aged 66 years.

0689 Died at Arthursburgh, September 12th, Jane, wife of
Samuel T.[sic] Dorland, aged 50 years old.

0690 Died at Arthursburgh, September 22d, Mary Dorland,
aged 71 years.

0691 Died at Riverton, New Jersey, September 28th, Peter
Van Wyck, aged 85 years.

0692 Died in Fishkill Village, September 27th, Gracie May,
infant daughter of John L. and Maria Kniffen, aged 1
year, 11 months and 20 days.

0693 Died near Fishkill Village, September 27th, Gilbert
Knapp, in the 79th year of his age.

0694 Died at Sylvan Lake, Dutchess county, N.Y., on
Monday, September 27th, Moss Kent, youngest son of

the late Morris M. Davidson, in the 24th year of his age.

0695 Died at Wappingers Falls, on Sunday, September 18th, infant son of John and Elizabeth Cary, aged 1 year and 8 months.

0696 Died in Poughkeepsie, on Tuesday, September 21st, Dr. Milton S. Van Duser, aged 42 years, of typhoid fever.

0697 Died at Moore's Mills, September 22d, Mrs. Rebecca L. Gracey, in the 69th year of her age.

SATURDAY, OCTOBER 9, 1875

0698 Andrew J. Higgs, of Matteawan was struck by a locomotive, while at work at Sing Sing, on Thursday, and was instantly killed. Mr. Higgs was a stonemason by trade, and was in the employ of the Hudson River Railroad. On Thursday he was engaged with a gang of men, in unloading a train of stone, preparing to do some stone work there. Evidently not hearing the approaching train, stepped in front of the morning express, and was caught by the advancing locomotive. Mr. Higgs was 49 years of age, and leaves a wife and five children, one daughter being married, and two of the boys well grown up. He was a member of the Matteawan Methodist Episcopal Church. He served in the late war, having been attached, we believe, to the Nineteenth Regiment.

0699 Rev. J. Millard, father of Rev. C.W. Millard, was on a visit to his son, at Matteawan, a few days ago.

0700 Mr. Henry B. Alden was interred in the Episcopal Cemetery, Matteawan, last Sunday afternoon.

0701   Married October 5th, at the M.E. Parsonage in
        Matteawan, by Rev. C.W. Millard, Eugene Lounsbury
to Sarah M. Milspaugh, both of Matteawan.

0702   Married on Thursday, September 30th, at the residence
        of the bride's father, by Rev. Asher Anderson, A.
Butler Anderson, of Hopewell, N.Y., to Susan, daughter of
Henry Van Wyck, of Fishkill, N.Y.

0703   Married on the 6th, by Rev. Dr. Wheeler, George F.
        Nostrand, of Fishkill, and Miss Hattie E. Smith, of
Moore's Mills.

0704   Married in Fishkill Village, October 2d, by Rev. W.F.
        Bush [sic], Courtland Hawks to Sarah C. Ireland, both
of Cold Spring.

0705   Married September 30th, by Rev. O.H. Hazard, at the
        residence of the bride's parents, Mr. James S. Pettit to
Miss Ella Flagler, daughter of Philip D. Flagler, of LaGrange.

0706   Married in the city of Brooklyn, September 14th, at the
        residence of the bride's parents, by the Rev. R.C.
Putney, James S. Duncan of Fort Union, New Mexico, to Mary
Lomas Wight, of Brooklyn. Newburgh papers, please copy.

0707   Died in Matteawan, October 2d, Ella, daughter of
        William and Harriet Roberts, aged 6 years and 9
months.

0708   Died at Poughkeepsie, October 1st, Charles D.,
        youngest son of John C. and Hannah E. McNeil, aged 9
years and 5 months.

106

0709   Died in Fishkill Landing, October 8th, Mrs. Phœbe
        Garrison, aged 81 years and 11 months. Relatives and
friends of the family are invited to attend the funeral on
Sunday, at 2 o'clock, from the Reformed Church, Fishkill
Landing.

0710   Died October 7th, Andrew J. Higgs, aged 49 years.
        Relatives and friends of the family are invited to attend
the funeral on Sunday, October 10th, at 4 o'clock, from the
M.E. Church, Matteawan.

SATURDAY, OCTOBER 16, 1875

0711   On Thursday, Mr. Thomas S. Dearing, of the National
        Bank of Fishkill, was united in marriage to Miss Mary
G. Smith, of the same village, at the residence of the bride's
parents. There was a large party present to participate in the
festivities of the occasion.

0712   It is befitting that a more detailed obituary should be
        given of the late Andrew J. Higgs to the sympathizing
public. Mr. Higgs enlisted in the summer of 1862, at
Poughkeepsie, in Company K, 150th New York State
Volunteers. He was in military service about two years and ten
months. His first battle was at Gettysburgh. He was disabled
from further active service by hernia after the battle at Dallas,
sent to the hospital, and eventually transferred to the Veteran
Reserve Corps, from which he was discharged by general order
in 1865. At his obsequies last Sunday afternoon, Post
Howland, G.A.R., E. Lewis, Commander, took an active part
in the ceremonies.

0713   Married at Fishkill Village, October 14th, by Rev. A.
        Anderson, at the residence of the bride's parents, Mr.

Thomas S. Dearing and Miss Mary G. Smith, all of the above place.

0714 Married in Newburgh, October 13th, by the Rev.
William K. Hall, James McGibbon, of Glenham, to Mary C. Miller, of Newburgh.

0715 Died at Riverton, N.J., September 28th, Peter S. Van Wyck, in the 86th year of his age. The funeral services were held on Friday, October 1st, in the house in which he was born, Van Wyck Place, Fishkill, and his remains interred in the family vault. He was received into the communion of the Presbyterian church under the pastoral care of Rev. Dr. Scott, in San Francisco, where he resided for eighteen years of his life.

SATURDAY, OCTOBER 23, 1875

0716 On Sunday night last, Elemuel Wixson, a resident of Glenham, was found this side of Red Rock hill. He was about 50 years of age, of intemperate habits, and died from the effects of the excessive use of liquor. Deceased leaves a wife and seven children, the youngest but two years of age.

0717 Mr. Charles F. Hunt, formerly of this village, having kept a lumber yard here for a couple of years, died at Carthage Landing on Sunday last, aged fifty-four years.

0718 Married on Wednesday, October 20th, at St. Luke's Church, Matteawan, by Rev. Edward T. Bartlett, Charles E. Tainter, of Worcester, Mass., to Helen, daughter of Judge Henry E. Davies, of New York.

0719 Married at Fordham, October 12th, at the residence of the bride's parents, by the Rev. H.W. Smuller, Jacob Horton, of East Fishkill, and Minnie J.V. Chapman, daughter of the late Rev. William Rogers Chapman, of New York, and step-daughter of W.J. Valentine, Esq., of Fordham. No cards.

0720   Married October 19th, at the bride's residence, by Rev.
        R. Roberts, Jacob Vail, of Fishkill-on-the-Hudson, to
Mary L. Davis, of Washington.

0721   Married at the residence of the bride's parents, October
        13th, by Rev. S. Hoyt, Mr. Franklin D. Ketchum, of
East Fishkill, and Miss Susie L. Humphrey, of Salt Point.

0722   Died in Fishkill Landing, October 18th, Bevenla [sic],
        daughter of William W. and Caroline Dunham, aged 7
years.

0723   Died at Glenham, October 17th, Charles F. Hunt, aged
        56 years.

0724   Died at New Hamburgh, on Saturday, October 9th,
        Walter, son of J.E. and Annie E. Millard, aged 7
months and 21 days.

SATURDAY, OCTOBER 30, 1875

0725   Father Sheehan, the Catholic clergyman at Wappingers
        Falls, was stricken with paralysis on Tuesday last, and
died the next day.

0726   At the marriage of Mr. Frederick Ireland and Miss
        Emma Morrison, in the Presbyterian Church,
Matteawan, last Saturday evening, at the conclusion of the
service, Mr. Willard H. Mase presented the parties with

some silver articles and one hundred dollars in money, the latter from the operatives of the hat works of the Matteawan Manufacturing Company.

0727   Mr. Charles L. Lyon, brother-in-law of Mr. L. Stevens, Jr., of this village, was nominated for the Assembly recently, by the Democrats of the Seventh Brooklyn district. Mr. Lyon is a practicing lawyer, about 43 years of age.

0728   The *Fishkill Journal* says: One of our oldest and most esteemed citizens, Mr. Coert A. Van Voorhis, died on Sunday morning last, in the seventieth year of his age. He had been in failing health for many months past. He was a director of the National Bank of Fishkill, and Trustee and Vice President of the Fishkill Savings Institute.

0729   Died at Matteawan, on Tuesday, October 26th, of diphtheria, Laura, only child of John E. and Louisa Selden, aged 3 years and 3 months.

0730   Died at Fishkill Village, October 24th, Coert A. Van Voorhis, in the 70th year of his age.

0731   Died on Monday, October 25th, in the city of New York, Charles Chauncey, son of Robert G. and Laura W. Rankin.

0732   Died at Channingville, on Wednesday morning, October 27th, the Rev. Dennis [sic] Sheehan, Catholic Pastor, in the 64th year of his age.

0733   Married in the Presbyterian church, Matteawan, on Saturday evening, October 23d, by Rev. J.L. Scott, Mr. Frederick Ireland, of Matteawan, and Miss Emma Morrison, of

Fishkill Landing.

0734   Married at Fishkill Landing, October 24th, by the Rev.
       Charles W. Fritts, assisted by Rev. Wendell Prime,
Lewis D. Bogardus to Lorretta R. Wiltsie, both of Fishkill
Village.

SATURDAY, NOVEMBER 6, 1875

0735   The *Fishkill Journal* says: William Ladue, one of the
       oldest citizens of East Fishkill, died on Wednesday of
last week, aged 77 years. Some months ago he was seized with
apoplexy, and his death had been long anticipated. He was an
active member of the Methodist church.

0736   On Saturday last, Matthew I. Snook, an aged citizen of
       Low Point, while at the funeral on Mr. William Ladue,
at Fishkill Hook, was suddenly stricken with paralysis during
the services, becoming entirely unconscious. On Sunday he
was conveyed to his residence at Low Point. There were
scarcely any hopes for his recovery.

0737   Married at the parsonage of the Pilgrim Baptist Church,
       Matteawan, on Wednesday, November 3d, by Rev. F.
Kratz, Mr. Mandeville Wallace, of Hyde Park, and Miss
Evelena Garrison, daughter of William H. Garrison, of Fishkill
Landing.

0738   Married in Binghamton, Broome county, N.Y., October
       19th, at the residence of Welcome A. Thompson, by
the Rev. A.M. Brown, Mr. Alfred P. Rider, of Kirkwood, to
Miss Mary J. Thompson, of Alexandria, Va.

0739   Died at Fishkill Landing, on Monday, November 1st,

Joseph Bertie Perry, adopted son of Lewis B. and Antha J. Ferguson, aged 3 years and 3 months.

0740   Died in Matteawan, November 2d, Emma Elizabeth, infant daughter of Joseph and Emma Sunderland, aged 2 years, 9 months and 18 days.

0741   Died at Brynesville, October 21st, David Croffird [sic], in the 51st year of his age.

0742   Died on Friday, October 29, James Dart, aged 43 years, son of the late Russel Dart.

SATURDAY, NOVEMBER 13, 1875

0743   Matthew I. Snook, of Low Point, who was stricken with paralysis while attending the funeral of William Ladue at East Fishkill recently, died at his residence on Friday of last week. His funeral took place on Sunday, and he was interred in the Fishkill Rural Cemetery. He was 79 years of age.

0744   Mr. Robert Rozell, of Fishkill Village, father of Mr. Alson Rozell, of this village, died at his residence on Wednesday of this week, aged 81 years. He had been in feeble health for a long time, but was out and voted on election day.

0745   Married in Brooklyn, September 27th, by Rev. Edward S. Porter, George Henderson to Mary E. Sutton, both of Glenham.

0746   Died near Fishkill Village, November 9th, Henrietta Wiltsie, wife of John Van Vliet, aged 72 years and 10 months.

0747   Died in Fishkill Village, November 9th, Andrew H.
        Ladue, aged 27 years.

0748   Died at Carthage Landing, November 5th, Matthew I.
        Snook, aged 79 years.

0749   Died at LaGrangeville, November 9th, John Upton,
        aged 28 years, 5 months and 22 days.

SATURDAY, NOVEMBER 20, 1875

0750   In the death of Miss Emma Sherwood, of Morristown,
        N.J., there is a bereavement felt, not only by an
affectionate father, mother and brother, but by a large circle of
friends. Miss Sherwood is a niece of Mrs. Dr. S. Mapes, of this
village. Her disease proved to be a serious attack upon the
heart and lungs, which suddenly terminated her earthly career.

0751   Married at St. Joachim's Church, Matteawan, on
        Thursday, November 4th, by Rev. Father McCourt,
James H. Owens to Annie Higgins, all of Matteawan.

0752   Married on Wednesday, November 10th, at the
        residence of the bride's parents, Hughsonville, by Rev.
E.P. Ackerman, Mr. William J. Hadden, of Wappingers Falls,
to Miss Lucy Ackerman, of the above place.

0753   Died in Poughkeepsie, November 12th, Myron H., son
        of Peter and Catharine E. Dorland, aged 20 years.

0754   Died at the United States Hotel, Morristown, N.J.,
        November 7th, Emma J., only daughter of B.F. and the
late Kate Townsend Sherwood.

SATURDAY, NOVEMBER 27, 1875

0755 The *Albany Journal* says that Mrs. General Hendrick
Van Rensselaer, formerly of Albany, celebrated her one
hundredth birthday at Randolph, Cattaraugus county, a few
days since, at the residence of her son, Dr. D.S. Van
Rensselaer, with whom she has resided for the last forty years.
Dr. Van Rensselaer is now in his eightieth year.

0756 Captain Benjamin H. Hart, a well-known resident of the
Town of LaGrange, died very suddenly on Friday
morning of last week. The cause of death was paralysis. He
was sixty years of age. - *Poughkeepsie Eagle.*

0757 Married at Fishkill Landing, November 24th, at the
residence of Mr. F. Van Voorhis, by Rev. C.W. Fritts,
Mr. Oakley Pugsley, of this village, and Miss Eva Van
Voorhis, of Peekskill.

0758 Married at the residence of the bride's parents,
Hughsonville, on Tuesday, November 16th, by Rev. Dr.
Sturges, Clinton Burroughs, of Wappingers Falls, to Minnie,
daughter of Isaac O. Norris, Esq.

0759 Married at New Hackensack, N.Y., by the Rev. H.
Ward, November 9th, Mr. William Smith to Miss Josie
Dutcher, both of Wappingers Falls.

0760 Died in Fishkill Landing, November 23d, Mrs. Mary
McLaughlin, aged 71 years.

0761 Died in Matteawan, November 22d, Mrs. Amy
Williams, aged 36 years, 2 months and 24 days.

0762 Died near Fishkill Village, November 18th, Sarah, widow of the late William C. Van Voorhis, aged 60 years.

0763 Died at Millbrook, November 20th, Walter W. Way, aged 20 years, 3 months and 13 days.

SATURDAY, DECEMBER 4, 1875

0764 Mr. Richard Pattleton, of Colusa, California, whose marriage we record this week, was formerly employed in the Rothery file works, Matteawan. He is Deputy Town Marshall of Colusa.

0765 The father of the wife of William B. Astor, the New York millionaire who died last week, was Major John Armstrong, the man who wrote the Newburgh letters urging Washington to make himself king at the close of the Revolution.

0766 Married at Colusa, California, November 8th, by Rev. J.C. Hyden, Richard Pattleton, formerly of Matteawan, N.Y., to Miss Delia Frances Sullivan, of Colusa.

0767 Married November 24th, at the M.E. Parsonage, North Newburgh, by Rev. R. Kerr, Mr. George M. Seaman, of East Fishkill, N.Y., to Miss Maud A. Rea, of Poughquag, Dutchess county, N.Y.

0768 Died at Fishkill Landing, November 24th, May Tracy, aged 4 months and 1 day, daughter of John and Elizabeth Tracy.

0769 Died in Brooklyn, December 1st, Mrs. Cornelia

Polhemus, widow of the late Joseph G. Van Wyck, of Fishkill, in the eighty-first year of her age.

0770 Died in Brooklyn, N.D. [sic], Sunday morning, November 28th, 1875, Jane, widow of the late James McAlpine, in the 90th year of her age.

SATURDAY, DECEMBER 11, 1875

0771 Married in Newburgh, December 8th, by Rev. William H. Gleason, George Root to Emma Light, both of that city.

0772 Married at the Reformed Church, Fishkill Village, December 2d, by Rev. Asher Anderson, Alfred T. Gibbs, of New York city, to Miss Sarah E. Graham, of Fishkill Village.

SATURDAY, DECEMBER 18, 1875

0773 Mr. Garret B. Brinckerhoff, brother of Mr. John Henry Brinckerhoff, of this village, and formerly a well-known resident here, died in New York one day this week, at an advanced age. Years ago he was connected with the freighting business on the Long Wharf.

0774 Mr. Samuel J. Owen, District Attorney of Putnam county, died at his residence in Cold Spring on Tuesday evening of last week. He had been indisposed for some time, and but little hopes were entertained for his recovery. He was elected to his present position in 1870, and re-elected in 1873. His unexpired term will be filled by appointment by Governor Tilden. Deceased was about thirty-five years of age, and leaves a wife and two children.

116

0775   Mr. Isaac H. Shurter, uncle of Mr. James E. Shurter, of
           this village, died at Poughkeepsie on Monday last, in
the 71st year of his age. He had been a resident of
Poughkeepsie forty-five years, having moved there from
Fishkill in 1830, when he engaged in the grocery business. For
the past forty years he was a member of the Washington street
M.E. Church.

0776   Married at St. Joachim's Rectory, Matteawan, January
           6th 1875, [sic] by Rev. Peter McCourt, William Grey
to Miss Mary Walsh, both of Matteawan.

0777   Died in Poughkeepsie, December 13th, Isaac H.
           Shurter, in the 71st year of his age.

0778   Died at Wappingers Falls, on Tuesday, December 7th,
           Rachel I., daughter of Webster A. and Sarah J.
Tompkins, aged 6 years, 11 months and 7 days; of dropsy.
Putnam county papers, please copy.

SATURDAY, DECEMBER 25, 1875

0779   Mrs. Elizabeth H. Forman, widow of the late L.S.
           Forman, died at Matteawan, on Monday.

0780   Mr. John B. Heroy, son of Mr. M. Heroy, of this
           village, died on Sunday morning last, after a brief
illness, of cerebro-spinal meningitis, commonly known as
spotted fever. He was buried on Monday afternoon, the
Denning Guard, of which he was a member, turning out and
escorting his remains to the cemetery.

0781   Married by the Rev. F. Kratz, at the residence of Mr.

Conklin, Wednesday evening, December 22d, Mr. Isaac B. Beckwith to Francis [sic] A. Welch, both of Matteawan.

0782   Married on December 11th, by Rev. W.G. Hillman, at the residence of the bride's mother, Mr. Edward Odell, of Fishkill Landing, to Miss Alfretta Fogg, of Wappingers Falls.

0783   Married December 21st, at the residence of the bride's father, by the Rev. R. Stewart, D.D., Mr. Albert A. Bensell, of Newburgh, to Miss Josephine W. Lomas, of Fishkill Village.

0784   Married at the residence of the bride's parents, on Wednesday, October 27th, by the Rev. J.C. Van Deventer, Walter W. Way, of Millbrook, to Henrietta, youngest daughter of Albert Weeks, of Glenham.

0785   Married at Middletown, N.Y., December 22d, by Rev. E.H. Beattie, D.D., assisted by Revs. W.B. Darrach and Charles Beattie, Hector Craig, of New York, and Mary W., only daughter of Mr. James Darrach, and grand-daughter of the late Dr. Bartow White, of Fishkill Village.

0786   Married in Poughkeepsie city, December 22d, by Rev. P.R. Hawxhurst, Mr. James E. Monfort to Miss Sarah E. Delamater, all of Beekman.

0787   Died in Fishkill Landing, December 14th, Emma, infant daughter of Frank H. and Christiana Hanson, aged 9 months.

0788   Died in Fishkill Landing, December 19th, John B. Heroy, aged 24 years and 9 months.

118

0789   Died in Fishkill Landing, December 21st, Ann Riley, aged 65 years.

0790   Died in Fishkill Landing, December 21st, at the residence of his son, A. Hill, Hezekiah D. Hill, formerly of High Falls, Ulster county, aged 74 years and 6 months.

0791   Died in Matteawan, December 20th, Elizabeth H., widow of the late L.S. Forman, aged 57 years and 9 months.

0792   Died in Fishkill Village, December 20th, Mrs. Jane Hunt, aged 76 years.

0793   Died in East Fishkill, December 21st, Ella L., daughter of John Phillips, aged 20 years, 4 months and 21 days.

0794   Died at Johnsville, December 14th, Martha, wife of William S. Serrine, aged 31 years.

0795   Died at Millbrook, November 20th, Walter W. Way, aged 20 years, 3 months and 13 days.

0796   Died in the Town of Washington, on the 17th of December, Rachel, widow of the late Stephen Sackett, in the 79th year of her age.

SATURDAY, JANUARY 1, 1876

0797   The death of Mr. Charles R. Owen, which took place so suddenly this week, is one of the saddest events that have ever occurred in our midst. On Thursday of last week, he went to New York on business, returning in the evening, with an attack of intermittent fever. A day or two afterward he was

119

attacked with pleurisy, in a very severe form. He sank rapidly, and at twenty minutes past nine on Tuesday evening, he died.

Mr. Owen was a member of the Matteawan M.E. Church; of Beacon Lodge, F. & A.M.; and of Beacon Light Council, O.U.A.M. His funeral took place on Friday afternoon, at one o'clock, from the above church. He was buried with Masonic honors.

0798 On Saturday morning last, Mrs. Lucy B. Cromwell, wife of Mr. Walter Cromwell, who resides opposite the little school house, on the Poughkeepsie road, about two and a half miles north of this village, committed suicide by hanging herself, at about half past seven o'clock, and while in a temporary fit of insanity. She had been subject to these spells for some years, at times being very gloomy and despondent, and then rallying. She was found hanging in the garret by her husband, who at once cut her down, but life was extinct. Mr. Cromwell was alone, and his mother's family living nearest, he proceeded there for help. She was a member of the Reformed Church at Glenham. Her funeral took place on Tuesday, and her remains were interred in the Fishkill Rural Cemetery. Mrs. Cromwell was about forty-three years of age, and leaves no children.

0799 *The New York Sunday Courier* announces that Miss Clara Louise Kellogg is announced to be married to Mr. Bradish Johnson Smith, a wealthy New Yorker. Mrs. Smith? Ah, the name is not un-American.

0800 Mr. Peter Evens, of Matteawan, who has been sick of consumption and recently went south for the benefit of his health, died at Savannah, Georgia, on the 18th ult. His body was brought home for interment, and the funeral took place at the Presbyterian Church on Sunday last. He was nearly 43 years of age, and a brother of Mr. Buel Evans.

0801   Married in Newburgh, December 25th, by Rev. L.H.
King, Charles Terbush to Rebecca Vanderwerker, all of
Peekskill.

0802   Died at Fishkill Landing, December 27th, Fanny, wife
of Mark Mohurter, aged 37 years.

0803   Died in Matteawan, December 28th, Charles R. Owen,
aged 36 years and 5 months.

0804   Died at Savannah, Georgia, December 18th, Peter
Evens, aged 42 years, 10 months and 16 days.

SATURDAY, JANUARY 8, 1876

0805   The Rev. John Brown, of St. George's Episcopal
Church, Newburgh, preached his sixtieth Christmas
sermon on the 25th ult. Mr. Brown is eighty-four years old.

0806   Married at the house of the bride's uncle, Samuel H.
Abbott, Coldwater, Michigan, December 21st, Mr.
William C. Harris, of Matteawan, N.Y., to Miss Jennie M.
Stevenson, of the former place.

0807   Married at Glenham, in the Free Church of St. John
Baptist, January 1st, by the Rector, Rev. John R.
Livingston, Theodore Lovell Adams, of New York, to Sarah
Louisa Pierce, of Glenham.

0808   Married at the M.E. Parsonage, Johnsville, December
22d, by Rev. G. Daniel, Alexander Smith of Newburgh,
to Adeline Harris, of Johnsville.

0809   Married at the Clinton Avenue Reformed Church, Newark, N.J., Thursday, December 30th, by the Rev. W.J.R. Taylor, D.D., Herbert Van Wyck to Anna E., daughter of George H. Lee; both of Newark.

0810   Died at the residence of A.V. Knevels, Fishkill Landing, Dutchess county, N.Y., Isaac A., son of the late Isaac Adrian Knevels, of St. Johns, West Indies, in the 72d year of his age.

0811   Died in Newburgh, January 3d, Morris S. Smith, aged 54 years, formerly principal of the Union Free School in the village of Fishkill.

0812   Died at Glenham, December 31st, Edwin Elmer, son of Charles and Ruth W. Heaton, aged 2 years, 11 months and 23 days.

0813   Died at Hopewell, December 29th, Elizabeth Mary, wife of William F. Jackson, aged 52 years.

0814   Died at Highland Falls, N.Y., on Saturday, January 1st, George, youngest son of George and Mary Sinclair, aged 2 years and 8 days.

SATURDAY, JANUARY 15, 1876

0815   John Matthews, a young man who had been employed at Groveville as a mason, but who resided at Rondout, started to go home on Friday evening of last week, by the six o'clock train of the Hudson River Railroad, at this depot. He was a little late, and tried to cross the track in front of the locomotive, which struck him. He was fatally injured, his skull being fractured. He was taken to Flannery's Hotel. His parents and brother came down, and the next morning he was taken home on a mattress. He died on Tuesday.

0816   Mr. Charles DuBois, who resided below Dutchess Junction, died on Wednesday of this week, after an extended illness, in the 63d year of his age. Mr. DuBois is a native of this place, a prominent and well-known citizen. He was engaged in the nursery business. His funeral will take place today, at 11 a.m., from his late residence.

0817   John W. Amerman, of Brooklyn, brother of Rev. O.V. Amerman, formerly of this village, died on Thursday night of last week, aged sixty-seven years. He was a printer, and for more than thirty years did business in New York city. He was associated with P.T. Barnum, who was his brother-in-law, in conducting the pioneer illustrated newspaper in that city.

0818   Mrs. Townsend, wife of George W. Townsend, of the firm of Homer Ramsdell & Company, died very suddenly at her late residence in Newburgh, on Friday evening of last week. Mrs. Townsend had been an invalid for some time, but was not considered dangerously ill.

0819   Mrs. Ellen Freeman, aged one hundred one years, two months and four days, died at Highland Falls on Monday. She was born on the King farm, east of Peekskill, in 1774.

0820   S.S. Wood, of New York city, formerly publisher of Wood's Household Magazine, was presented with twin boys, on Christmas Day. — Both stockings full.

0821   James Hamill, the well-known Pittsburgh oarsman and

123

ex-champion sculler, died on Monday.

0822   Married at the Rectory of the Free Church of St. John
            Baptist, Glenham, January 5th, by Rev. John R.
Livingston, Rector, Jeremiah E. Travis to Mary F. Mosher, all
of Glenham.

0823   Married in New York city, January 1st, by the Rev.
            William Lloyd, Harry Passmore to Lizzie Gray,
daughter of John Gray, of Fishkill.

0824   Died near Fishkill Landing, on Wednesday, January
            12th, Charles DuBois, in the 63d year of his age.
Relatives and friends of the family are invited to attend the
funeral from his late residence, on Saturday, 15th, at 11
o'clock, a.m.

0825   Died near Dutchess Junction, January 5th, Mr. Coles
            Mosier, aged 64 years.

0826   Died at Gayhead, East Fishkill, January 6th, Mrs. Abby
            Emans, in the 81st year of her age.

SATURDAY, JANUARY 22, 1876

0827   The late Guernsey Smith left $2000 to the Reformed
            Church at Glenham, of which he formerly was a
member and an officer.

0828   Married by Rev. Philip Germond, at the home of the
            bride, East Coldenham, N.Y., January 12th, Henry M.
Mosher, of Fishkill Landing, and Hattie N. Horton, of East
Coldenham.

0829 Married at Fishkill-on-Hudson, by Rev. Philip
Germond, January 18th, Emile Parmentier, of Paris,
France, and Ellen Boyce, of Glenham, N.Y.

SATURDAY, JANUARY 29, 1876

0830 Jacob B. Jewett, a prominent and influential citizen of
Poughkeepsie, died on Sunday last, in the 51st year of
his age.

0831 Mrs. Roxanna M. Drew, wife of Daniel Drew, died in
New York city on Thursday, aged 77 years. She was an
invalid for several years, suffering from paralysis of the spine.
She was born in the town of South East, Putnam county, N.Y.,
and was married to Mr. Drew, who was then a poor young
man, in 1820. She had been a member of the Methodist
Episcopal Church for thirty-six years, and was a very charitable
woman. Her remains were taken to Brewsters, for burial in the
family cemetery.

0832 Samuel Brown, one of the oldest and most highly
esteemed citizens of Wappingers Falls, died on
Saturday of last week. Years ago he was a prominent Whig,
but left that party when it dropped its name for that of
Republican, and become a Democrat. During his public career,
he was Overseer of the Poor of the Town of Poughkeepsie,
Town Auditor, and Justice of the Peace. At the time of his
death, we believe he was one of the Trustees of Wappingers
Falls, also a Director of the Wappingers Falls bank.
Mr. Brown was a native of Scotland and a resident of the
above village between forty and fifty years.

0833 Married on Wednesday, January 26th, by Rev. Charles
W. Fritts, James H. Hedges to Martha Barrett, both of

Matteawan.

0834   Married in Fishkill Village, January 23d, by the Rev.
          W.F. Brush, Charles H. Giddings, of LaGrange, to
Kattie [sic] E. Way, of Fishkill.

0835   Married at Millerton, January 20th, at the residence of
          the bride's parents, by the Rev. Robert Hunt, Mr.
James Sowdan to Miss Eva Hutchinsen, both of Millerton.

0836   Died in Brooklyn, on Monday, January 24th, Carrie A.,
          youngest daughter of Oscar and Cornelia A. Schenck,
aged 11 years and 2 months. The remains were brought to this
village for interment.

0837   Died at Glenham, January 24th, Maria, wife of John
          Brown, aged 75 years.

0838   Died in Poughkeepsie, January 23d, John B. Fleet, only
          child of John J. and Ida Fleet, aged 2 months and 21
days.

0839   Died at Verbank, January 1st, Phebe Jane Sherman,
          wife of Leonard B. Sherman, aged 48 years and 3
months.

SATURDAY, FEBRUARY 5, 1876

0840   Mr. Frederick Butterfield, son-in-law of Mr. John
          Falconer, head of the Seamless Clothing Manufacturing
Company at Matteawan, is the largest creditor of the concern,
which failed this week.

0841   Rebecca Thurston died at Lambertville, N.J., on the

26th of December, aged eighty-one years. She is said to have been well-known to the early settlers of the town of Fishkill, and to have joined the first cold water society in the town, some fifty years ago.

0842   Married at the residence of James M. Armstrong, Morrisania, Westchester county, by the Rev. J.L. Beman, D.D., LL.D., James Armstrong, Jr., to Miss Louise Nesbitt, both of that place. Attendants — Charles LaCoste, Jennie Armstrong, John Ernst, Lillie Merritt, Frank Gleasen, Lina Daniels.

0843   Died at his late residence in Kingston, N.J., on Saturday, January 29th, William A. Pierce, aged 61 years, 2 months and 29 days.

SATURDAY, FEBRUARY 12, 1876

0844   Judge Barnard has granted an absolute divorce to Alonzo Mabie from Catharine A. Mabie, both of Peekskill. Cause, adultery.

0845   Leonard Carpenter, a prominent business man of Poughkeepsie, having been a grocer there for over forty years, died on Tuesday, aged seventy-five years.

0846   Rear-Admiral Silas Horton Stringham, of the United States navy, died at his residence in Brooklyn, on the 7th of February, aged seventy-eight years. He was a native of Wallkill, Orange county, in this State.

0847   Rev. Christopher A. Farrell, formerly pastor of St. Joachim's Catholic Church, Matteawan, died at Savannah, Georgia, on Sunday last. His remains were brought

to New York for interment. Mr. Farrell was pastor of Thomas'
Church, Mamaroneck, Westchester county, N.Y. He went
south for his health, and died the day after his arrival in
Savannah.

0848   Married on Saturday, February 5th, in Free Church of
          St. John Baptist, at Glenham, by the Rector, Rev. John
R. Livingston, Owen Normanton to Celia Kerney.

0849   Married February 3d, at the house of Miss Melissa J.
          Velie, of Freedom Plains, by the Rev. John S. Gilmor,
Mr. William F. Cary, of East Fishkill, to Miss Carrie Pells, of
Freedom Plains.

0850   Died in Matteawan, February 7th, Sylvester H.
          Woolhiser, aged 35 years, 9 months and 7 days.

0851   Died at East New York, February 7th, Miss Sarah A.
          Bailey.

0852   Died at Prattsville, Greene county, N.Y., February 5th,
          Willard E. Mase, of consumption, aged about 24 years.

SATURDAY, FEBRUARY 19, 1876

0853   Died on Sunday afternoon, February 13th, in Fishkill
          Village, Josie, daughter of John L. and Maria Kniffen,
aged 3 years, 10 months and 11 days.

SATURDAY, FEBRUARY 26, 1876

0854   Married at Fishkill, N.Y., on Thursday, February 24th,
          by Rev. Asher Anderson, assisted by Rev. F.W.
Shelton, Robert N. Verplanck to Kate, daughter of Matthew

V.B. Brinckerhoff.

0855   Married on Saturday, February 19th, at the Free
           Church of St. John Baptist, Glenham, by the Rector,
Rev. John R. Livingston, Charles Henry Henian to Harriet A.
Cable.

0856   Married at the residence of the bride's father, Mr. Elias
           LaForge, by Rev. A.L. Culver, Thursday, February
24th, Mr. Albert B. Tuthill, of New York city, to Miss Francis
[sic] LaForge, of Cold Spring, N.Y.

0857   Died in Fishkill Landing, February 21st, Jane E., wife of
           Peter Rodgers, aged 42 years.

0858   Died in Stapleton, Staten Island, on Wednesday,
           February 16th, John Dodridge, aged 76 years, formerly
a resident of Matteawan; his remains were interred in St.
Luke's Cemetery, Matteawan.

0859   Died in Fishkill Village, on Tuesday night, February
           22d, Miss Hannah Brinckerhoff, in the 88th year of her
age.

0860   Died at Mott Haven, N.Y., February 19th, Mrs. Sarah
           Leach, widow of Charles Leach.

SATURDAY, MARCH 4, 1876

0861   Henry S. Van Etten, a well known Ulster county hotel
           proprietor, was found dead in [blank] on Saturday last,
from apoplexy. He was sixty years of age.

0862   Richard J. Garrettson, a prominent young man of

Rhinebeck, died on the 26th ult. He was the son of Hon. Freeborn Garrettson, and represented his town as Supervisor, in the fall of 1860; in the same year he was elected Member of Assembly, and had been selected as a candidate for other responsible positions by the Democratic party of this county.

0863 Mr. John G. Halsted, Sheriff of this county, died at Poughkeepsie, on Wednesday morning, in the 54th year of his age, of general debility of the digestive organs. He was born in the town of Clinton, and was the son of David Halsted, a noted Quaker preacher. He represented his native town as Supervisor in 1857 and 1858; in 1862 he was a candidate for the Assembly, but was defeated; was deputy under Sheriff Lamoree, under Sheriff for Sheriff Kenworthy, deputy Sheriff for Sheriff Pitcher, and elected Sheriff in 1873. He had been delegate to the Republican State Convention several times.

0864 We find the following biographical sketch in the *Albany Evening Journal Almanac*: B. Platt Carpenter (Rep.) of Poughkeepsie, was born in Stanford, Dutchess county, May 14, 1837. He graduated Union College 1857; is a lawyer; was elected District Attorney of Dutchess county in 1858; was Internal Revenue Assessor for the Twelfth District of New York 1865-'69; Member of New York Constitutional Convention in 1867, 1868; Delegate to the last two Republican National Conventions, and temporary Chairman of the Republican State Convention in 1872. He was elected to the Senate by a majority of 3,610 over James Mackin (Dem.).

0865 On Saturday evening last there assembled at the residence of Mr. Edward Remsen, in this village, his family and a few friends to celebrate his seventy-sixth birthday. Among those present was General Jacob L. Scofield, who has just passed his eighty-first birthday.

0866   Married at Poughkeepsie, February 26th, by the Rev.
        J.F. McClelland, William A. Mosher, of Matteawan,
and Anna Hawkes, of Carthage Landing.

0867   Died in Matteawan, March 2d, Lucy, daughter of
        Gilbert E. and Hetty Gregory, aged 3 months and 8
days. Friends and relatives of the family are respectfully invited
to attend the funeral from the residence of her parents, Cottage
Place, on Saturday afternoon, March 4th, at 2 o'clock.

0868   Died at Millbrook, February 24th, Jane A. Tompkins,
        aged 58 years and 2 months.

SATURDAY, MARCH 11, 1876

0869   John S. Smith, a youth about 18 years of age, living at
        Fishkill, and employed in the *Journal* office, died quite
suddenly on Saturday last.

0870   Jesse Wells, oldest man in Albany county, aged
        ninety-eight years, died at his residence at the Shakers,
last week, while on his knees in prayer. He was the last of a
family of nine, all of whom died at the Shakers at an average
age of over seventy-five years.

0871   Mrs. Sarah Dougherty, of the town of Cochecton,
        Sullivan county, is ninety-one years of age on the first
of next April. She was born in Dutchess county, married and
had two children, daughters. She was lived a widow seventy
years. She has eighteen living grandchildren, one hundred and
one great-grandchildren, one twenty-four and one twenty-six
years of age.

0872   Mr. C.W. Tompkins, the newly elected Supervisor from

131

this town, is a son of Mr. Solomon Tompkins, and was a member of the late firm of S. Tompkins and Son, grocers, Matteawan.

0873 Between 7 and 8 o'clock on Wednesday morning, the body of Richard Kain was discovered lying on the rocks in the creek, below the upper dam, at the raceway at Matteawan. Mr. Kain was of intemperate habits, and had been in poor health. He was about 50 years of age, a file forger by trade, and had worked for the Messrs. Rothery for the past twenty years. The jury rendered a verdict of accidental drowning. He was buried on Friday, in the Catholic Cemetery. He leaves a wife and several children. It was his boy who was so badly hurt at the file works some months since, by having a hot file thrust into him. His brother, Bernard Kain, resides at Patterson, N.J.

0874 Died at Glenham, March 9th, Mrs. Martha Van Amburgh, widow of the late David H. Van Amburgh, in the 74th year of her age. Relatives and friends are invited to attend the funeral, from her late residence, Glenham, on Monday, 13th inst., at 2 p.m.

0875 Died in Fishkill Village, March 4th, John S., son of John and Mary A. Smith, aged 18 years.

0876 Died in Fishkill Village, March 4th, Josiah Hustis, aged 59 years.

0877 Died near Fishkill Village, March 2d, Mrs. Elizabeth Shaw, aged 78 years.

0878 Died in East Chatham, March 7th, John G. Dorland, aged 75 years and 2 months.

SATURDAY, MARCH 18, 1876

0879   John B. McKinnon, of Greenpoint, L.I., formerly of
Wappingers Falls, died on the 3d inst. His remains were
taken to Wappingers Falls for interment.

0880   Mr. John Greenwood, Jr., formerly manager of
Barnum's Museum, but recently American Consul to
Germany, died at Brunswick, Germany, on the 12th of
February, aged about 54 years. His remains were brought to
this country, and on Wednesday of last week were interred at
Bethel, Connecticut. Mr. Greenwood was an uncle of Mr.
George W. Taylor, of this village.

0881   Mrs. Winifred Ward, wife of Isaac Ward, and mother of
the celebrated Ward brothers, Henry, Joshua, Gill and
Ellis, who were victorious in the great international regatta, at
Saratoga, died on Monday at the residence of her son, Joshua,
in Cornwall. Mrs. Ward was about seventy-two years old, and
a very remarkable lady, having given birth to fourteen children,
nine boys and five girls, all of whom are yet living, John, aged
about fifty-four, and Ellis the youngest. Isaac Ward, the
husband and father, is yet in good health.

0882   Married on Monday, March 13th, by Rev. Mr. Shelton,
at the parsonage, Miss Ella G. Collins, of Carthage
Landing, to Mr. Charles Constantine, of New York city.

0883   Died in Matteawan, March 12th, Carrie, infant
daughter of Charles and Elizabeth Robertson, aged 6
years and 5 months.

0884   Died at Paris, France, February 21st, of pneumonia,
Miss Lucy E. Selden, sister of Mr. J.E. Selden, of

Matteawan, N.Y.

0885   Died at Hopewell, March 9th, Aletta Rapelje, in the 70th year of her age.

SATURDAY, MARCH 25, 1876

0886   Captain Anning Smith, a well-known river captain, died at New Paltz Landing on Saturday of last week. An injury two weeks previous resulted in erysipelas, which finally attacked the brain, causing death.

0887   Beyond a doubt, says the *Troy Times*, Valley Falls enjoys the honor of having for one of its residents the oldest woman in Rensselaer county, in the person of Mary Wallace. Her maiden name was Northrop, and she was born in Poughkeepsie in 1773.

0888   Died at Matteawan, on Tuesday, March 21st, of consumption, Lyman P. Mase, aged 59 years.

0889   Died at Glenham March 15th, Miss Ann Pine, aged 74 years.

0890   Died in Brooklyn, N.Y., March 15th, William H., son of William Knapp, of Glenham.

0891   Died at Millbrook, March 16th, Anna J. Lane, wife of John G. Lane.

0892   Died at Lumberville, Delaware county, March 7th, Harriet Myers, in the 76th year of her age, formerly of Dutchess county.

0893   Married at the residence of the bride's parents, Orange
         Lake, February 22d, Theodore Miller to Annie F.,
eldest daughter of Edward E. Traver, formerly of Fishkill
Landing.

0894   Married at Johnsville, East Fishkill, at the Parsonage,
         March 20th, by Rev. George Daniel, Joseph Vernol, of
Fishkill, to Maria Knapp, of East Fishkill.

SATURDAY, APRIL 1, 1876

0895   Mrs. William P. Bickel, late of this village, died
         recently, in Florida.

0896   Died in Matteawan, March 29th, Mrs. Jane Mason,
         wife of David Mason, aged 75 years.

0897   Died at Fishkill Landing, on Sunday, March 26th, Eva
         W. Quick, daughter of Joseph and Sarah M. Quick,
aged 8 years, 1 month and 12
days.

0898   Died in Fishkill Village, March 24th, Catharine Ann,
         wife of Elisha Bailey, in the 73d year of her age.

0899   Died in Fishkill Village, March 24th, Ann, widow of the
         late James Ladue, in the 60th year of her age.

0900   Died in Fishkill Hook, March 22d, Mrs. Margaret
         Winslow, aged 70 years.

0901   Died February 6th, at Hughsonville, Frederick H.
         Traver, aged 81 years, 6 months and 14 days.

0902 Died at Wappingers Falls, on Monday, March 27th,
Josiah Faulkner, in the 65th year of his age.

SATURDAY, APRIL 8, 1876

0903 Mrs. W.P. Bickel, whose death we announced last
week, did not die in Florida, as we were informed, but
at Stapleton, Long Island, on the 21st of March.

0904 Mr. Allan S. Campbell, long a resident of this place,
and organist at St. Luke's church, died quite suddenly
on Tuesday morning, of apoplexy, aged forty-two years.

0905 Married at the residence of Mr. Joseph Metcalf,
Matteawan, April 1st, by Rev. J.L. Scott, Mr. Elmore
Mann, of Glenham, and Miss Ellen Surrine, of Johnsville, N.Y.

0906 Died at Fishkill Landing, April 4th, Allan S. Campbell,
aged 42 years.

0907 Died at Matteawan, April 6th, Mrs. Margaret Purdy,
aged 85 years.

0908 Died in Matteawan, April 2d, Robert Brown, aged 29
years.

0909 Died at Glenham, April 5th, of apoplexy, Mr. Zacheus
Marsh, in the 62d year of his age. Funeral on Saturday,
8th inst., at 2½ o'clock from the house, and 3 o'clock from the
Reformed Church. Friends and relatives are invited to attend.

0910 Died at Glenham, April 3d, Edward, infant son of
Nathaniel and Lavina Ladue, aged 7 months and 9 days.

0911   Died at Arthursbugh, April 4th, Rosanna, wife of Peter I. Vermilyea, aged 53 years.

SATURDAY, APRIL 15, 1876

0912   The wife of Rev. J. Howard Suydam, formerly of this village, died at Jersey City on Tuesday.

0913   Mr. John F. Warner, formerly proprietor of the Irving House, in this village, died quite suddenly, at Tarrytown, on Monday.

0914   Married at Verbank, April 8th, by C.P. Colwell, Esq., Walter Fervis, of Rockland, Sullivan county, to Miss Jennie E. Brown, of Beekman, Dutchess county.

0915   Died at Fishkill Landing, April 11th, Darius Thorne Glover, son of Darius and Deborah A. Glover, aged 12 years, and three months.

0916   Died at Fishkill Landing, April 10th, Justina Clareta Adkins, aged four years and eleven months.

0917   Died at Fishkill Landing, April 14th, Annie M. Keene, aged sixteen years. Funeral from St. Joachim's Church, Matteawan, at 2 ½ o'clock on Sunday. Relatives and friends are invited to be present.

0918   Died at Matteawan, April 14th, Mr. John Page, aged 77 years and 8 months. Funeral from St. Luke's Church, on Monday, at 2½ o'clock, p.m. Relatives and friends are invited to attend.

0919   Died suddenly, on Wednesday, April 12th, Catharine

137

Storm Teller, relict of Henry S. Teller, in the 78th year of her age. Funeral at Presbyterian Church, Matteawan, on Saturday, 15th inst., at 2½ o'clock p.m.

0920   Died in Fishkill Hook, April 11th, James E. Purdy, aged 28 years.

0921   Died at Stormville, April 11th, Charles H. Rogers, aged 54 years.

0922   Died at Rhinebeck, April 6th, Anne Elbertina Brownson, daughter of the Rev. H. Brownson.

0923   Died on Tuesday morning, April 11th, at her late residence in Jersey City, Sarah Augusta, the beloved wife of Rev. J. Howard Suydam, in the 42d year of her age.

SATURDAY, APRIL 22, 1876

0924   Died at Glenham, April 20th, Patrick Barron, aged 73 years. Funeral at St. Joachim's Church, Matteawan, on Saturday, April 22d, at two o'clock. Relatives and friends are invited to attend.

0925   Died at Carmel, Putnam county, on Monday, April 17th, John Foshay, aged 61 years, 4 months and 5 days.

SATURDAY, APRIL 29, 1876

0926   We give below a full list, as far as the committee has knowledge, of persons who have planted centennial trees, (in honor the one hundredth birthday of the United States.)

Alden, Henry A.   Beatty, Eliz. N.

Alden, George B.
Addington, Mrs. W.R.
Addington, Julia
Anthony, William N.
Anthony, Mrs. Annie W.
Anthony, Remsen
Briggs, Edw.
Brady, James

Booth, John
Beacon Light Council No. 52,
        O.U.A.M.
Brundage, Charles W.
Beardsley, H.S.
Brett, Walter
Brett, Caroline A.W.
Brett, Mrs. Cornelia

0927   Centennial Trees, cont.

Brett, Walter W.
Bogardus, Miss Elizabeth M.
Bogardus, John S.
Cook, J. Hervey
Clark, Bernard
Cook, Louisa W.
Cunningham, Matthew
Colwell, W. Scott
Colwell, Mrs. R.E.
Colwell, Frank S.

Cogswell, William
Curtiss, M.E.
DeWint, Arthur
Dietrich, M.E.
Duffy, Annie
Darragh, Robert
Darragh, James S.
Dunham, William
Fitzpatrick, Mary Annie
Friese, John

0928   Centennial Trees, cont.

Fishkill Young Men's Association
Flaherty, Laurence
Greenwood, Mrs. J.R.
Goodrich, F.B.
Green, Joseph I.
Garrison, George
Garrison, William H.
Hopper, Nicholas
Hills, Miss Sarah
Hustis, H.H.

Haver, James W.
Heston, Ephraim
Jones, William A.
Kittredge, C.M.
Kittredge, Marcia E.
Kittredge, George D. [sic]
Knevels, Adrian V.
Knox, Starr B.
Lomas, Joseph
Lester, Anna R.

139

0929   Centennial Trees, cont.

Leverich, Mrs. J.B.	Meyer, Carrie
Lorenz, John	Meyer, William N.
Monell, John J.	Miller, Amand
Monell, Caroline E.	Martin, Charles E.
Monell, Mary G.	Manes, Stephen
Meyer, Mrs. Mary	Moith, A.T.
Meyer, Minnie	Moith, J.E.
Meyer, Phenie	Member, James E.
Meyer, Willie	Member, George A.
Meyer, James	Member, Edward J.

0930   Centennial Trees, cont.

Mackay, Alexander Rufus	Member, Ralph
McManus, Catharine C.	Nelson, Mrs. Charlotte
McManus, James	O'Sullivan, Bernard
McManus, Mary	O'Sullivan, Mrs. Mary
McManus, John	O'Sullivan, James J.
McManus, Edw.	O'Sullivan, Mary Agnes
McManus, Mary A.	O'Sullivan, Eugene
Morrison, John	O'Hara, Peter
Morrison, William	Phesay, John
Mohurter, Mark	Place, John

0931   Centennial Trees, cont.

Pralatowski, Wladyslaf J.	Rozell, William H.
Pralatowski, Mary E.	Rozell, Mrs. W.H.
Pollock, Mary A.	Rogers, James
Pollock, Fred.	Rogers, Dewitt C.
Ryan, James	Rogers, Samuel B.
Remsen, Edward	Rogers, Joseph J.
Remsen, Matilda W.	Stotesbury, Helen
Remsen, Sarah	Stotesbury, Charlotte F.
Remsen, Bartow W.	Spaight, J.W.

Remsen, Livingston   Spaight, Eliza J.

0932   Centennial Trees, cont.

Scofield, J.L.   Sage, Milo
Scofield, Mary C.   Sage, William F.
Scofield, Sidney   Smith, Silas G.
Scofield, Eliza V.   Smith, John T.
Scofield, Frank G.   Shurter, James E.
Sewell, Mrs. Jennie   Sturges, John
Swift, H.N.   Seaman, George A.
Swift, Mrs. E.L.   Seaman, Mrs. Mary C.
Schlosser, J.F.   Stebbins, Joseph
Strong, Benjamin   Stebbins, Jessie W.

0933   Centennial Trees, cont.

Theall, Frank   Verplanck, Samuel
Tompkins, Lewis   Verplanck, William S.
Talbot, Benjamin M.   Van Buren, Willis
Tracy, John   Van Voorhis, William H.
Underhill, Samuel   Vail, Mrs. M.E.
Van Rennselaer, Mrs. E.   Whittemore, J. DeWint
Van Tine, John   Williams, George B.
Van Tine, Arabella   Wolcott, Charles M.
Van Tine, Robert T.   Washington, Amos
Van Vliet, Sylvanus   Wilcox, E.M.
Van Buren, Lorenzo   Way, Miss Jennie E.
Van Voorhis, Frederick   Youmans, P.D.

0934   At the West Point Foundry, on Wednesday afternoon
last, a mortar burst on firing, into four or five pieces,
one of which, weighing about sixty pounds, killed Mr. Colin
Tolmie, Jr., instantly.

0935   Mr. Joseph I. Green, one of our most aged native

citizens, is in his 89th year.

0936   Married at Johnsville, April 19th, by Rev. G. Daniel,
          Mr. William Hasbrook, of New Hamburgh, to Mrs.
Catharine E. Peter, of East Fishkill.

0937   Died near Myers' Corners, April 13th, Mrs. Ann
          Phillips, wife of John R. Phillips, aged 56 years.

0938   Died at Amityville, L.I., April 27th, Alfred Saxton, in
          the 76th year of his age.

SATURDAY, MAY 6, 1876

0939   The death of John A. Bolding, a colored man, at
          Poughkeepsie, revives the story of his capture, about a
quarter of a century ago, under the Fugitive Slave act: — John
A. Bolding, in 1845 or 1846, was a slave in Charleston, South
Carolina. He was sold to a Mrs. Dickinson, who shortly
afterward came north, and Bolding escaped and located in this
city. Mrs. D. also came to this city, and under the Fugitive
Slave law, sold him to a planter in Charleston. When his
capture became known, a crowd of abolitionists hurried to the
depot, too late to purchase Bolding's freedom. The city was
determined to purchase his freedom, and raised $2,000 for him;
he was brought back again, and he came to reside here
permanently.
   Before he was taken sick, he worked at tailoring for Hayt
and Lindley. He died of consumption. *-Poughkeepsie Eagle.*

0940   The names of the following persons have been added to
          the list of those who have planted centennial trees:
George C. Smith, Wilbur F. Hopper, Alonzo S. Wiltse, Miss
Julia Dean, Miss A.M. Dean, Miss M. Dean, Lizzie C. Rogers,

142

Anna M. Rogers, James Ackerman, Mrs. Mary Ackerman, Mrs. Mary Hobart Verplanck, Mrs. E.A. deWint, Mrs. Rebecca Lester, Jefferson B. Schenck, James Smith.

0941 Married at the residence of the bride's mother, Newburgh, May 3d, by Rev. John Gray, Mr. Isaac H. Van Wagner, of Fishkill, Dutchess county, to Miss Sarah E. Many, of Newburgh.

0942 Married in Newburgh, May 4th, by Rev. J.L. Scott, Mr. Andrew M. Grier to Miss Anna Mason, both of Matteawan.

0943 Died at Matteawan, May 4th, Robert Johnston, aged 72 years. Relatives and friends of the family are invited to attend the funeral on Saturday, May 6th, at four o'clock, from his late residence.

0944 Died near Fishkill Village, May 2d, Samuel M. Stevens, in the 78th year of his age.

SATURDAY, MAY 13, 1876

0945 The names of James E. Thompson and Guydon Yale have been added to the list of those who have set out Centennial trees.

0946 Died in Brooklyn, May 9th, Sarah A., wife of William H. Van Vliet, in the 63d year of her age.

0947 Died at Middletown, Orange county, N.Y., May 7th, 1876, Sarah, widow of the late Absalom Barker, aged 76 years and nine months; formerly of Matteawan.

0948   Died at Glenham, May 8th, Eliza, widow of the late Peter Cromwell, aged 87 years.

SATURDAY, MAY 20, 1876

0949   Died in Fishkill, May 15th, Mrs. Lucia Annan, wife of the late General Theodorus Annan, and daughter of Mr. Samuel S. Myrick, deceased, of Carmel, Putnam county, aged 67 years, 6 months and 20 days.

0950   Died in Upper Hopewell, May 10th, Henrietta, daughter of Tunis B. Adriance, aged 42 years.

0951   Died near Stormville, May 11th, Charity, wife of George R. Ladue, in the 47th year of her age.

0952   Died at Albany, May 12th, Geraldine, wife of Thomas Kenworthy.

0953   Died at Elizabeth, N.J., April 28th, Sarah E. Chatterton, aged 77 years, 8 months and 14 days, formerly of this town.

SATURDAY, MAY 27, 1876

0954   John P. Nelson, one of the oldest and most respected citizens of Poughkeepsie, died quite suddenly at Kingston, whither he had gone visiting, on Monday.

0955   The M.E. Church, Matteawan, was crowded Wednesday evening, with persons desirous of witnessing the marriage ceremony of Mr. Bissel Tompkins and Miss Agnes Williams. The ushers were Messrs. Edward Taylor, A.W. Merritt, Albert Townsend, and A.G. Ormsbee.

The ceremony was conducted by the pastor, Rev. C.W.
Millard. The bridal party left the same evening for Philadelphia.

0956   Died at New York, May 26th, Mrs. Charlotte
           Partridge, wife of Frederick Partridge, and daughter of
Lorenzo and Charlotte Van Buren, of this place, aged about 35
years. Relatives and friends of the family are invited to attend
the funeral on Saturday, 27th inst., at 11 o'clock, from the
residence of her parents. Interment at Fishkill Rural Cemetery.

0957   Died in Fishkill Landing, May 22d, Lavina, wife of
           Henry Mosher, aged 59 years and 3 months.

0958   Died at Wappingers Falls, May 18th, John DuBois,
           aged 51 years, of inflammation of the lungs.

0959   Died at Binghamton, May 6th, Richard Downing, aged
           64 years and 3 months, formerly of LaGrange,
Dutchess county.

0960   Married at the M.E. Church, Matteawan, by Rev. C.W.
           Millard, Mr. Bissel Tompkins and Miss Agnes
Williams, all of the above place.

SATURDAY, JUNE 3, 1876

0961   Charles J. Gaylord, son of George R. Gaylord, and an
           attache of the *Poughkeepsie Daily Press*, died last
week, aged thirty-six years.

0962   William Brewer, one of the oldest members of the bar
           of this county, died at his residence at Bangall, on
Saturday last, from an attack of paralysis.

0963 Ira Hasbrouck, of Poughkeepsie, was drowned in the river at that place, on Monday evening, by the upsetting of a single shell boat, in which he was practicing. He was but seventeen years of age.

0964 Among the persons who celebrated Decoration Day, and followed the procession, was Mrs. Catharine Reynolds, a colored woman whose age is authenticated at one hundred and six years. Mr. John D. Pitts took her over the route in his wagon. Mrs. Reynolds is a native of St. Thomas, one of the West India isles, and has been a resident of this village over sixty years.

0965 The Decoration Day parade marched to the Episcopal Cemetery in this village, where exercises were conducted at the grave of Lt. Col. Davies.

0966 On Sunday evening last, Timothy Ryan, a young man residing with his father in the brick building, Glenham, while returning home at a late hour, fell from the bridge crossing the railroad track near his residence, and sustained injuries from which he died on Wednesday.

0967 Married May 31st, at the Presbyterian Church, Monroe, N.Y., by Rev. D.N. Freeland, the bride's father, assisted by Rev. J.H. Duryea, D.D., the groom's uncle, Walter L. Thompson, Esq., of Fishkill, N.Y., to Miss Annie E. Freeland, of the former place.

0968 Died at Glenham, May 31st, Timothy Ryan, aged 24 years.

SATURDAY, JUNE 10, 1876

0969   The Reformed Church of this village was filled with a
            large assemblage on Thursday afternoon, for the
marriage of Mr. Henry B. Schenck, of the firm of John B.
Schenck's Sons, Matteawan, and Miss Mary F. Bartley, of this
village. Messrs. John F. Schlosser, George A. Alden, Charles
E. Martin, and William F. Sage acted as ushers, and were in
full dress. At five o'clock the bride arrived on the arm of her
brother-in-law, Mr. John Place, and the groom arrived with his
brother, Mr. William T.Y. Schenck. The bride wore a travelling
suit of brown silk. Rev. Charles W. Fritts was the officiating
clergyman. Miss Nellie Rankin presided at the organ, and the
music was excellent. The wedded pair left on the 6 o'clock
train, going north, we believe intending to visit Lake George.

0970   Mr. William R. Scofield died at the residence of his
            brother-in-law, Mr. Dubois Brinckerhoff, near this
village, from hemorrhage, June 7th. He had been an invalid for
many years, from an injury received in his
boyhood in the Fishkill mountains, while battling a fire, from
which he never fully recovered. He retired from active business
in 1871, and the winter of 1874 and 1875 was passed in Aiken,
South Carolina. He spent last winter in Lower California, and
had but recently returned.

He was a son of Gen. Jacob L. Scofield, of this village, and
was born August 9, 1832, in Glenham. While in active business
in New York, he united with the Presbyterian church, Rev. Dr.
Hatfield's, there some twenty years ago. He afterward united
with the Ross street Presbyterian church, where his
membership still continued. He was a member, also, of the
Masonic fraternity. He married, some sixteen years ago, a lady
in Brooklyn, a daughter of Judge Boswell, who deeply mourns
her great loss.

147

0971   We learn from the *Middletown Argus* that the marriage
of Mr. Walter L. Thompson, of Fishkill, with Miss
Annie E., daughter of Rev. D.N. Freeland, the able and popular
preacher of the Presbyterian Church at Monroe, on
Wednesday, 31st ult., drew out a large congregation to witness
the interesting ceremony, which was performed by the bride's
father, in his own church, assisted by Rev. Mr. Duryea, of
Paterson. Mr. McGarrah presided at the organ. The bridal
party started in the evening for New York, on their way to
Saratoga, Niagara Falls, and Washington.

0972   Married on Thursday, June 8th, at the Reformed
Church, Fishkill Landing, by the Rev. Charles W. Fritts,
Henry B. Schenck, of Matteawan, to Mary F. Bartley, of
Fishkill Landing.

0973   Died in Fishkill Landing, June 7th, William R. Scofield,
in the 44th year of his age. Relatives and friends are
invited to attend the funeral on Saturday, June 10th, at eleven
o'clock, from the residence of his brother-in-law, Mr. Dubois
Brinckerhoff.

0974   Died at Fishkill Landing, May 31st, at the residence of
her son-in-law, Mr. A. Miller, Mrs. Esther, widow of
the late Morris Davenport, of Cold Spring, aged 81 years and
21 days.

SATURDAY, JUNE 17, 1876

0975   The Rev. Marvin Richardson, the oldest member of the
New York Annual Conference of the M.E. Church,
died at the residence of his son-in-law, Rev. L.M. Vincent,
Poughkeepsie, on Wednesday evening, in his eighty-eighth
year.

148

0976   Married in Fishkill Village, June 7th, at the house of the
       bride's parents, by Rev. Asher Anderson, Mr. Sylvester
Southard to Miss Sarah Frances Storm, daughter of Mr. John
V. Storm, all of that village.

0977   Married June 13th, at the M.E. Parsonage, Walden,
       Orange county, N.Y., by the Rev. J. Millard and the
Rev. C.W. Millard, A.C. Dwight, of the Coxsackie National
Bank, and Hattie L. Millard, of the former place.

0978   Died at Shenandoah, June 14th, Nathaniel Sprague,
       aged 66 years.

SATURDAY, JUNE 24, 1876

0979   We are informed that Miss Amelia B. Johnson, of
       Newburgh, formerly a teacher in the public school of
this village, died very suddenly in Newburgh, a few weeks ago.

0980   Lester Winfield, of the *Montgomery Standard*, refuses
       to pay a judgment of $300 and costs, and will go to jail.
His paper will be published during his absence by his wife and
friends.

0981   We had the pleasure of seeing the Republican nominee
       for Vice President, Hon. William A. Wheeler, at
Garrison, a few days ago. He had been stopping at the
residence of his brother-in-law, Mr. Henry W. Belcher.

0982   Mr. W.S. Colwell, son-in-law of Mr. H.N. Swift, has
       taken the machine shop in Matteawan, and is engaged
in the manufacture of hat formers and hat machinery.

0983   Married on Sunday, June 18th, in the Free Church of

St. John Baptist, Glenham, by the Rev. John R. Livingston, Missionary, assisted by the Rev. Mr. Sartwell, of Texas, William Henry Lobdell to Charlotte Hultz; all of Cold Spring.

0984   Died at Shenandoah, June 14th, Nathaniel Sprague, aged 66 years.

0985   Died at Jamaica, L.I., June 14th, Charles A. Ketcham, aged 24 years and 2 months.

SATURDAY, JULY 1, 1876

0986   On Monday afternoon last, an Englishman, whose name is unknown, was killed on the Hudson River Railroad, about a mile above this village. He was a tailor by trade, and had been at work for Mr. Leon Pralatowski, for ten days previously, but would not give his name to anyone, but said he had a family in England. He was a middle-aged man.

0987   On Friday evening of last week, John Hadfield, a lad about seven years of age, and son of Levi Hadfield, of Matteawan, was drowned in a well on Walsh's brewery premises, in that village. It seems that the children of that neighborhood have been in the habit of playing on the premises, against the orders of the proprietor and the warning of parents. The well is twelve feet in diameter, and contains about six feet of water. The premises are also enclosed by a high board fence, over which the boys would climb.

0988   An exhibition of relics, held by the Young Men's Association, of this village, is being held. We give a partial list of the many articles exhibited:
John S. Bogardus, Bible, 1728.
Sidney Scofield, Dutch Bible of 1741.

150

W.J. Pralatowski, a Polish book of 1782.

Walter Brett, large Dutch Bible, printed in 1710.

Mrs. Van Rennselaer, Dutch Bible, 1718; a Hebrew book, 355 years old.

Dr. John Young, diploma of Gululmas Young, 1776.

Mrs. Walter Brett, the family china of her grandfather, Martin Wiltse, Sen., more than 100 years old.

Mrs. Mary M. Alden, a child's dress, 125 years old, worn by Col. Jonathan Barret, of Revolutionary fame; a breadth of dress skirt over 100 years old, spun and woven by Urania Locke and her sisters — the stamps for the figures were made by their brother, and the dyes were of their own invention.

Joseph Howland, a part of the wedding silver of Mr. and Mrs. Joseph Howland, married in 1772.

0989   Died at Groveville, June 28th, William Shuttleworth, aged 52 years.

0990   Died at Glenham, June 25th, Ann Augusta, wife of Albert W. Patterson, aged 42 years.

0991   Died at New Windsor, Orange county, on Tuesday, June 27th, Rebecca, youngest child of Jennie A Northrop and Oliver Cromwell, aged 3 years, 11 months and 9 days.

SATURDAY, JULY 8, 1876

0992   The Hon. Peter B. Gates, Mayor of Schenectady, N.Y., died suddenly in the Saratoga special train on the Hudson River Railroad, Tuesday, near this place, while on his way home from the Centennial Exhibition. The cause is supposed to have been heart disease.

0993   Mrs. Catharine Reynolds, the old colored woman of
        whom we have made mention several times, died quite
suddenly on Monday, and was buried on Tuesday afternoon.
She was very old, good authorities putting it at one hundred
and six to one hundred and eight years.

0994   Married July 4th, by the Rev. Charles W. Fritts, Dewitt
        Dolsen to Emma Wilson, both of Brynesville

0995   Married July 3d, at the M.E. Parsonage, Fishkill
        Landing, by Rev. A. Coons, George E. Cullen to
Martha Page, both of Glenham, N.Y.

0996   Married July 3d, at the M.E. Parsonage, Fishkill
        Landing, by Rev. A. Coons, Charles A. Van Voorhis to
Anna Van Tassel, both of Cold Spring, N.Y.

0997   Died in Jamaica, Long Island, June 24th, Annie E.,
        daughter of Henry M. and Annie J. Knowles, aged 16
years, 3 months and 13 days.

SATURDAY, JULY 15, 1876

0998   Mr. Josiah Fuller died at his residence, on his farm near
        Matteawan, on Friday morning, aged seventy-three
years.

0999   A car load of convicts from Sing Sing, on their way to
        Auburn, passed through this village, on the 8:03 train
on Thursday evening. It is understood that Edward S. Stokes,
the murderer of James Fisk, Jr., was among them.

1000   Married at Matteawan, July 12th, by Rev. J.L. Scott,
        Mr. William Brown, of Matteawan, and Miss Mary E.

Kane, of Pine Bush, Orange county, N.Y.

1001 Married June 14th, in the town of Washington, at the residence of the bride's parents, James H. Hayt to Miss Georgianna Thorne.

1002 Died at Matteawan, July 14th, Josiah Fuller, aged 72 years, 5 months and 10 days. Relatives and friends of the family are invited to attend the funeral, on Sunday, July 16th, at half-past three o'clock, from the M.E. Church, Matteawan.

1003 Died at Cold Spring, on Thursday, July 6th, Burtis D. Ferguson, in the 67th year of his age.

1004 Died in the town of Washington, July 11th, Mrs. Walter Wodell.

SATURDAY, JULY 22, 1876

1005 On Saturday evening last, William Teschke, twenty-one years of age, and nephew of Mr. Hermann [sic] Shrayer, overseer of the weaving department in the Glenham mill, accompanied by a son of the latter, named Albert, twelve years old, went bathing in the Jones Bend part of Fishkill creek. Teschke, while attempting to swim across the stream with the boy upon his back, was taken with cramps, and both drowned before they could be rescued. The funeral took place on Monday afternoon, from the Reformed Church of Glenham, and was largely attended.

1006 Rev. Dr. Snodgrass, of Goshen, has reached the age of eighty years. He is the oldest clergyman in Orange county in active service.

1007   Peter S. Cramer, for forty years a citizen of
Poughkeepsie, committed suicide last Sunday night by
jumping into the Hudson. His body was found next morning.
Financial embarrassment and illness was the cause of the rash
act.

1008   Mr. William T. Garner, who was drowned in New
York bay on Thursday, was only thirty-three years of
age, and a son of the late Thomas Garner, an Englishman who
came to this country when a young man, and began the
manufacture of print-cloths, of which, at the time of his death
in 1865, he was the largest producer in the world. The son
entering the establishment of his father, at his father's death
inherited a fortune, valued at from $15,000,000 to
$20,000,000. Mr. Garner was the head of the firm of Garner &
Johnson. At his cotton mills he employed from 7,000 to 8,000
persons.

1009   Mr. Benjamin Elsden, the policeman who was shot at
Newark, and killed, by the Thielhausens, was a brother
of Mr. Robert F. Elsden, of Matteawan. His funeral took place
at Newark on Sunday last, from the residence of his father. His
funeral procession included one hundred and thirty-five
policemen, and about four hundred members of the
Independent Order of Odd Fellows — of which he was a
member. The remains were taken to the Second Reformed
Church, with interment in Fairmount Cemetery.

1010   Married at the parsonage of the M.E. Church, Walden,
July 11th, by Rev. C.W. Millard, and Rev. J. Millard,
William R. Church, of the firm of Church & Powell,
Coxsackie, N.Y., and Mrs. F.M. Keeler, daughter of the last
named clergyman.

1011   Died at Matteawan, July 19th, James Leslie, aged 70 years.

1012   Died at Glenham, July 15th, H. Albert, son of C. Herman [sic] and Louisa Shrayer, aged 12 years.

1013   Died at Glenham, July 15th, F. William Teschke, aged 21 years.

1014   Died at Fishkill Village, July 15th, Matilda Gould, aged 46 years.

SATURDAY, JULY 29, 1876

1015   William M. Whritner, a brother of Mrs. William Gildersleve, of this village, is supposed to have been drowned near Unionville, Long Island, last Saturday night. He went out fishing with a party in a yacht, and sometime during the night is presumed to have fallen overboard. Young Whritner was about twenty-six years of age, a machinist, and formerly worked in the Schenck Machine Shop at Matteawan.

1016   Married at Matteawan, June 28th, by Rev. C.W. Millard, George P. Wilman, of Auburn, N.Y., to Belle Hamlin, of Matteawan, N.Y.

1017   Married at Matteawan, Sunday, July 23d, by Rev. R.F. Elsden, Elizabeth Nichol to Henry Sutcliffe, both of Groveville, N.Y.

1018   Died at Palmyra, Wayne county, at the residence of his son, July 12th, William Pettit, formerly of LaGrange, Dutchess county, in the 83d year of his age.

SATURDAY, AUGUST 5, 1876

1019   The body of William M. Whritner, who was
accidentally drowned near Unionville, L.I., recently, has
been found, thus clearing up a part, at least, of the mystery of
his disappearance.

1020   William Shuttleworth, late of this village, died on
Tuesday morning last. From the time of the conversion
of the Clinton Mills into carpet works, up to last year, he was
the respected manager under the late firm of Messrs. Firth,
Willans & Co., now Messrs. T. F. Firth & Co. Mr.
Shuttleworth left this village in the summer of last year for the
purpose of starting a large carpet manufacturing concern in
America for the celebrated firm of A.T. Stewart & Co. Friends
of the deceased in this village and neighborhood feel very
deeply for his widow and family. *-Brighouse and Rastrick
Gazette*, England, July 15th.

1021   Died in Fishkill Landing, August 2d, William B. Chase,
aged 30 years and 10 months.

1022   Died in Fishkill Village, on Monday, July 31st, Abbe
Knapp, wife of Israel Knapp, aged 51 years.

SATURDAY, AUGUST 12, 1876

1023   Secretary of State Fish was 67 years of age last Friday.

1024   Mrs. Caroline Husted, mother of Hon. James W.
Husted, Speaker of the Assembly, died at the family residence,
Bedford, Westchester county, on Friday of last week, at the
mature age of 78 years.

1025   The wife of William H. Gildersleve, baker of this
          village, died on Wednesday. She had been sick for
several weeks. The funeral took place on Friday, at Fishkill
Village.

1026   General Philip Lasher died suddenly at the residence of
          his son-in-law, Dr. Brewster, in Brooklyn, last Tuesday
morning, of apoplexy. Gen. Lasher was formerly postmaster at
Madalin, and has filled many public appointments in the town
of Red Hook, where he resided for many years. He was a
Brigadier General in the State Militia. -*Poughkeepsie Eagle*.

1027   John Barton, sick from the effects of cholera morbus,
          died in the barn of James Hall, July 17th. He had been
intoxicated since July 4th, and was weak and prostrated. He
was deemed not strong enough to be moved to the Highland
Hospital by Dr. J.P. Schenck, M.D.

1028   Died in Fishkill Landing, August 9th, Mary Smith, wife
          of William H. Gildersleve, aged 51 years.

1029   Died in Newburgh, August 10th, Caroline M., wife of
          Charles W. Teller, aged 72 years. Friends and
acquaintances are invited to attend the funeral from her late
residence, No. 118 Smith street, on Saturday after- noon, at
2½ o'clock, and from St. George's Church at 3 o'clock.
Interment at Rural Cemetery, Fishkill Village.

1030   Died at Carthage Landing, August 3d, Willie J., child of
          Sebring and Sarah C. Ackerman, aged 1 year, 3 months
and 9 days.

1031   Died at Sandy Hill, Washington county, N.Y., August
          7th, Richard, son of Ann and the late Richard Burton,

157

formerly of Glenham, aged 26 years.

SATURDAY, AUGUST 19, 1876

1032   Rev. John Hendricks, of Rhinebeck, died on Saturday, the 6th inst., at the advanced age of 94 years.

1033   Naugatuck, Ct., August 14th: Editor of the *Fishkill Standard*, Dear Sir, I just learned by telegram that my wife, Lucy A., died this morning at your place. Having been sick for some months, she insisted upon going to Fishkill, her native place, where she has been kindly cared for by her sister. Although her absence was grievous to me, I consented, and hope all will remember her kindly, as well as her afflicted and bereaved husband. My own feeble state of health prevents my attendance at her funeral. -[signed] W. Valentine.

1034   Died at Fishkill Landing, August 14th, at the residence of her brother, Mr. Daniel Leach, Lucy A. Leach, wife of William Valentine, late of Albany, aged 72 years.

1035   Died at Matteawan, on the 12th inst., Annie Mitchell, aged 20 years.

SATURDAY, AUGUST 26, 1876

1036   The wife of Rev. M.L. Berger, formerly of this village, died at Santa Barbara, California, on the 31st of July.

1037   Rev. William A. Cornell, a minister of the Reformed Church, living in LaGrange, committed suicide by hanging a few days ago. He had been suffering from temporary insanity.

1038   Died in Fishkill, August 20th, Miss Sarah Rogers, aged
78 years.

1039   Died on Monday, August 21st, in New York, Rebecca
H. Roosevelt, wife of James Roosevelt, and daughter of
the late Gardner G. Howland.

1040   Died at his residence near Millbrook, August 5th,
Joseph Bartlett, aged 74 years.

SATURDAY, SEPTEMBER 2, 1876

1041   Mr. W.G. Van Buskirk, soon after his return from
Canada, was called to Fort Miller, Washington county,
where his sister had been suddenly struck with paralysis, and is
not expected to recover. She was been unconscious ever since
the attack.

1042   Miss Deborah Tillott, one of our oldest and best known
lady residents, died at her home in this village on
Monday. Her funeral took place on Thursday, from the
Protestant Episcopal Church, Matteawan. She was 80 years of
age, and one of a numerous family, all of whom have departed,
except one brother, Mr. Caleb M. Tillott, of this village.

1043   Died in Fishkill Landing, August 28th, Miss Deborah
Tillott, aged 80 years.

1044   Died at Ashley, Michigan, August 22d, Mrs. Helen M.
Pollock, wife of the late Jacob Pollock, formerly of
Dutchess county, in the 73d year of her age.

SATURDAY, SEPTEMBER 9, 1876

1045   Mr. W.G. Van Buskirk's sister, whose sudden illness
       we mentioned last week, has since died, at her
residence at Fort Miller.

1046   Mr. Oscar Schenck, formerly of this village, but of late
       years connected with the Third National Bank of New
York city, and residing in Brooklyn, died at his residence on
Monday last, of heart disease, with which he had been afflicted
for some time. His funeral took place on Thursday, from the
Reformed Church of this village. Mr. Schenck was a son of the
late Abraham H. Schenck, and a brother of the late Dr. John P.
Schenck. He was the last surviving member of the family. As a
young man he associated himself with his brother Charles in the
machine finding business. During a part of the war, he was with
Col. Stewart Van Vliet, in the quartermaster's department in
New York city. He leaves a wife and seven children.

1047   Married at the residence of the bride, Fishkill Landing,
       Sept. 7th, by Rev. C.W. Fritts, Mr. Edward Lowden
Parris, of New York, to Miss Mary Ida DuBois, daughter of
the late Charles DuBois.

1048   Died at Fishkill Landing, September 7th, William, son
       of Lemuel and Cornelia Hallock, aged 1 year and 6
months.

1049   Died at Fishkill Landing, September 6th, Charles, son
       of Isaac Fisher, aged 4 years.

1050   Died in Brooklyn, on Monday morning, September 4th,
       of heart disease, Oscar Schenck, in the 59th year of his
age.

1051   Died at Washington Heights, New York city,
        September 6th, T. Ransom, infant son of George S. and
Eunice R. Allan, aged 12 days.

1052   Died at Fort Miller, on Friday, September 1st, Rebecca
        Van Buskirk, about 58 years of age.

1053   Died at Fishkill Plains, September 4th, Phebe A., wife
        of Albert D. Hitchcock, aged 30 years.

1054   Died at Peekskill, August 28th, Mrs. Phebe Whitney, in
        her 87th year, daughter of Levi Owen, deceased.

1055   Died at Norfolk, Virginia, August 27th, Mrs. Sarah
        Cole, aged 72 years, daughter of Levi Owen, deceased,
of Peekskill.

SATURDAY, SEPTEMBER 16, 1876

1056   Rev. Charles C. Keys, who died in New York city last
        February, in the fifty-ninth year of his age, was for over
forty years a member of the New York Conference of the
Methodist Episcopal Church. In 1854-'55 he was stationed in
this village, the Methodists of Matteawan and Fishkill Landing
having but one church at the time.

1057   Mr. Charles L. Strong, of New York city, died at his
        residence on Sunday last, after a brief illness, aged
forty-four years. His body was brought to this village on
Tuesday, and funeral services held at the Methodist Episcopal
Church. He was buried in the Episcopal Cemetery at
Matteawan. Mr. Strong was a native of Lyons, Wayne county,
N.Y., and in his earlier years was a school teacher. He came
from Ulster county to this village in 1860, to take charge of the

161

public school. In 1864 he engaged in the stone and marble business. He was quite prominently connected with the M.E. Church, of which he was a licensed exhorter. He leaves a wife and four children.

1058　Died in New York, September 10th, Charles L. Strong, formerly of this village, aged 44 years.

1059　Died at Millbrook, N.Y., September 7th, Esther L. Swift, wife of Nathan G. Swift, aged 56 years.

SATURDAY, SEPTEMBER 23, 1876

1060　In the death of Charles Davies, LL.D., one of our most eminent citizens has passed away. Prof. Davies was for some years one of the trustees of our village public school and took a deep interest in its welfare. He had a genius for mathematics, and was unquestionably great. He was a graduate of West Point, and we think one of two, if not the only one, of the oldest living graduates. In beautiful Matteawan cemetery his remains on Wednesday were laid away by his old comrades and friends.

1061　Rev. William Goss, of Poughkeepsie, Presiding Elder of this district, has been seriously ill for a couple of weeks, but is now recovering.

1062　We are sorry to learn that Rev. P. McCourt, pastor of St. Joachim's Catholic Church, Matteawan, is confined to the house by a severe and painful affliction of a mysterious character. He was taken with a pain in the ankle, which extended to the knee, but without soreness or swelling.

1063　Died at Fishkill on the Hudson, September 18th,

Charles Davies, in the 79th year of his age.

1064   Died in Jamaica, Long Island, George L., infant son of
            Henry M. and Anna J. Knowles, aged 7 months and 10
days. [No date given.]

SATURDAY, SEPTEMBER 30, 1876

1065   Mr. and Mrs. Gilbert D. Theall left town on Thursday,
            for a brief bridal tour, and may possibly take in the
Centennial.

1066   Rev. William Goss, Presiding Elder of the
            Poughkeepsie District, New York M.E. Conference,
died at his residence in Poughkeepsie on Tuesday morning.

SATURDAY, OCTOBER 7, 1876

1067   William Watson, of Glenham, aged 42 years, died on
            Thursday of last week. Mrs. Watson returns her sincere
thanks to Messrs. N.B. Hustis, Joseph Sunderland, William
Harris, and others, for their kindness during her recent
troubles.

1068   Rev. Father Edward S. Briady, pastor of St. Patrick's
            Church, Newburgh, celebrated the twenty-fifth
anniversary of his priestly ordination, on Monday last, by
appropriate ceremonies in that church.

1069   Ex-Sheriff Moses C. Sands died in Poughkeepsie on
            Wednesday of last week. He was about sixty-two years
of age. He was first a Justice of the Peace in the town of
Stanford, and he was afterwards elected Justice of Sessions. In
1854 the Republicans elected him Sheriff of Dutchess county.

163

He was in the New York Custom House for two years, and afterwards for six years a doorkeeper in the House of Representatives in Washington.

1070   [paraphrased] Mrs. Adelia Wixon was awarded $800 and five per cent. allowance, from a jury in Poughkeepsie, in her civil court case against Michael McCabe, a saloon keeper in Matteawan, in the death of her husband November last. Mr. Wixon, of Glenham, had gone into McCabe's saloon, had five glasses of apple whiskey; went out, and lying down under a tree, died. His wages had been $1.50 a day.

1071   Married at Wappingers Falls, October 1st, by Rev. J.H. Hawxhurst, Mr. Edward Meeks to Miss Estella Kipp, both of Matteawan.

1072   Died at Glenham, September 28th, William Watson, aged 42 years.

1073   Died at Glenham, September 28th, Angeline, wife of John Moshier, aged 54 years.

SATURDAY, OCTOBER 14, 1876

1074   The *Poughkeepsie Eagle* gives the testimony of the witnesses in the Wickson [sic] - McCabe Case: His family was composed of his wife, Adelia Wickson, and six or seven children. They had been married for 27 years. Mr. Wickson, of Glenham, had gone into McCabe's saloon, had five glasses of whiskey; went out, and lying down under a cedar tree, died. Mr. Wickson was about 49 years of age, was the sole support of his widow. The jury returned a verdict of "death from intoxication," and the amount of damages claimed in this suit was fixed at $5,000. Judge Barnard delivered the charge, as stated last week.

1075   Mr. William Lottimer, a resident of this village for the
            past sixteen or seventeen years, and for a long time one
of the leading dry goods merchants of New York city, died at his residence in this village on Saturday last.

1076   There died at Union Corners, Warwick, Orange county,
            on the 2d inst., a colored woman named Hannah
Freeman, said to be one hundred and seventeen years of age. Elder Roberts, a colored preacher, who preached her funeral sermon, stated that there was no doubt whatever that this was her real age.

1077   Mr. John B. Seaman, who has been sick for nearly two
            years past, died on Thursday noon. Mr. Seaman was
born at Keane, New Hampshire, in October 1802, and in two weeks more would have been seventy-four years of age. He was the youngest of four children, the others surviving him, although each of them is over four score years of age. — Mr. Seaman removed to this village from New York city in 1859. He has been for a number of years Vice President of the First National Bank of Fishkill Landing, and was Senior Warden of St. Luke's Church, Matteawan. He was first attacked by disease, a congestion of the lungs, twenty months ago. His wife died between three and four years ago.

1076   Married on Thursday, September 21st, at the residence
            of the bride's father, by the Rev. J.S. Gilmore, Mr.
Henry T. Berry, of Roselle, N.J., to Miss Sarah A. Van Kleeck, daughter of Mr. Monfort Van Kleeck, of LaGrange, N.Y.

1079   Married at Washington, Dutchess county, Thursday,

165

October 5th, by Friends' ceremony, J. Henry Cooley, of Corning, Steuben county, to Mary, the eldest daughter of Justus C. Haviland, of the former place.

1080   Died at Fishkill Landing, October 12th, Mr. John B.
          Seaman, aged 74 years. Relatives and friends of the family are invited to attend the funeral, at St. Luke's Church, Matteawan, on Monday, October 16th, at 3 o'clock p.m., without further notification.

1081   Died at Fishkill Landing, October 7th, William
          Lottimer, aged 61 years. His remains were taken to New York for interment.

1082   Died at Matteawan, October 8th, Annie O'Brien, aged
          31 years.

1083   Died in Matteawan, October 7th, Thomas Moran, aged
          40 years.

1084   Died in Matteawan, October 6th, Jane Wanzer, aged 83
          years, 8 months and 22 days.

1085   Died in Paterson, N.J., October 1st, Mr. Watts Cooke,
          formerly of Matteawan, aged 84 years.

1086   Died in Newburgh, October 4th, William Edward, son
          of Justus E. and Virginia C. Ralph.

SATURDAY, OCTOBER 21, 1876

1087   Mr. David G. Warwick, of Highland Falls, who left for
          the old country two or three months ago to visit relatives there, returned on Wednesday, the 11th inst., in good

166

health. He visited his mother, brother, sisters, and other relatives in County Antrim, Ireland, and had a very pleasant time. Twenty-four years had passed since he left his home last.

1088 Died at Matteawan, October 18th, Mary Ella, daughter of Benjamin and Mary Hubbell, aged 8 years, 8 months and 6 days.

1089 Died at Matteawan, October 18th, John O'Mara, Jr., aged 16 years and 4 months.

1090 Died at the residence of her son-in-law, Rev. W.F. Brush, in Fishkill Village, October 15th, Mary A., wife of Barton Wood, in the 55th year of her age.

1091 Died at New Hackensack, October 10th, of consumption, Belle Ferdon, aged 24 years.

1092 Married at Cold Spring, Sunday, October 15th, by the Rev. F.T. Williams, Mr. Arthur Naylor, of the above place, to Miss Salemma Mosher, of Fishkill Landing.

1093 Married in Newburgh, October 16th, at the residence of the bride's parents, by the Rev. Charles Cuthbert Hall, William J. Whited and Kate Moore.

SATURDAY, OCTOBER 28, 1876

1094 Justice T.J.B. Schenck, Esq., of this village, died about half past eight o'clock last Tuesday evening. He had been sick but a short time, having been confined to the house only four or five days. — He was a native of New York city, having been born there on the 30th of November, 1814. He was engaged in business in Newbern, North Carolina; then in

167

Mansfield, Massachusetts, in company with his brother Samuel
B. In 1851 the machinery manufactory moved to Matteawan.
After Samuel died in 1861, he acted as administrator of the
estate. He became associated with the late John B. Schenck,
also a brother, in the machine business in 1865. About four
years ago he was elected Justice of the Peace, and afterward
was appointed Police Justice of the village, both of which
offices he held at the time of his death. He leaves a widow and
five children, one of them being married. Mr. Schenck's funeral
took place on Friday, and his remains were interred in the
Episcopal Cemetery.

1095   William S. Reynolds, a well-known coal dealer, and a
            gentleman universally respected for his integrity and
other virtues, died in Poughkeepsie on Saturday last, in the
56th year of his age.

1096   Rev. William P. Thomas, for many years a resident of
            Poughkeepsie, and a minister of the Episcopal Church,
died suddenly on Sunday night at Havana, Ohio. He preached
in the morning at that place. He was 79.

1097   Married at the parsonage in Johnsville, N.Y., Oct. 8th,
            by Rev. T.S. Lent, Theodore Knapp, of Poughkeepsie,
to Phebe Jane Smith, of Phillipstown, N.Y.

1098   Married at Green Haven, N.Y., Oct. 17th, by Rev. T.S.
            Lent, D.W. Jackson, of Johnsville, to Emma Lee, of
Green Haven.

1099   Married at home, Oct. 18th, by Rev. T.S. Lent, Thomas
            D. Hughson, of Fishkill, N.Y., to Alida, daughter of
Thomas Cary, of Fishkill.

1100   Married at the Reformed Church, New Hackensack, by
Rev. Henry Ward, Mr. John P. Monfort, of Fishkill
Plains, and Miss Gertrude Myers, of Fishkill. [No date given.]

1101   Married Oct. 19th, at the house of the bride's parents,
by Rev. F.T. Williams, of the Presbyterian church, Mr.
Henry Hustis to Miss Jennie Stevenson, both of Nelsonville,
Putnam Co., N.Y.

1102   Married at the house of the bride's mother, Garrisons,
Oct. 16th, by Rev. J.H. Loomis, Mr. Hiram E. Reeve,
of Germantown, N.Y., to Miss Carrie Hopper.

1103   Married Oct. 15th, at the North Highlands M.E.
Parsonage, by the Rev. R. Decker, Charles Lozier, of
East Fishkill, to Miss Melissa Gorham, of Fishkill.

1104   Married at Rochester, Ulster county, Oct. 23, at the
house of the bride, by the Rev. Mr. Broom, Miss Carrie
A. Tanner to Mr. Abm. D. Hyzer, of LaGrange, Dutchess
county.

1105   Died in Fishkill Landing, Oct. 24, T.J.B. Schenck, in
the 62d year of his age.

1106   Died in Fishkill Landing, Oct. 25, Lottie Meyer, widow
of the late William Stotesbury, Jr., aged 28 years and 8
months. Relatives and friends of the family are invited to attend
the funeral on Sunday, the 29th, at 2 o'clock, from the
Reformed Church.

1107   Died near Fort Montgomery, October 25th, John
Rodgers, son of Peter Rodgers, of this village, aged
about 26 years.

169

1108   Died in Fishkill village, Oct. 20, Annie May, daughter
of Rev. W.F. and Jennie A. Brush, aged 1 year and 3
days.

1109   Died at Millbrook, Oct. 22d, Howard T. Tripp, in the
51st year of his age.

1110   Died at Millbrook, tenth month, 23d, Sarah M. Smith,
aged 60 years.

SATURDAY, NOVEMBER 4, 1876

1111   Spencer C. Brooks, of the firm of Brooks &
Schoonmaker, Newburgh, died quite suddenly last
week, at his residence at Cornwall.

1112   Mr. George Moore, Jr., formerly of Newburgh, but for
a couple of months past engaged in the meat business at
Terbush's old stand, in this village, died of typhoid fever on
Monday morning last. He had been sick nearly a week. He was
thirty-one years of age, and leaves a family. His body
was taken to Newburgh on Wednesday, for interment.

1113   John Jay Smith, who claims to be a native of Dutchess
county, is a prisoner in the jail at Matamoras, Mexico,
on a charge of sympathizing with the revolutionary movement
led by Cortina. He denies the truth of the charges, and has
appealed to Secretary Fish for relief. He is a resident of
Matamoras, a civil engineer; and is a disabled Union soldier.

1114   Hon. Charles DeLong, a native of Dutchess county,
died at Virginia City, Nevada, on the 27th of October,
of typhoid fever. Mr. DeLong was a lawyer by profession, and
about forty-five years of age. He was a member of the

170

Constitutional Convention of 1859, and represented Yuba county, California, in both branches of the State Legislature. When Nevada was admitted to the Union, Mr. DeLong moved to Virginia City. Subsequently, he was appointed Minister to Japan from 1869 to 1873.

1115 Married at Chatham, N.Y., October 24th, Daniel Y. Bayley, of Matteawan, and Miss Mary Park, of the former place.

1116 Married at Hughsonville, October 21st, by the Rev. Dr. Sturges, at the residence of Mr. Frances [sic] I. Hasbrook, Zachariah Chase, of New Hamburgh, to Hattie Hawks, of Hughsonville.

1117 Died at Matteawan, November 3d, Samuel Higgs, aged 24 years, 11 months and 23 days. Funeral on Sunday, at 2 o'clock, from the house of Gilbert Wood, and at 2½ o'clock from the Protestant Church, Matteawan.

1118 Died at Fishkill Landing, October 30th, George Moore, Jr., aged 31 years. His body was taken to Newburgh for interment.

SATURDAY, NOVEMBER 11, 1876

1119 Frederick D. Emigh, of Lagrangeville, fell from a wharf at Newark, N.J., on Friday of last week, and was drowned. He was about twenty-four years of age.

1120 Cornelius H. Reynolds, of Pine Plains, died very suddenly on Tuesday night. He had been engaged at the polls all day, and in the evening was taken with a fit that ended his life. He was Under Sheriff to both Pitcher and Halstead, and was a faithful, capable officer, as well as a respected citizen.

1121   Pompey Graham, an old colored gentleman living in
        Montgomery, Orange county, is one hundred and seven
years old. He was born a slave and owned by General Johnson,
of Ulster county. Johnson sold him to Dr. Graham, of
Shawangunk. When the slaves were declared free, he moved
into the town of Montgomery. It is said he recollects well when
Independence was declared.

1122   Married in Jersey City, November 2d, by Rev. W.P.
        Corbit, of Trinity M.E. Church, George B. Seaman to
Mattie Strong, both of Matteawan, N.Y.

1123   Died in Fishkill Landing, November 4th, Elizabeth
        Ratigan, aged 82 years.

1124   Died at his residence in Millbrook, Dutchess county,
        N.Y., November 6th, of pneumonia, Isaac Merritt, in
the 78th year of his age.

SATURDAY, NOVEMBER 18, 1876

1125   Lawrence Zahn, who conducted the coal yard in this
        village, had a fall down stairs and killed himself. He was
a single man, aged 46 years, a German, and lived with his
brother-in-law, Fred Narius, on Broad street. He rose from his
bed between 12 and 1 o'clock, and was heard to fall heavily
down stairs. He died about 4 o'clock Tuesday morning. The
coroner's jury said he "came to his death by the rupture of an
aneurism." -*Fishkill Journal.*

1126   Married at Santa Cruz, California, November 4th,

1876, at the residence of the bride's cousin, by Rev. Chauncey Parks, William H. Chickering, formerly of Pittsfield, Mass., to Caroline A., daughter of George M. Clapp, Esq., of Brooklyn, N.Y.

1127   Married at the residence of the bride's parents,
            Matteawan, November 5th, by Rev. S.B. Almy, Mr.
Charles W. Wilson and Miss Mary E. Robinson, all of that village.

1128   Married November 9th, at Newark, New Jersey, by the
            Rev. H. Kastendieck, George Vanderburgh to Miss
Emma A. Conklin, of Newark.

1129   Married at Astoria, Long Island, on Thursday,
            November 9th, by Rev. H.W. Harris, D.D., Stephen B.
Halsey to Addie, daughter of J.B. Vandervoort, and grand-daughter of the late John C. Van Wyck, of Fishkill.

1130   Died at Glenham, Nov. 10th, Mrs. Anna O'Leary, aged
            52 years.

1131   Died in Fishkill Village, on Tuesday morning,
November 14th,
            Lawrence Zahn, aged 46 years.

SATURDAY, NOVEMBER 25, 1876

1132   Rev. R.F. Wile died at Highland last Sunday, aged
            about seventy-three. He was pastor of the Presbyterian
Church at Pleasant Valley, Dutchess county, for thirty-nine years, and of that at Highland since 1865.

1133   Died at Matteawan, November 19th, Walter E., son of

173

Walter Forbes, aged 3 years, 6 months and 24 days.

SATURDAY, DECEMBER 2, 1876

1134   Patrick Carligan, ragman at the entrance to Breakneck
tunnel in the Highlands, who held the distinction of
being the longest in the service of the Hudson River Railroad
Company in that capacity, met with his death on Friday
morning of last week. He was struck by the Poughkeepsie
special, bound south. Carligan had been in the employ of the
Company since the opening of the road, and was an attentive
and reliable servant. Deceased some year since was struck by a
train and lost a leg.

1135   The *Hudson Republican* says of the late Rev. Joseph
Scudder, D.D.: "He had been out of health for several
months. Dr. Scudder was the third son of the late Rev. John
Scudder, D.D., who was for many years the distinguished
missionary of the Reformed Church in India. He was born in
that country; graduated at the Rutgers College in 1848, and at
the New Brunswick Theological seminary in 1851. He spent
seven years as a missionary in India; shortly after his return the
late civil war commenced, and Dr. Scudder undertook a
chaplaincy in the army. Two or three years later he was elected
Secretary of the American and Foreign Christian Union,
Several years later he assumed the pastorate of the Reformed
church of Glenham until 1875, when he received and accepted
a call from the Reformed church at Upper Red Hook, and was
installed as pastor, May 26th, 1875.

1136   Married at the residence of Mrs. Camack, Fishkill
Landing, N.Y., November 27th, by Rev. A. Coons,
Richard V. Fountainville de Guinon, Esq., of New York city,
and Miss May E. Wood Benson, of Fishkill Landing.

1137   Married at the Methodist Parsonage, Wappingers Falls,
            on Saturday, November 4th, by the Rev. J.H.
Hawxhurst, Mr. Joseph W. Knapp to Miss Elizabeth Weed;
both of East Fishkill.

1138   Died in Fishkill Landing, November 30th, Ann, wife of
            William Carmichael, aged 83 years, 4 months and 15
days. Funeral services on Saturday, at ten o'clock, from her
late residence. Friends of the family are invited.

1139   Died at Matteawan, November 24th, Albert Gregory,
            son of Gilbert E. and Hattie [sic] Gregory, aged 4
years, 4 months and 4 days.

1140   Died in New York city, November 26th, R. Wiley
            Wing, in the 49th year of is age, formerly a resident of
Dutchess county.

SATURDAY, DECEMBER 9, 1876

1141   Joseph Van Anden, one of the oldest residents of
            Poughkeepsie, died on Saturday last, in the 75th year of
his age.

1142   Married in Poughkeepsie, December 6th, by Rev. J.F.
            McClelland, William A. Lawson, of New Hamburgh,
and Miss Sarah A. Gee, of Fishkill.

1143   Married at Matteawan, December 6th, by Rev. R.F.
            Elsden, Caroline Augusta Croft to Charles Frost, both
of Glenham, N.Y.

1144   Married on Thursday, November 30th, at the home of
the bride's parents, by the Rev. John R. Livingston, Frank

Marquet to Elizabeth Frost, of Glenham.

1145   Married Thursday, November 30th, at his residence, Poughkeepsie, N.Y., by the Rev. Asher Anderson, of Fishkill, G.D. Anderson to Emily L. Clement.

SATURDAY, DECEMBER 16, 1876

1146   Another of our elderly citizens has passed away. Smith T. Van Buren came into our vicinity not many years ago. He was the last surviving son of Martin Van Buren, who came up from the humble walks of life, and took his place among the Governors of New York, and Presidents of our country, and a brother of John Van Buren. He was born in Albany in 1817. He was buried in St. Luke's Churchyard last Wednesday.

Smith T. Van Buren was married to a daughter of the late William James, of Albany. After her death he moved to his father's residence in Kinderhook. There he married a daughter of Gabriel F. Irving, of New York city. After the death of his father he removed to Fishkill-on-the-Hudson, where he resided ever since. For a number of years he suffered from ill health. His widow, four daughters and a son survive him.

1147   Captain John S. Scofield, one of the oldest of our native citizens, and brother to General Jacob L. Scofield, of this village, died at the residence of his son-in-law, Charles E. Bartow, Esq., Glenham, on Monday last, in the seventy-second year of his age. He was born near Fishkill Village, June, 1805. For many years he was Superintendent at the Glenham Company; at the time of his death he was in the employ of A.T. Stewart & Co. as a master mechanic. He had been Town Collector and Supervisor of the Town, and Chairman of the Board of Supervisors.

176

He was a Colonel of the 149th Regiment of New York State
Militia for a number of years. In 1862 he raised a Company of
Volunteers, of which he was elected Captain, and which was
attached to the 150th Regiment. He was a member of the
Ancient Free and Accepted Order of Masons and of the
Independent Order of Odd Fellows. He leaves two daughters,
Mrs. Charles E. Bartow, Glenham, and Mrs. C.A. Vickery,
Rochester. His funeral was on Thursday afternoon. His body
was placed in the Receiving Vault at the Fishkill Rural
Cemetery. Members of Beacon Lodge, F. & A.M. acted as pall
bearers, and a detachment from Post Howland G.A.R. acted as
an escort, and fired a volley at the close of the service in the
Cemetery.

1148   Mr. J.W. Wiley, for three years one of the publishers of
         the *Amenia Times*, died last Saturday of hemorrhage of
the lungs.

1149   Cadet Smith, the colored youth over whom so much
         controversy occurred at West Point, died of
consumption at his father's residence in Columbia, S.C., on the
29th ult. He married Miss Elizabeth Simpson, of Highland
Falls, who was with him at his death, but expects to return
soon.

1150   Mr. Dewitt Dubois, of this village, died on Thursday,
         after a very severe and lingering illness, at the age of 65
years. He was a son of the late Peter C. Dubois, and brother of
the late Charles Dubois. He was of a quiet and retiring
disposition, and never took an active part in the affairs of the
public.

1151   Died near Fishkill Landing, December 14th, Dewitt
         DuBois, aged 65 years. Relatives and friends of the

177

family are invited to attend the funeral on Sunday, December 17th, at 2 o'clock from his late residence.

1152   Died December 10th, Smith T. Van Buren, in the 60th year of his age.

1153   Died in Matteawan, December 10th, Jennie M. Yates, wife of Crawford C. MacNeil, aged 28 years.

1154   Died at Newburgh, Orange county, N.Y., December 10th, Lizzie Hiser, wife of Harry Greenfield, aged 23 years, 8 months and 13 days.

1155   Died at Johnsville, December 7th, Susan A., wife of George Townsend, aged 22 years.

1156   Died near Fishkill Plains, December 8th, Mary, wife of Henry Musterman, aged 37 years.

1157   Died at Brooklyn, December 8th, Charlotte B., daughter of the late Henry A. and Charlotte A. Charlock, aged 35 years.

SATURDAY, DECEMBER 23, 1876

1158   The funeral of Rev. Peter McCourt, pastor of St. Joachim's Church, Matteawan, who died last Tuesday, took place this Friday morning. There was a solemn Requiem Mass. Rev. M. Phalen, of St. Mary's Church, Newburgh, delivered the panegyric. Rev. James Dougherty, of St. Joseph's, Kingston, was celebrant of the Mass; Rev. Bartholomew Galligan, of Cold Spring, deacon; Rev. M.C. O'Farrel, of New York, sub deacon; Rev. Joseph Byron, of New York, Master of Ceremonies. His remains were deposited in a vault on the parsonage grounds, adjoining the Church, under the shade of several beautiful trees.

1159   Married at the parsonage of the Methodist Episcopal
         Church, Fishkill Landing, December 13th, by Rev. A.
Coons, Mr. Charles Haight and Miss Louisa Reinhart, both of Matteawan.

1160   Married at the Episcopal parsonage, Matteawan, on
         Wednesday evening, December 20th, by Rev. E.T.
Bartlett, Mr. J. Sebring Cromwell, and Miss Grace McFarlane, of the above village.

1161   Died in Fishkill Landing, December 19th, Mary Ann
         Burns, wife of Thomas Burns, aged 28 years, 7 months
and 26 days.

1162   Died at Newburgh, Sunday, December 17th, Henry H.
         Felter, aged 8 years, eldest son of George H. and
Antoinette Felter, formerly of Matteawan.

1163   Died at Cold Spring, Phebe, relict of the late John
         Laforge, aged 87 years. [No date given.]

SATURDAY, DECEMBER 30, 1876

1164   Mr. William Teller, who died on Sunday last, was in the
eighty-fifth   year of his age. Mr. Teller was a native of this
place, a son of the late Oliver Teller, and was born near
Tioronda. He has been best known to our citizens as a grocer
and dry goods dealer at the Corners. He was been a Director of
the Bank ever since its organization, and for a great many years
one of the Deacons of the Reformed church. He leaves an only
daughter. His funeral took place on Thursday afternoon, from

179

the above church.

1165   Married on Christmas day, at the home of the bride's
        parents, by the Rev. John R. Livingston, Thomas
Farror, of Glendale, N.Y., to Laura Ann Frost, of Glenham.

1166   Married in Fishkill Village, December 24th, by Rev.
        W.F. Brush, Vincent Horton to Emma Smith; both of
that village.

1167   Died in Fishkill Landing, December 24th, William
        Teller, aged 84 years and 11 months.

1168   Died in Fishkill Landing, December 24th, Miss Adaline
        Van Amburgh.

1169   Died at Fishkill Landing, December 28th, Mrs.
        Elizabeth Murray, aged 86 years.

1170   Died at Fishkill Landing, December 26th, Mrs.
        Catherine Faherty, wife of John Faherty, aged 23 years.

1171   Died November 24th 1876, at Oakland, California,
        Anna H. Bartley, wife of Jerome F. Kendall and
youngest daughter of Catharine and the late Edgar Bartley,
aged 29 years, formerly of this place.

1172   Died at Matteawan, December 24th, Edgar Manning,
        aged 21 years.

1173   Died at Matteawan, December 25th, Edna, daughter of
        John and Mary Harris, aged 2 months and 17 days.

SATURDAY, JANUARY 6, 1877

1174   In our remarks on Mr. William Teller last week we
should have said he had been for a long time one of the
Elders of the Reformed Church of this village, instead of
Deacon.

1175   Mr. George M. Sullivan, formerly of Matteawan, was
in town this week. He is engaged in business in
Cincinnati, Ohio, with his brother- in-law, Mr. Lyon, and is
doing well.

1176   Married at the parsonage, Matteawan, January 3d, by
the Rev. S.B. Almy, Andrew Delahay to Minnie
Collins, both of Fishkill Landing.

1177   Died at Newburgh, January 2d, Nettie May, daughter
of George H. and Nettie Felter, aged 6 months.

1178   Died at Hopewell, December 31st, Dora, daughter of
Charles and Sarah Stockholm, aged 1 year, 3 months
and 17 days.

SATURDAY, JANUARY 13, 1877

1179   On Saturday afternoon of last week, Mr. James E.
Burhans, station agent of the Poughkeepsie, Hartford
and Boston Railroad Company, at Pine Plains, in this county,
left home for Poughkeepsie, informing his wife that he would
return in the evening. — At an early hour in the evening he
telegraphed and informed her he would return the next
morning. Nothing has since been heard of him, although
diligent search has been made for him. He is not quite 30 years
of age, been married about six years, and was living happily

181

with his wife and one child, a little girl, of whom he was very fond. He is a member of the Odd Fellows at Poughkeepsie, a member of the Masonic Order, and a member of the Scott Guard. Information of him may be sent to Peter Burhans, 92 Cannon street, Poughkeepsie.

1180 Married December 27th, in Middletown, Orange
    county, by Rev. J.K. Wardle, Harvey Sheppard, of
Matteawan, to Fannie Cooper, of Middletown.

1181 Died at Fishkill Landing, January 10th, Edward
    Hamsher, aged 36 years.

1182 Died at LaGrangeville, January 7th, Archibald Colwell,
    aged 82 years.

1183 Died at Myers Corner, December 23d, John Phillips,
    aged 86 years.

SATURDAY, JANUARY 20, 1877

1184 Hon. Stewart L. Durland, Assemblyman from the
    Second District of Orange county, died at Middletown
on Wednesday morning.

1185 Mr. Charles H. Perrine, of Rondout, formerly of this
    village, has just lost a little girl by death from that
fearful disease, diphtheria. — Two other children are very sick
of the same disease; also Mrs. Perrine, who is getting better,
however.

1186 Died at Poughkeepsie, January 17th, Louie, only son of
    Louis and Lizzie Meyer, aged 2 years and 10 months.

1187   Died at Rondout, January 14th, Cattie Jane, daughter
of C.H. and C.E. Perrine, aged 2 years, 2 months and
24 days.

SATURDAY, JANUARY 27, 1877

1188   Mysterious disappearances are getting to be quite
common. Mr. Burhans, of Pine Plains, has not been
heard of yet; Mr. Perry Knickerbocker, of Matteawan, is
reported among the missing; and Mr. Charles Luyster, of East
Fishkill, has been gone for ten days past. Mr. Luyster was here
on Tuesday, 16th, at the trot on the ice, and was last seen here
about half past seven that evening at the Long Wharf. The pilot
of the ferryboat saw a man going toward Newburgh on the ice,
and warned him to keep farther north, above the track of the
boat. That same evening, the watchman at the Newburgh
plaster mills saw a man approaching the shore, and called to
him to go father North to avoid the ferryboat track made in
front of the city, but the man evidently misunderstood, and
started south. It is possible that both men were Mr. Luyster,
who fell into the track, among the jagged pieces of ice, sank
and was drowned.

1189   We are sure our readers will join us in expressions of
profound sorrow to Mr. and Mrs. Charles H. Perrine, in
the loss of all their children, four in number, from diphtheria,
all within eight days. Cattie Jane died on the 14th inst., and on
the 21st their only little boy, Ralph, a little over five years, was
called away. On Monday, Sarah Bell, aged about four, and
Emma, an infant of ten months, died within a few hours of each
other. The funeral of the trio of deceased little ones was held
from the desolated home of the parents, on Wednesday
afternoon. -*Rondout Freeman.*

183

1190   Last fall Mr. William Thompson sold his harness shop,
         in Jackson's building, on the Matteawan road, to Mr.
Perry Knickerbocker, of Millerton, who immediately took
possession. Last Wednesday Mr. Knickerbocker suddenly and
mysteriously disappeared. On that morning he went to
Newburgh, and is known to have received a check for $23
from Col. Isaac Wood, Jr., and that he had the same cashed at
the Quassaick Bank, in that city. Since then, there is no trace of
him. He was married, had one child, and his relations with his
family are said to have been of the pleasantest character. He is
about 35 years old, medium size, light complexioned, good
looking and wore a mustache. The initials P.K. are marked on
his arm in India ink. His wife went to Millerton on Thursday to
make enquiries of him.

1191   Married January 20th, by the Rev. John R. Livingston,
         at the house of Mr. Whittle, Mr. Peter Gilberts, of
Matteawan, to Catherine A. Purdy, of Glenham.

1192   Died at Fishkill Landing, N.Y., January 24th, Mrs.
         Ellen Adkins, aged 38 years.

1193   Died at Matteawan, January 23d, Mrs. Lorena
         Luddington, aged 68 years and 16 days.

1194   Died near Fishkill Village, January 20th, H. DuBois
         Knapp, aged 32 years.

1195   Died at Stormville, January 21st, Maggie, daughter of
         the late Charles H. Rogers, aged 26 years.

1196   Died at Rondout, January 21st, 1877, Ralph Lefever,
         only son of C.H. and C.E. Perrine, aged 5 years, 10
months and 16 days; also on January 22d, 1877, Sarah Bell

184

Perrine, aged 3 years, 11 months and 12 days, and Emma M. Perrine, aged 10 months, all of diphtheria.

SATURDAY, FEBRUARY 3, 1877

1197   Mr. Perry Knickerbocker returned on Thursday night, but enquiries failed to elicit any satisfactory information as to where he had been or what he has been doing. It is said he went as far West as Utica, stopping at the various stations west of Albany. His stock of harness, etc., was sold at constable's sale on Friday afternoon.

1198   Howard Barnes, son of O.S. Barnes, a wealthy farmer of East Fishkill, left home about ten days ago, and nothing has been heard from him since. He is about seventeen years of age, and about 5 feet 8 inches in height. No cause is known for his disappearance, as he had no trouble with any of the family.

1199   The silver wedding anniversary of Mr. and Mrs. William J. Norris was celebrated at their residence at Carthage Landing, on Friday evening, 19th ult.

1200   Miss Martha Forbus, the last of her family, noted in the annals of Poughkeepsie, died in that city, on Saturday last. She was in the eighty-third year of her age.

1201   Died at Glenham, January 30th, Angeline, wife of Charles N. Gerow, aged 35 years.

1202   Died in Fishkill Landing, January 24th, Carrie A., child of Lewis H. and Mary E. Ladue, aged 5 months and 14 days.

SATURDAY, FEBRUARY 10, 1877

1203   Thomas Shaw, one of Newburgh's oldest citizens, died in that city on Tuesday last, aged seventy-seven years.

1204   The *Poughkeepsie Press* notices an old couple, George Badgley and wife, aged respectively eighty-six and eighty-three, now living in the town of Clinton, who were married in 1815 in Pleasant Valley. They are keeping house by themselves, doing all their own housework, and are on the same farm where they first commenced keeping house in 1816.

1205   Retributive justice has overtaken Rothlin, the soldier who, while on guard at West Point, early last summer, shot and fatally wounded Washington Putnam. He was transferred to Willet's Point, where he has been convicted of stealing. The court martial placed him on the retired list for three years, with the moderate service of carrying the ball and chain as an ornament of special merit.

1206   Died in Fishkill Landing, February 7th, Edna, infant daughter of Thomas and Mary A. Aldridge, aged eight months. Funeral services from the residence of her parents, on Saturday, February 10th, at 10½ o'clock. Relatives and friends are invited to attend.

SATURDAY, FEBRUARY 17, 1877

1207   Another of the "drowned men" has returned home safe — Charles Luyster. He went to Newburgh and got on an extended spree.

1208   Married February 13th, at the parsonage of the M.E. Church, Fishkill Landing, N.Y., by Rev. A. Coons, Mr.

186

Michael P. Holland, of Rockaway Beach, to Miss Julia F. Hughson, of Poughkeepsie.

1209   Married at the M.E. Parsonage, in Fishkill Village, January 28th, by Rev. W.F. Brush, Morton Barton, of Cold Spring, to Sarah A. Burrows, of Fishkill.

1210   Married at Ludingtonville, February 3d, by Justice F.J. Sprague, James H. Dakin and Ophelia J. Ballard, both of East Fishkill.

1211   Died at Matteawan, February 15th, Mrs. Mary Horton, in the 85th year of her age.

1212   Died at Low Point, on Friday, February 9th, Mrs. Jane Adriance, wife of Capt. Charles Adriance, age 73 years.

SATURDAY, FEBRUARY 24, 1877

1213   We are sorry to say that our informant was in error last week, when he reported that Mr. Charles Luyster has returned home, safe and well. We learn from his brother that nothing has been heard from him since his absence was first noted.

1214   Noah Hanson has passed away. For over forty years he has been among us. His sickness was brief. On Friday last he took the mail to the depot, but was attacked by a severe chill and prostration, and had to be brought home. He took to his bed, and on Thursday last, at about seven o'clock, he passed away.
   Mr. Hanson was born in Kennebec, Maine, in 1811. His ancestors were among the original settlers of that state. At the age of eighteen, Noah came to Poughkeepsie, and learned the

soap and candle trade. In 1834 he came to this village, and started the same business on his own account. Mr. Hanson has been connected with politics, and has held quite a number of local offices. He has been County Superintendent of the Poor, from 1847 to 1852; also, Poor Master of the town, Constable, Road Commissioner, Police Officer, etc.

By his first wife, Mr. Hanson had five children, four girls and a boy, all of whom are living, with one exception. His second wife is still living.

1215   On Monday afternoon of this week, at Swartwoutville, in this town, William H. White, aged thirty-two years, a young farmer, committed suicide by hanging. He was the only son of Mr. Alfred White. The young man had been suffering from mental depression the greater part of a year. He ran the dairy on his father's extensive farm, and had a wife and three children.

1216   General Jacob L. Scofield was 82 years of age on Wednesday.

1217   James E. Post, a well-known horseman of Middletown, Orange county, died suddenly on Saturday morning last, of heart disease, while sitting in his chair at the Grand Central Hotel, in that place.

1218   Died in Fishkill Landing, February 20th, Noah Hanson, aged 66 years.

1219   Died at Matteawan, February 19th, Mrs. Margaret Scott Brown, aged 69 years and 2 months.

1220   Died at Swartwoutville, February 19th, Lebbeus S. Charlock, aged 63 years.

1221   Died at Swartwoutville, February 19th, William H., son of Alfred and Eliza White, aged 32 years.

1222   Died in LaGrange, February 9th, William, oldest son of Cornelius Phillips, aged 26 years.

SATURDAY, MARCH 10, 1877
(Issue of March 3 found in Appendix C)

1223   Mr. James W. Mowatt, who was next to the oldest person living in this village, was called away, after a long period of weakness and gradual failing. He had been confined to the house but a short time. He finally breathed his last near midnight on Tuesday.

   Mr. Mowatt was born in the town of Blooming Grove, near Craigville, Orange county, in 1793. He learned the trade of millwright from Mr. Benjamin Brown, and moved with him to Glenham. He later moved to Matteawan, and then to Fishkill Landing, a hamlet of a few houses and but one store. Mr. Mowatt was a member of the Reformed Church of this village; and the last surviving charter member of Beacon Lodge, No. 283, F.& A.M.

1224   Mr. George D. Kittredge died in Andover, Mass., on Tuesday morning. He had been an invalid for some time, from an affection of the lungs. He came to our village a few years since, and was engaged in business with his brother, Dr. C.M. Kittredge. During the last year he was a member of the Village Board of Trustees. He was an active member of the Young Men's Association. He was liberally educated at Amherst College.

1225   Mr. Joseph R. Green is the oldest man in our village. He is nearly ninety years of age.

1226   Joseph W. Powell, a prominent citizen of Newburgh, was found dead in his room at the United States Hotel, in that city, last Saturday morning. He retired the previous night in good health. It is supposed death was caused by apoplexy. The deceased was long connected with the fire department of Newburgh, and at one time was foreman of Cataract No. 3. He was aged fifty-eight years and was a bachelor.

1227   Mr. Edmund Luyster, of East Fishkill, offers one hundred dollars reward for the recovery of the body of Charles Luyster, his brother, who it is supposed was drowned in crossing the river at this place on the night of the 18th of January. The missing man was forty years of age, of a sandy complexion, and wore a full beard. When last seen he had on a dark water-proof overcoat and a dark suit of clothes, with heavy boots.

1228   Married on Tuesday, March 5th [sic], at Rectory, in Glenham, by the Rev. John R. Livingston, John M. Hill, of Rhode Island, to Margaret J. Miller, of Glenham.

1229   Married on Wednesday, March 7th, at the residence of the bride's father, by Rev. W.W. Sever, James D. Swift, of Millbrook, Dutchess county, to Emma E., second daughter of John C. Carson, of New York city.

1230   Died in Fishkill Landing, March 6th, James W. Mowatt, aged 83 years and 8 months. Relatives and friends of the family are invited to attend the funeral on Saturday, March 10th, at ten o'clock, from the Reformed Church.

1231   Died in Fishkill Landing, March 3d, Alvaretta, aged 4 years and 1 month; March 5th, Samuel, aged 8 months, children of Samuel J. [sic] and Laura A. Mathews.

1232   Died in Fishkill Landing, March 3d, Deborah, wife of
          John Gee, aged 70 years.

1233   Died at Glenham, March 4th, of congestion of the
          lungs, Ellen, wife of John Phillips, in the 31st year of
her age.

1234   Died at Andover, Mass., March 6th, Mr. George D.
          Kittredge, of this village.

1235   Died at Matteawan, March 7th, Mrs. Mary Anne, wife
          of Mr. George Broad, aged 49 years, 7 months and 12
days.

1236   Died at Poughkeepsie, March 3d, Mrs. Annette Horn,
          aged 57 years.

1237   Died on Friday, March 2d, at the residence of his son,
          Rev. O. Haviland, Tuckahoe, N.Y., Horace J. Haviland,
in the 70th year of his age.

SATURDAY, MARCH 17, 1877

1238   Captain Lahrbusch, said to be the oldest person in
          America, last week celebrated his one hundred eleventh
birthday. He is put down as a *protege* of General J. Watts de
Peyster, of Red Hook.

1239   The funeral of Mr. James W. Mowatt took place last
          Saturday morning. The services were held in the
Reformed Church, under charge of Rev. Mr. Fritts, assisted by
Rev. A. Coons. Beacon Lodge, F. & A.M., attended as a body.

The deceased was buried in the Methodist Cemetery of this village.

1240   Rev. Uriah Messiter died on Friday of last week, 9th inst. His funeral took place at Cold Spring on Thursday afternoon. Mr. Messiter had for nearly thirty years been a faithful minister of the Methodist Episcopal Church. He began preaching in 1848, when he was stationed at Glenham; in 1852 - 1863 he was at Fishkill. His present assignment was at Coeyman's Hollow.

1241   Mr. J. Hervey Cook left on Tuesday afternoon to attend the funeral of his father-in-law, Hon. Peter Smith, of Waterloo, N.J., who died on Monday. Mr. Smith has been President for a long time of the Hackettstown National Bank, a member of the State Senate, and a trustee of the Hacketts- town Seminary. He was also an active member of his church (Methodist Episcopal).

1242   George Dimick Kittredge, of this village, who died in Andover, Mass., at the house of his brother-in-law, Rev. C.F.P. Bancroft, on the morning of the sixth, instant, was the second son of the late Captain Timothy and Mrs. Fanny (Marsh) Kittredge, and was born in Mount Vernon, N.H., January 9th, 1841. He graduated from Amherst College in 1865. In 1870 he joined his brother, C.M. Kittredge, M.D., in a private Sanitarium in this place. He was a member of the Congregational Church. His remains were taken to his native place for interment.

1243   Died in Fishkill Landing, March 13th, Joseph, son of Daniel and Elizabeth Dwan, aged 6 years and 6 months.

1244   Died at Glenham, on Wednesday, March 14th, of

typhoid fever, Herbert Wickson, son of the late Lemuel
Wickson, aged 17 years.

1245 Died in New York city, March 13th, Lela, infant
        daughter of Willis and M. Louise Van Tine, aged 1 year
and 3 months. Interment at Matteawan.

1246 Died at Liberty, Sullivan county, N.Y., March 6th, Ai
        Gildersleve, aged 56 years.

1247 Died at Fishkill Landing, March 14th, Jane Walsh, aged
        21 years.

SATURDAY, MARCH 24, 1877

1248 Miss Amelia Van Vliet, eldest daughter of Mr. John
        Van Vliet, of this village, died on Wednesday morning
after a brief illness.

1249 Stephen Cooper, aged sixty-two, of the town of Dover,
        in this county, was convicted of the murder of his son,
Steve, aged twenty-three, last February. The jury brought in a
verdict of manslaughter in the third degree, for the shooting,
and Cooper was sentenced to imprisonment in the Albany
Penitentiary for three years. Young Steve had been accused of
beating his father, mother and eighty-two year old
grandmother, on several occasions.

1250 Died on Wednesday, March 21st, Miss Amelia Van
        Vliet, aged 37 years.

1251 Died at Matteawan, March 22d, Mrs. Mary Fitzgerald,
        aged 79 years.

1252   Died at Paterson, N.J., March 19th, of diphtheria, after
two days' illness, Fanny, eldest child of John S. and
Lucy Matilda Richards, aged 7 years, 9 months and 11 days.
The body was brought to this village for interment in the vault.

SATURDAY, MARCH 31, 1877

1253   The last full-blooded Indian of the tribe of
Schaghticook Indians in this county, was the locally
famous Eunice Manwee. She lived on a State reservation, and
died in 1859, aged about 104 years. She was intelligent and
accustomed to talk, and remembered many curious things.

1254   Married in Poughquag, by Rev. B.W. [sic] Lewis,
March 10th, Mr. James W. Brett to Miss Hannah
Ladue, both of Fishkill.

1255   Died at Matteawan, March 24th, Lewis Francis, infant
son of Lewis and Ellen Klenke, aged 1 month and 3
days.

1256   Died at Newburgh, March 25th, suddenly, Rachel,
widow of the late Barlow Green, aged 54 years.

1257   Died in Wappingers Falls, on Tuesday, March 20th,
John, son of John and Phœbe Acheson, aged 5 years
and 9 months.

1258   Died in New York city, March 25th, Mrs. Emeline
Miller, aged 68 years.

SATURDAY, APRIL 7, 1877

1259   The *Fishkill Journal* says a baptismal font of Italian marble has been placed in the Hopewell Reformed Church, bearing the inscription: "In Memoriam, M.K. Davidson, Anno Domini, September, 1875." It was presented by the brothers and sisters of the deceased.

1260   Divorced. — In the city of Poughkeepsie, on the 31st day of March, 1877, by the Hon. Joseph H. Barnard, Justice of the Supreme Court, Anna Virginia Green from Willis Van Buren, both of this village.

1261   Samuel McLaughlin, a well-known Orange county horseman, died in the town of New Windsor, near Little Britain, on Thursday of last week.

1262   Captain M.B. Michaels, some years ago captain of the ferryboat between this place and Newburgh, died in that city last Saturday morning, in the sixty-third year of his age.

1263   Married in Fishkill Village, March 25th, by Rev. W.F. Brush, Austin P. Russell to Maggie M. Smith.

1264   Married at the residence of the bride's parents, in Hughsonville, March 27th, by Rev. E.S. Bishop, Mr. Albert Hitchcock, of Fishkill Plains, to Miss Mary L. Van Nosdall, of the former place.

1265   Died in Newburgh, April 1st, Sarah L., wife of N.B. Beede, aged 43 years and 1 month.

1266   Died in Fishkill Village, April 1st, Mrs. Sarah P. Tibbals, in the 77th year of her age.

SATURDAY, APRIL 14, 1877

1267 Mr. Charles Carman, a native and continual resident of
Poughkeepsie for seventy-eight years past, and
well-known in business and social circles, died at his residence
on Wednesday morning of this week.

1268 Died at Fishkill Landing, April 8th, Hattie E., eldest
daughter of Edward J. and Mary Frances Member,
aged 4 years, 1 month and 5 days.

1269 Died in East Fishkill, April 4th, William, son of
Catherine E. and the late William Porter, aged 23 years.

SATURDAY, APRIL 21, 1877

1270 Sergeant Peattie's recent marriage to a cousin of
Captain Forrestal, was quite a noted social event.

1271 Mr. William Schram, of Newburgh, is probably the
oldest effective practical printer on the Hudson river.
He celebrated his seventieth birthday on Wednesday of this
week.

1272 The death of Mr. Joseph Bartlett, of Poughkeepsie, is
announced, at the ripe age of almost 78 years. He went
to that city, says the *Eagle*, in 1840, and was engaged in active
business for about twenty-five years, being the founder of the
cracker and cake business now carried on by William H. Broas
& Co. He was a prominent member of the Presbyterian
Church, having been an elder for a number of years. Mr.
Bartlett leaves a wife and one daughter, the wife of Otis
Bisbee, and five sons, two of whom are active workers in the
ministry. He had been married for over fifty years.

196

1273   Married at St. Stephen's Church, New York city, April
         10th, by Rev. Father McCready, James Peattie, of
Fishkill Landing, to Anastasia Forrestal, of New York.

1274   Married at Newburgh, Monfort Waldron to Maggie
         Magar, both of Matteawan.

1275   Married April 5th, at the residence of the bride's
         parents, Hopewell, N.Y., by Rev. Graham Taylor,
Charles S. Hawes, of Brooklyn, N.Y., to Sarah A., daughter of
Peter Luyster.

1276   Died at the residence of DuBois Brinckerhoff, near
         Fishkill Landing, April 19th, Harriet, wife of
Washington Van Pelt, aged 33 years and 9 months.

1277   Died April 6th, 1877, at the house of Oliver Cromwell,
         in the town of New Windsor, N.Y., Yoner Clauson,
colored, born at Fishkill, at the late Francis Purdy's.

SATURDAY, APRIL 28, 1877

1278   The wife of Rev. William Goss, deceased, has moved
         from Poughkeepsie to Sing Sing.

1279   Eli Benjamin, aged eighty-four years, turns the wheel of
         The New Paltz Times press.

1280   The Rev. Thomas Keating, D.D., pastor of St. Mary's
         Catholic Church of Hudson, died last Monday evening.

1281   Captain George Barker, who died at Hudson on
         Sunday morning last, in the eighty-fourth year of his
age, had been a Master Mason since 1814, and an Odd Fellow

since 1815.

1282   Rev. Joseph Wickham, D.D., of Manchester, so many
          years the efficient Principal of Burr Seminary, received
with his honored wife, on the 4th inst., — it being the
completion of the eightieth year of his age — marked tokens of
love and respect from their elderly friends and the citizens of
Manchester, in an unexpected gathering and gifts. -*Vermont
Chronicle.*
  Dr. Wickham was the first settled pastor of the Presbyterian
Church, Matteawan, being installed forty-four years ago.

1283   Married April 25th, at the bride's home in Hillsdale, by
          Rev. A. Coons, assisted by the Revs. William E. Clarke
and J. Grimes, the Rev. E.H. Roys, of Florida (N.Y.)
Conference, to Miss Hattie Tipple.

1284   Died near Fishkill Village, April 24th, Emma Jane, child
          of John J. and Lavina Wood, aged 1 year, 8 months and
3 days.

1285   Died at Fishkill Plains, April 19th, Phebe E. Van Wyck,
          daughter of Elizabeth and the late R.S. Van Wyck.

1286   Died at Sandown, Isle of Wight, March 28th, Adelia
          Emans, wife of R.W. Gordon, Sr., in the 53d year of
her age.

SATURDAY, MAY 5, 1877

1287   Officer John Nelson, of the Newburgh police force, was
          suddenly taken ill while coming down Western Avenue
on Friday night of last week, and died in about ten minutes
after, on the sidewalk.

1288 One of the largest funeral processions ever seen in
       Florida, Orange county, was that of old colored Chloe.
She was the nurse of the late Hon. William H. Seward; in his
life time he made provision for her while she should live.

1289 Mr. Hugh Wallace, whose decease we record today,
       was well-known, having been long identified with
several organizations. He was a veteran of the late war—a
member of the Denning Guard; a comrade of Post Howland,
G.A.R.; a member of Plano's Brass Band; a brother in the
Independent Order of Odd Fellows, etc. By trade he was a
mason. He had been attacked by consumption.

1290 Rev. Hector Brownson, the well-known agent of the
       American Bible Society, and a minister of the
Methodist Church, died on Sunday morning last, at his
residence in Rhinebeck village. He had attained to the ripe age
of 86 years.

1291 Married May 3d, at the residence of the bride's parents,
       by the Rev. J.R. Livingston, William Sutcliffe to Mary
Eliza Townsend, all of Glenham.

1292 Married at Matteawan, April 27th, by the Rev. S.B.
       Almy, Charles Leach to Sarah E. Sheerer, both of
Wappingers Falls.

1293 Married at Matteawan, April 28th, by the Rev. S.B.
       Almy, Jeremiah P. Mead to Ann Barkley, both of Port
Jervis.

1294 Died at Matteawan, May 2d, Hugh Wallace, aged 36
       years, 4 months and 15 days. Relatives and friends of
the deceased are invited to attend the funeral on Sunday, at 2

p.m., at the Presbyterian Church, Matteawan.

SATURDAY, MAY 12, 1877

1295 George W. Vail, of Verbank, in this county, son of
Elias Vail, lost his life by an accident at Verbank, in this
county, last Sunday evening. Young Vail was about fifteen
years, and was one of a pair of twins. He and his brother were
going after some rats who were among the eggs and the young
chickens. George, in advance of his brother, climbed the fence,
dragging the loaded gun after him, muzzle first. By some
means, the gun was discharged, the load entering his breast and
piecing his lung. He died almost instantly. -*Poughkeepsie
News.*

1296 George Booth, a printer who used to work in the
Fishkill Journal office, some years ago, but latterly
employed in New York, but recently unemployed, committed
suicide by hanging himself on Thursday morning of this week.
He had recently become unemployed. *The Sun* says he lived
with his mistress, Annie Harrington, with whom he had a
quarrel on Wednesday morning; he knocked her across the
bed, and she locked him out of their rooms. After battering on
her door for three quarters of an hour, he climbed into the
room through the fanlight. He talked lovingly to Annie, saying
he would marry her; at 2 o'clock Thursday morning, he went
into an outer room, knotted his shirt about his throat, and hung
himself from the crossbar of the door to the bedroom. He was
26 years old. His aged mother lives in Fishkill Village.

1297 Married at Matteawan, May 9th, by the Rev. J.J. Dean,
Andrew W. Smith, of Monticello, N.Y., to Lizzie
Ladue, of Matteawan.

1298   Died at Fishkill Landing, May 10th, Katie D., infant
          daughter of John and Mary E. Sewell, aged 1 year, 11
months and 21 days. Relatives and friends of the family are
invited to attend the funeral on Saturday, May 12th, at 2½
o'clock, from the residence of her parents.

1299   Died at Fishkill Landing, May 4th, Susan Elizabeth,
          daughter of John W. and Martha A. Stevenson, aged 11
years, 4 months and 8 days.

1300   Died at Brooklyn, May 8th, Mrs. Gertie Brush,
          daughter of J.H. Gesner, of Fishkill Landing, aged 22
years.

1301   Died at Matteawan, May 7th, Kate S. Smith, wife of
          Everett B. Smith, aged 34 years, 3 months and 2 days.

1302   Died at Matteawan, May 4th, Carrie M. Christ, wife of
          Herman Christ, aged 24 years, 5 months and 24 days.

SATURDAY, MAY 19, 1877

1303   Married on Wednesday, May 9th, at the residence of
          the bride's parents, by Rev. P.C. Archer, William H.
Masters, of Matteawan, N.Y., to Helen M., eldest daughter of
Williamson Wynne, Esq., of Huntsville, Texas.

1304   Married at Brookfield Centre, Conn., at the residence
          of the bride's mother, Mrs. C.V.B. Booraem, by the
Rev. E. L. Whitcome, Anna H., daughter of the late Dr. A.C.
Booraem, of New York city, to Caswell L.
Higby, of Fishkill Landing.

1305   Died in Fishkill Landing, May 16th, Frankie, son of

201

J.W. and Martha Stevenson, aged 6 years, 9 months and 6 days.

1306   Died at Fishkill Landing, May 13th, Mrs. Rhoda
        Ackroyd, aged 71 years, 9 months and 28 days.

1307   Died in Fishkill Landing, May 16th, John Wiltsie, aged
        71 years.

1308   Died in Matteawan, May 17th, Ann, widow of the late
        James McArdle, aged 40 years. Relatives and friends of
the family are invited to attend the funeral on Saturday, May
19th, at ten o'clock, from St. Joachim's Church, where a
requiem and high mass will be held.

SATURDAY, MAY 26, 1877

1309   Rev. C.W. Millard preached the funeral sermon of Mrs.
        Samuel Rogers, Sr., at the Matteawan M.E. Church, on
Thursday. There were also present Rev. Messrs. Dean, Scott,
and Fritts.

1310   Mrs. P.W. Hitchcock died, at Omaha, on Tuesday
        evening, 15th inst. She was the daughter of Dr. Gilbert
C. Monell, and niece of Hon. John J. Monell, of this village,
and was born in Newburgh. The family removed to Omaha in
1857, and in the fall of 1858 she was married, in her 19th year,
to Hon. P.W. Hitchcock.

1311   Mr. Frederick Pugsley, son of Mr. Charles B. Pugsley,
        died on Friday morning, at the parsonage of the
Reformed Church in this village. He had been sick just a week,
and was not thought to be in any special danger, until his
disease developed into pneumonia, congestion of the lungs,

and finally typhoid fever set in. He was a member of the Reformed Church; and was connected with the Sunday school. Mr. Pugsley was about 23 years of age. For two years past he had been engaged with Mr. Stephen Schouten, in the under-taking business.

1312   Married at the Presbyterian Parsonage, Wappingers
        Falls, April 14th, by the Rev. J.O. Denniston, William
Hall, of Hughsonville, to Sarah A. Terwilliger, of Fishkill-on-Hudson.

1313   Married by the Rev. L.H. King, in Newburgh, April
        15th, Albert Townsend to Lillie Wood, both of
Matteawan.

1314   Married in Poughkeepsie, May 19th, by Rev. J.R.
        Kendrick, D.D., Mr. Josiah S. Budd, of Matteawan,
and Miss Gertrude E. Stanford, of Poughkeepsie.

1314   Married at the residence of the bride, Albany, N.Y.,
        May 17th, 1877, by the Rev. Merritt Hulburd, of St.
Paul's Church, Lowell, Mass., Mr. Eleazer J. Knowles and Miss Jennie Lord, both of Albany, N.Y.

1315   Died in Fishkill Landing, May 25th, Frederick Pugsley,
        aged 23 years and 3 months. Relatives and friends of
the family are invited to attend the funeral on Sunday, May 27th, at 2½ o'clock, from the Reformed Church.

1316   Died at Matteawan, May 21st, Catharine Rogers, wife
        of Samuel Rogers, Sr., aged 68 years, 1 month and 25
days.

SATURDAY, JUNE 2, 1877

1317   Bennie Havens, of Highland Falls, a noted character
          and the original of the class song, "Bennie Havens, O,"
died there Wednesday morning, aged ninety-one years. He was
always a great favorite among the cadets.

1318   The funeral of Mr. Frederick Pugsley took place on
          Sunday afternoon last. The body was interred in the
Presbyterian Cemetery.

1319   Married in Brooklyn, N.Y., May 17th, 1877, by the
Rev. A.O. Connell,   James A. Cull, of Brooklyn, to Mary E.,
daughter of W.H. Mosher, formerly of Matteawan, N.Y.

SATURDAY, JUNE 9, 1877

1320   Married at Poughquag, May 30th, by Rev. B.N. [sic]
          Lewis, Egbert L. Berry, of East Fishkill, and Gertie
Hall, of Poughquag.

1321   Married at North Woodstock, Conn., May 30th, by
          Rev. E.H. Pratt, T.H. Meek, of East Douglas, Mass., to
Millie S. Childs, of North Woodstock, Conn.

1322   Died at Lagrange, May 29th, Ralph Phillips, aged 76
          years, 5 months and 20 days.

SATURDAY, JUNE 16, 1877

1323   The body of John [sic] Luyster, of East Fishkill, who
          has been missing since last January, was found in the
water near New Windsor, on Wednesday of last week. He was

last seen on the ice upon the occasion of a horse trot, and it is
supposed he must have accidentally fallen into the ferry track.

1324   Married on Thursday, June 14th, at the residence of the
           bride's mother, Mrs. Adelia DuBois, by Rev. C.W.
Fritts, George P. Alden to Cornelia DuBois, all of Fishkill
Landing, N.Y.

SATURDAY, JUNE 23, 1877

1325   William H. Odell, of Low Point, "borrowed" a buck
           saw from his brother-in-law, John Higgs, of this village,
and refused to return it. He was arrested and taken before
Justice Harris, who suspended sentence, upon promise of Odell
that he would return the saw.

1326   Henry D. Varick, a prominent and esteemed citizen of
           Poughkeepsie, died there on Monday. He had held
various positions of responsibility during his life.

1327   David Ticehurst, of Matteawan, who died on Thursday,
           June 21st, was a member of the Grand Army of the
Republic, who will attend his funeral on Saturday afternoon.
Mr. David J. Ticehurst was aged 34 years, 9 months and 25
days.

1328   Died at Matteawan, June 16th, Wm. Davis, aged 72
           years.

1329   Died at Matteawan, June 20th, Charles, son of Thomas
           and Bridget Cleary, aged 9 years and 8 months.

1330   Died in East Fishkill, June 15th, Geneva B., infant
           daughter of Robert T. and Melissa B. Knapp, aged 7

months and 9 days.

1331 Died in Troy, June 17th, Mrs. Sarah Wood, aged 38 years.

SATURDAY, JUNE 30, 1877

1332 Married in St. Paul's P.E. Church, Bridgeport, Conn., Wednesday, June 20th, by Rev. N.S. Richardson, D.D., Thomson E. Goring, of Wappingers Falls, N.Y., to Mary J., only daughter of James Myatt, Esq., of Bridgeport, Conn.

1333 Married at Wappingers Falls, in Zion P.E. Church, on Wednesday, June 20th, by Rev. H.Y. Satterlee, Mr. Frank Wiedener, of Philadelphia, Pa., to Miss Elizabeth DuBois, of Wappingers Falls.

1334 Died at Matteawan, June 22d, George Broad, aged 49 years, 7 months and 25 days.

1335 Died in Phillipston, Putnam county, June 23d, Elizabeth Ann, widow of Josiah Hustis, in the 63d year of her age.

SATURDAY, JULY 7, 1877

1336 William P. Thorne and his wife Lettie, whose troubles we published a couple of weeks ago, have parted, she returning to her parents' home at Glenham with the little girl, while he retains possession of the two boys. Mr. Thorne forbids all persons trusting his wife on his account.

1337 On Monday of this week, Mr. Buel Evans, of Matteawan, received an envelope by express,

206

containing $200. It came from J.G. Smith, Charleston, S.C. The same day he received a letter, written in a disguised hand, which stated he had taken the money from Mr. Buel's brother who died in his presence, and that "Smith" had taken it for safekeeping. The brother spoken of was undoubtedly Peter Evans, who died at Bresnan's European House, Savannah, Georgia, on the 18th of December, 1875.

Mr. Evans thinks the money he received is only a part of what was taken from his brother's person or trunk by the person who sent the money. Mr. Peter Evans went South for the benefit of his health, being consumptive, and died as stated above.

Mr. Evans had two brothers die away from home. About twenty-eight years ago, one of his brothers started for California, and was never heard from. It is supposed he died at the South, but this is not positively known.

1338 We understand that Rev. J.R. Livingston, of Glenham, has been taken to the Hudson River Hospital for the Insane, at Poughkeepsie, for treatment.

1339 Mrs. Longbottom, formerly of Groveville, and one of the passengers in the delayed *"City of Brussels,"* died very suddenly of apoplexy, at Sun Inn, Light Cliff, England, a few days ago, only a day or two after the arrival there of her husband.

1340 Married at Matteawan, July 3d, by Rev. A. Coons, Mr. Alfred Hulse, of Newburgh, and Miss Anna Terwilliger, of Matteawan.

1341 Died July 4th, at the residence of her brother, Mr. Joseph Lomas, Amelia Lomas, widow of the late Joseph Simpson, aged 70 years.

1342   Died July 1st, at Fishkill Landing, Susie, daughter of
        Thomas and Ann Haigh, formerly of Middletown, aged
22 years.

1343   Died at Fishkill Landing, July 2d, Joseph B. Whiting,
        from near Boston, aged 36 years and 4 months.

1344   Died at Fishkill Landing, July 5th, Mrs. Mary Schutt,
        aged 70 years. Friends and relatives are invited to
attend the funeral on Saturday, the 7th, at 3 o'clock, from the
Reformed Church, Fishkill Village.

1345   Died in Poughkeepsie, July 4, William Whitehouse,
        aged 26 years.

SATURDAY, JULY 14, 1877

1346   Mr. and Mrs. John Peatie, of Rhinebeck, formerly of
        this village, celebrated their twentieth wedding
anniversary last Monday. Quite a number of friends from this
neighborhood were present.

1347   Mr. Richard Hopper, brother of Mr. Nicholas Hopper,
        of this place, died in New York city, on Friday of last
week, 6th inst., in the 49th year of his age. Mr. Hopper has
been for nearly twenty years Janitor of the General Theological
Seminary of the Protestant Episcopal Church in that city. His
funeral service on Sunday afternoon, in the Chapel of the
Institution, were conducted by the Dean. Mr. Hopper's
remains were brought to Garrisons on Monday for interment.

1348   On Friday afternoon of last week, Thomas Stevenson,
        of this village, being under the influence of liquor for
some days, attempted to kill himself by cutting the veins in his

right wrist, with a razor. He called to his wife, formerly Mrs. Griffin Snook, to bid her farewell, when efforts were made to stop the flow of blood, and bind the wound. He is now recovering.

1349   Married on Saturday, June 30th, at Hopewell Parsonage, by Rev. Graham Taylor, Charles H. Richmond, of Matteawan, to Mattie LeFevre, of Glenham.

1350   Died at the General Theological Seminary, New York city, July 6th, Richard Hopper, in the 49th year of his age, for twenty years the highly esteemed janitor of the institution.

1351   Died in New York city, July 7th, of consumption, Miss Mary Weller, daughter of the late Captain William Weller, aged 23 years. Interment last Monday, in the Fishkill Rural Cemetery.

SATURDAY, JULY 21, 1877

1352   On Tuesday, Patrick Murphy, of Matteawan, was taken to the Hudson River Hospital for the Insane, in Poughkeepsie. We understand that Rev. J.R. Livingston, of Glenham, also was recently taken there for treatment.

1353   The remnant of the Broad family, consisting of three girls and one boy, have left Matteawan for England, where they have relatives who are well off.

1354   Mr. Robert P. Newcomb, who purchased the Dr. Montagnie place a year or more ago, died at Newark, N.J., on Saturday of last week, aged 43 years. His complaint was heart disease. He formerly resided at Glenham. His body

209

was brought to this village, the funeral services taking place at his late residence. The interment was in the Fishkill Rural Cemetery.

1355   Died at Matteawan, July 18th, Mary, daughter of George Davidson, aged 10 months.

1356   Died at Groveville, on the 14th inst., William Shuttleworth, aged 28 years.

1357   Died at Newark, N.J., July 14th, Mr. Robert P. Newcomb, aged 43 years.

1358   Died in the town of Washington, July 10th, George H., son of Charles and Mary Jane Ladue, in his 22d year.

SATURDAY, JULY 28, 1877

1359   Mr. and Mrs. Bartow Vandewater, Matteawan, are to celebrate their silver wedding on the 10th of August.

1360   Mr. and Mrs. William Romain Edmond, Matteawan, are to celebrate their silver wedding on the 23d of August.

1361   Miss Helen V. Osborne, formerly organist in the Reformed Church of this village, was married last week to Mr. H.E. Kriebiel, of Cincinnati, Ohio, and has been visiting friends in this neighborhood.

1362   Died at Fishkill Landing, July 25th, George W. Beebe, aged 39 years. Interment at Danbury, Conn.

1363   Died in Matteawan, July 23d, Willie, son of Charles and

Mary Gerow, aged 4 months and 6 days.

SATURDAY, AUGUST 4, 1877

1364   The remains of the late General Custer have been
            brought to Poughkeepsie, for interment in the receiving
vault, until the funeral takes place next October.

1365   Married at Hughsonville, on Wednesday, August 1st,
            by Rev. R.M. Brown, D.D., at the residence of the
bride's mother, Charles D.B. Monfort, of Fishkill Plains, to
Hattie M. Hasbrook, of the former place.

1366   Died at Fishkill Landing, July 30th, Agnes, daughter of
            Eugene B. and Margaret O'Sullivan, aged 3 months
and 5 days.

1367   Died at Matteawan, August 2d, Daisey May, infant
            daughter of J.T. and Kate Oliver, aged 15 days.

1368   Died at Matteawan, July 30th, Enos Scholefield, aged
            78 years, 2 months and 21 days.

1369   Died at Middlebush, July 21st, Mrs. Jane Conover, wife
            of Benjamin Conover, aged 77 years.

SATURDAY, AUGUST 11, 1877

1370   By the swamping of the flat-bottomed boat in which
            they were taking a pleasure sail last Saturday evening,
six Newburgh men were precipitated into the water, near
Denning's Point, and one, a young man named Walter S.
Bennett, was drowned, while attempting to swim ashore. His
body was recovered on Monday. He formerly worked for Mr.

211

Samuel McKee, of Matteawan, when that gentleman was in business in Newburgh.

1371   Under our matrimonial heading is recorded the marriage of Captain Charles W. Brundage, of this village, and Miss Ella E. Murphy, of Matteawan. This happy event took place on Wednesday, at the residence of Prof. Murphy, of Harpersfield, Delaware county, in this State. After a short bridal tour, the newly wedded pair will take up their residence in this village.

1372   Mr. Lynde Belknap, formerly proprietor of the flour mill at Matteawan, died at Westfield, N.J., on Friday of last week. His health had been very poor ever since his removal from Matteawan, but there were no symptoms of immediate danger until six weeks ago. At that time his trouble assumed the form of a heart affection. His sufferings were continuous and severe until about nine o'clock on Friday morning, when death suddenly came to his relief. The burial took place in the family ground near Little Britain, on last Tuesday afternoon.

1373   Philip Smith, a dissolute fellow, was found dead in Mr. Beecher's blacksmith shop, on the Matteawan road, on Wednesday evening. He had been very feeble of late. In the afternoon he came to the shop, and was helped in, being intoxicated, and lay down on the floor. Shortly afterward, he was found to be dead. He was about 55 years of age, and in his younger days was a gardener for Mr. H.W. Sargent. He leaves a wife and several children, from whom he has been separated for many years. They live at Cohoes, in Columbia county. His children are all grown up. He was a volunteer during the late civil war, and expected soon to come into possession of about $1500, due him for services or bounty. The funeral took place on Friday afternoon, from the residence of his brother, Patrick

Smith, in this village.

1374   A very heavy thunderstorm visited a portion of Ulster
            county about 7 p.m. on Tuesday, and raged with great
fury for a short time. The barn of Dubois Elting, a farmer,
situated about half a mile from Gardiner Station, was struck by
lightning and burned to the ground. Mr. Elting was instantly
killed. John Fallon, also in the barn, was stunned and knocked
down.

1375   Married at the residence of the bride's parents,
            Harpersfield, N.Y., on Wednesday, August 8th, 1877,
by the Rev. F. Duncan Janden, Rector of St. Peter's Church,
Hobart, N.Y., Miss Ella E. Murphy, to Captain Charles W.
Brundage, of Fishkill Landing.

1376   Married July 31st, in Chester, by Rev. George Clarke,
            pastor M.E. Church, Ira J. Dolson, of East Fishkill,
Dutchess county, N.Y., to Miss H. Lizzie Dains, of Chester.

1377   Died in Fishkill Landing, August 7th, Phœbe
            Townsend, wife of Edwin Jewell, aged 53 years and 3
months.

1378   Died at Fishkill Landing, August 4th, Mabel Helena,
            daughter of William H. and Helena A. Rozell, aged 10
months and 17 days, of infantum.

SATURDAY, AUGUST 18, 1877

1379   Hon. Allard Anthony died suddenly at a quarter to six
            o'clock Sunday evening, at his residence, corner of
Market and Montgomery streets, aged about 30 years. He had
been ill for a week or ten days with dysentery, but was able to

attend to his law business. His illness becoming worse, Mrs. Anthony, becoming alarmed, sent one of the children for Dr. J.C. Payne, and another for Hon. John Thompson, her father. He expired just as they both arrived. Cause of death was sudden and severe congestion of the brain.

Allard Anthony came to this city from Union College when he was 20 years of age, and entered John Thompson's law office to study law. In 1859 he was appointed to fill the unexpired term of District Attorney for Hon. B. Platt Carpenter, who resigned; in 1861 and 1864 he was elected to that position. In 1867 he was elected County Judge by the Republican party.

Deceased leaves a wife and two children (a boy and a girl) behind. His mother and brother reside at Newburgh. Judge Anthony's funeral took place on Wednesday. His body was interred in the Fishkill Rural Cemetery.

1380   Benjamin Conover, formerly a resident of Fishkill Village, died at Wappingers Falls on Friday of last week, aged 89 years.

1381   The funeral of Mrs. John Kimbark took place from the Glenham M.E. Church, last Sunday afternoon. The services were conducted by Rev. E.S. Bishop, of Fishkill Village.

1382   Charles T. Bennett, postmaster at Fulton, in this State, and editor of the *Fulton Patriot*, died on Tuesday. He was formerly from Peekskill, and a young man of excellent qualities and fine business abilities, as well as a successful editor.

1383   Died at Fishkill Landing, August 9th, Mary, wife of B. Manning, aged 66 years.

1384   Died at Glenham, August 10th, Mrs. John Kimbark, in
the 59th year of her age.

1385   Died in Fishkill Village, August 9th, Carrie E., daughter
of Albert and Eliza L. Meeks, aged 1 year, 3 months
and 10 days.

1386   Died in Fishkill Village, August 8th, Freddie, child of
John and Laura Losee, aged 1 year, 11 months and 8
days.

SATURDAY, SEPTEMBER 1, 1877
(no issue of August 25)

1387   John J. Roche, a Newburgh auctioneer and
saloon-keeper, suddenly fell dead while out riding in
that city, last Saturday morning, from heart disease.

1388   Died in Fishkill Landing, August 28th, Elizabeth
Bowne, widow of the late Peter Laforge, aged 85 years
and 3 months. Relatives and friends of the family are invited to
attend the funeral on Saturday, September 1st, at 2½ o'clock,
from the M.E. Church, Fishkill Landing.

1389   Died at Fishkill Landing, August 26th, May, daughter
of Edward J. and Mary Frances Member, aged 4
months and 8 days.

1390   Died at Fishkill Landing, August 24th, Samuel
Sampsen, colored, aged 55 years.

1391   Died at Matteawan, August 29th, Grace, daughter of
Isaac and Minnie Harris, aged 1 year and 10 months.

1392   Died at Glenham, August 26th, Addie D., daughter of
Charles D. and Sarah Cooper, aged 12 months and 14
days.

1393   Died at Binghamton, N.Y., Sunday, August 19th, Eliza,
wife of Howard H. Harris, formerly of Matteawan,
aged 30 years.

1394   Died at Fishkill Village, August 25th, Sarah, wife of
Derrick Brinckerhoff, in the 83d year of her age.

1395   Died in New York city, August 24th, suddenly, Frank
Sleight, of Fishkill Village, in the 60th year of his age,
second son of the late Benjamin A. Sleight, of Fishkill

1396   Died at Williamstown, Mass., on Monday, August
27th, Thomas Alfred, fourth child of Julien T. and Alice
M. Davies, aged 4 years.

SATURDAY, SEPTEMBER 8, 1877

1397   The funeral of Mr. Emans took place on Monday
afternoon, from his late residence, and then from
Hopewell Church. The attendance was large, many men of
prominence, including a number of county officers, being
present.

1398   Brooks Hughes, a well-to-do farmer of the town of
Hyde Park, in this county, and a prominent Democrat
and active politician, committed suicide by hanging himself in
his barn, early on Tuesday morning of this
week. He appears to have been suffering from a depression of
spirits for some time.

1399   On Saturday afternoon, September 1st, John Seymour
       Emans, of East Fishkill, died at his residence, aged 52
years, 8 months and 13 days. His illness was short, and his
death very sudden. He had typhoid fever.

   John S. Emans was born on the farm where he died. He was
a prominent Democrat. He was once Member of Assembly,
was twice elected Justice of Sessions, and several times
Chairman of the Board of Supervisors. He was a director of
the Dutchess and Columbia Railroad Company. At the time of
his death he held the position of Supervisor from his town. He
leaves a wife and two grown up sons. *-Poughkeepsie Eagle,*
September 3d.

1400   Died at Matteawan, September 3d, Ann, wife of
       William McEvoy, aged 43 years, 8 months and 10 days.

1401   Died at Williamstown, Mass., September 1st, Helen,
       daughter of Julien T. and Alice M. Davies, aged 5
years.

1402   Died in Poughkeepsie, September 2d, Carry [sic], infant
       daughter of Allie M. and Jonathan I. Gill.

1403   Died at Gayhead, on Saturday, September 1st, John S.
       Emans, in the 53d year of his age.

SATURDAY, SEPTEMBER 15, 1877

1404   The relatives of Mr. Solomon Tompkins, Matteawan,
       celebrated the sixty-seventh anniversary of that
gentleman's birthday, on Tuesday evening.

1405   The story has been started, and is perhaps not without
       foundation, that Governor Robinson is about to marry

the daughter of Hon. D.B. St. John, State Senator from the
Newburgh district.

1406   David Moore, one of Newburgh's most respected
            citizens and prominent business men, died at his
residence in that city, on Sunday evening last, after an illness
which had confined him to his bed for about a week.

1407   Rev. Edgar Brett, his brothers Harvey and Charles, and
t   he widow of his deceased brother William, have lately
each received as a gift, fifty shares of Hudson River Railroad
stock, valued at par at five thousand dollars. These gifts come
from the widow of the late Mr. Danforth, proprietor of the
Danforth Locomotive Works, Paterson, N.J., she being related
to the Brett family.

1408   The will of the late Zacheus Marsh, of Glenham, has
            been annulled by Surrogate Dorland, on the ground that
the testator was incompetent to make a valid will at the time it
was executed. His property is valued at
$25,000.

1409   Married at the residence of Vincent Woodhull,
            Glenham, on Thursday afternoon, September 13th,
1877, by the Rev. R.B. Van Kleeck, Jr., Erastus Henry
Woodhull, and Georgianna Trumper, both of Cornwall, Orange
county, N.Y.

1410   Married at Fishkill Village, September 12th, by Rev.
            Asher Anderson, Mr. Edgar Bergen, of Long Island,
and Miss Gertie E. Mathewson, of Fishkill Village.

1411   Married at LaGrange, by Rev. J.W. Felvus, pastor of
            Verbank, Sanford Martin to Sarah E. Madaugh, both of

LaGrange.

1412 Married in Poughkeepsie, September 9th, by Rev. J.R.
          Kendrick, D.D., Mr. William Seeley, of Poughkeepsie,
and Mrs. Elizabeth Drum, of Stanfordville.

1413 Married at New Hamburgh, by Rev. Chas. Sager, Aug.
          27th, Wm. H. Robbins, of Clarksburgh, and Matilda E.
Mount, of Perrineville.

1414 Died at Fishkill Landing, September 8th, infant child of
          John T. and Carrie Smith, aged 2 months and 14 days.

1415 Died at Matteawan, September 8th, William H.
          Lockwood, aged 13 years and 10 months.

1416 Died at Matteawan, September 9th, William Germond,
          aged 23 years, 4 months and 9 days.

1417 Died at his residence in the Town of Washington,
          September 10th, Andrew Haight, in the 73d year of his
age.

1418 Died at Manchester Bridge, August 26th, William E.,
          son of Charles and Mary Montfort [sic], aged 1 year
and 3 days. [See also #1422.]

SATURDAY, SEPTEMBER 22, 1877

1419 Derrick Brinckerhoff died at Fishkill Village, on Friday
          last, at the ripe age of nearly ninety-one years. His aged
wife died on the 30th [sic] of August, only about two weeks
previous. He was born in what is now the town of East
Fishkill. He was an efficient member of the Reformed Church.

219

1420   John Lawson, an employee of the Atlantic Dredging
        Company, of Brooklyn, who was at work on the ferry
improvements in this village, drowned about half past ten last
Saturday morning. He fell from a mud scow, and he could not
be reached before he sank. The deceased was about 26 years of
age, and a foreigner, a Swede it is thought. He was hired by the
dredging company at South Amboy, New Jersey, about six
months ago. He gives evidence of having an education, and had
probably seen better days. The remains were interred Saturday
afternoon.

1421   Did at Fishkill Village, September 14th, Derrick
        Brinckerhoff, in the 91st year of his age.

1422   Died at Manchester Bridge, Dutchess county, N.Y.,
        September 15th, Charles Irving, son of William and
Mary Monfort [sic], aged 1 year and 23 days. [See also #1418]

SATURDAY, SEPTEMBER 29, 1877

1423   At Birmingham, Oakland county, Michigan, on Friday,
        September 14th, John W. Cromwell, a son of the late
Squire Cromwell, of this village, died, after a long and painful
illness, in the sixty-third year of his age.
The *Birmingham Post* says he was born in the town of Fishkill,
Dutchess county, N.Y., on the 25th of December, 1814. He
was married in his native town to Louisa Bromfield, also of
Fishkill, on the 5th of October, 1836. He removed with his
family in 1845, to Ann Arbor, Michigan, where he engaged in
mercantile pursuits; they remained until moving to Detroit in
1851. As his health declined, he moved his family to a farm
situated in the town of Troy, Oakland county, about two miles
from Birmingham. As his disease assumed a mixed type of
paralysis of the lower extremities, with chronic rheumatism, he

220

sold the farm and located in this village, about three years ago. He leaves a wife and two daughters to mourn his loss.

1424 Married at Matteawan, September 22d, by Rev. S.B. Almy, Mr. M.A. Fuller and Mrs. P.J. Hyde.

1425 Married at the M.E. Parsonage, Fishkill Village, September 15th, by Rev. E.S. Bishop, Mr. Edward P. Lake, of Glenham, to Miss Jennie Conklin, of Matteawan.

1426 Married at the Baptist Parsonage, Ludingtonville, September 16th, by Rev. W.B. Harris, John F. Emans, of East Fishkill, to Emma Barrett, of Farmers' Mills.

1427 Died in Fishkill Landing, September 24th, Sarah J. Pollster, wife of Henry G. Jones, aged 39 years and 9 months.

1428 Died at Matteawan, September 26th, Mary McGinnis, aged 70 years.

1429 Died at Matteawan, September 17th, Lyman A., infant son of Milo and Kate Robinson, aged 3 months.

1430 Died at Brooklyn, September 19th, Emma F. Huggins, daughter of the late James Huggins, aged 24 years. Interment at Matteawan.

1431 Died at Hughsonville, September 21st, Joseph Vail, in the 75th year of his age.

1432 Died at Union Vale, September 18th, Anna Mary, daughter of Egbert S. Peckham.

SATURDAY, OCTOBER 6, 1877

1433   Gussie Jaycox drowned herself early last Sunday
         morning. Miss Mary Augusta Jaycox was about
twenty-six, daughter of David Jaycox, who for ten or twelve
years past has been a helpless invalid. They resided on South
street, Matteawan. When Mrs. Jaycox died a few years ago,
leaving the sole care of the invalid father and the property to
the daughter, the burdens of the two seem to have had a
depressing effect. She had been sick for about a month
previous with malarial fever, and had been attended by her
cousin, Mrs. Sarah J. Tompkins, of East Fishkill, who, with her
husband, Webster A. Tompkins, was in the house at the time of
the drowning. Gussie threw herself into the cistern about nine
o'clock in the morning.

1434   Married at the bride's residence, September 24th, by
         Rev. J.J. Dean, Mr. Salathiel O. Hyatt and Mrs. Annie
Hamlin, all of Matteawan.

1435   Married at the residence of the bride's mother, San
         Francisco, Wednesday evening, September 19th, by
Bishop Thomas Bowman of the M.E. Church, a cousin of the
bride, Rev. Martin L. Berger, pastor of Westminster
Presbyterian Church, San Francisco, formerly of Fishkill
Landing, to Mary Anna Keller.

1436   Died at Fishkill Landing, September 30th, Laura A.,
         wife of Samuel S. [sic] Mathews, aged 22 years.

1437   Died at Matteawan, September 30th, Josie, child of
         George Lockwood, aged 2 years and 8 months.

1438   Died at Matteawan, September 30th, Mary Augusta

222

Jaycox, aged 27 years, 6 months and 12 days.

1439   Died at Matteawan, October 3d, William Lane, aged 67
years, 11 months and 19 days.

1440   Died in Newburgh, September 30th, James Brown,
aged 79 years and 6 months, father-in-law of Mr. John
Van Tine. Remains brought to Fishkill for interment.

1441   Died in Medford, Mass., September 26th, Jane Dow
Peirce [sic], oldest child of J. Everett and Rebecca A.
Peirce, aged 4 years, 1 month and 27 days.

SATURDAY, OCTOBER 13, 1877

1442   Married at Glenham, by Rev. J.C. Van Deventer, Miss
Anna A. Wood, of Glenham, to Franklin Skidmore
Hoyt, of Newburgh. [No date given.]

1443   Married at the residence of the bride's father, October
7th, by Rev. Graham Taylor, William F. McCord, of
Beekman, to Harriet A., eldest daughter of Charles Stockholm,
of Hopewell.

1444   Died at the residence of Mr. Walter Van Amburgh,
near Matteawan, October 4th, Mrs. Mary Riley, of
New York, aged 60 years.

1445   Died at Carthage Landing, October 7th, Sophronia R.,
wife of John A. Taplin, aged 63 years.

1446   Died at Glenham, October 6th, Charles Herbert, son of
William Weeks, aged 4 years.

223

SATURDAY, OCTOBER 20, 1877

1447   On Thursday, workmen were engaged in erecting a
          monument in the grounds adjoining St. Joachim's
Church, Matteawan, to the memory of the late beloved pastor,
with the inscription: "Rev. Peter McCourt, born in
Roscommon, Id., 1839, died in Matteawan, Dec. 19th, 1876."
On another side are the words: "Ordained at Troy, June 1868,
Pastor of St. Joachim's Church from June 1871."

1448   John J. Bullock, uncle of the wife of Rev. Henry Ward,
          pastor of the Presbyterian Church of New Hackensack,
in this county, and uncle of ex-Governor Bullock, of Georgia,
died on Monday evening last, at the residence of Rev. Henry
Ward, from a paralytic stroke and apoplexy, in the
74th year of his age.

1449   Married at the Reformed Church Parsonage, Fishkill
          Village, by the Rev. Asher Anderson, October 10th,
Everet A. Smith to Violet Gordon, both of Matteawan.

1450   Married at the M.E. Parsonage, New Hamburgh,
          October 2d, by Rev. C. Sager, Charles McCarnac and
Amelia Edgar, both of Washington Hollow.

1451   Married at the house of the bride's father, Low Point,
          October 2d, by Rev. C. Sager, James H. Brower and
Mary E. Treadwell.

1452   Married at Harlem, September 5th, at the residence of
          the bride's brother, Mr. William Raynor, by Rev. D.C.
Ferris, Miss Julia Raynor, of Harlem, to Mr. John C. Haight, of
Fishkill.

224

THE FISHKILL STANDARD SATURDAY, OCTOBER 20, 1877

1453 Married in Fishkill Village, October 10th, by Rev. E.S.
Bishop, George E. Everett, of Wappingers Falls, to
Jennie H., daughter of Abraham Ladue, of Fishkill Village.

1454 Married on Thursday, October 11th, at the residence of
the bride's parents, by Rev. Graham Taylor, Stephen.
T. Van Voorhis to Anna C., daughter of Charles Hitchcock, all
of Fishkill Plains.

1455 Married at Mountain View, Poughkeepsie, October
10th, by the Rev. Francis B. Wheeler, D.D., Eugene N.
Howell, of Philadelphia, to Miss Mary Josephine, only
daughter of the Hon. John O. Whitehouse.

1456 Married at the house of the bride's father, October
10th, by the Rev. John S. Gilmour, James L. Velie, of
Poughkeepsie, to Susan E. Cornell, of Lagrange.

1457 Died at Matteawan, October 12th, Henry A. Ely, son of
Thomas C. and Anna Eliza Ely, aged 20 years.

1458 Died at Matteawan, October 15th, John M. Brower,
aged 55 years.

SATURDAY, OCTOBER 27, 1877

1459 Samuel J. Owen, a brother of the late Charles R. Owen,
and well known in the town of Fishkill, died at Cold
Spring on Sunday last, aged 34 years. He was a lawyer, and
District Attorney of Putnam county.

1460 Married at the residence of Mrs. Charles H. Sedgwick,
on Wednesday, October 17th, by Rev. Dr. Van
Gieson, Mr. Joseph Potter, of Lagrange, to Miss Hettie A.

Sedgwick, of Poughkeepsie.

1461   Died at Matteawan, October 12th, George Rothery, aged 46 years, 6 months and 21 days.

1462   Died at Cold Spring, October 21st, Samuel J. Owen, aged 34 years.

1463   Died in Fishkill Hook, October 22d, John C. Pollock, aged 56 years.

SATURDAY, NOVEMBER 3, 1877

1464   Walter C. Anthony, a native of the town of Fishkill, and a brother of the late Allard Anthony, is the Republican candidate for District Attorney in Orange county.

1465   Married on Wednesday, October 24th, by Rev. Dr. Duryea, Frederick B. Schenck, to Mary S., only daughter of Junius Gridley, all of Brooklyn.

1466   Died in Fishkill Landing, November 1st, Isabella F., wife of Jeromus Schouten, aged 53 years. Relatives and friends of the family are invited to attend the funeral on Sunday, November 4th, at 2 o'clock, from her late residence.

1467   Died in Fishkill Landing, October 29th, Bertie, infant son of Mortimer and Maria F. Cooper, aged 4 months and 2 days.

1468   Died in Fishkill Landing, October 29th, Stephen Howland, son of Andrew J. and Ann E. Ackerman, aged 11 years, 6 months and 27 days.

226

1469   Died at Matteawan, October 26th, Abbie Odell, aged
51 years, 9 months and 10 days.

SATURDAY, NOVEMBER 10, 1877

1470   B.F. Sherwood, of Morristown, N.J., a brother-in-law
of Dr. S. Mapes, of this village, lay at the point of death
on Thursday.

1471   Mr. Monfort Waldron, clerk in Dr. Wilson's drug store,
who has been sick of inflammatory rheumatism of the
heart, died early on Friday morning, in the 22d year of his age.
He leaves a wife and infant child.

1472   James Brown, founder of the New York banking house
of Brown Brothers & Co., and father of George H.
Brown, formerly President of the Dutchess and Columbia
Railroad, died in New York on the 1st inst., aged eighty-six
years. He was a native of Ulster, Ireland.

1473   Married by the Rev. Samuel Sprague, at his residence
in Kent, N.Y., August 26th, 1877, Mr. Alexander
Denton to Miss Emerett [sic] Roscoe, both of the Town of
East Fishkill.

1474   Married by the Rev. Samuel Sprague, at the residence
of Simeon Lee, East Fishkill, October 25th, Mr. Elias J.
Knapp to Miss Rinda J. Lee, of East Fishkill.

1475   Married at the residence of Daniel Smalley, November
3d, by Rev. Samuel Sprague, Mr. James Hadden to
Miss Mary F. Smalley, all of East Fishkill.

1476   Died at Rondout, November 5th, Harriet, wife of

Thomas Mellor, and daughter of the late Caleb Pierce, of East Fishkill, in the 35th year of her age.

SATURDAY, NOVEMBER 17, 1877

1477   Rev. Aaron L. Culver, son-in-law of the late Rev. J.B. Wakeley, died at Sing Sing on Sunday last, aged 37 years. Mr. Culver was well known in this section, having held an appointment at Fishkill Village for two years, from the spring of 1866 to the spring of 1868. He has been in delicate health for a number of years.

1478   Mrs. Mary Jane Winchell, wife of Mr. George W. Winchell, of the *Wappingers Era*, died on Monday, at Wappingers Falls. She was 36 years of age, had been married 19 years, and leaves six children, the eldest 13 years and the youngest three months old. She had been ill only seven days.

1479   Mr. B.F. Sherwood, a brother-in-law of Dr. S. Mapes, of this village, died at Morristown, N.J., on Friday of last week, aged 49 years. He was proprietor of the United States Hotel, and had been a hotel keeper for twenty years. He had been sick about three weeks, nicotine poisoning being the cause of his illness. He was buried at Newton, N.J., on Tuesday last, the bearers being members of the Resolute Hook and Ladder Co., of Morristown.

1480   Louis Goeltz, one of the editors of the *Republican*, of Hudson, N.Y., died at Colorado Springs, whither he had gone for his health, last Monday. Mr. Goeltz's parents were Polish exiles, and settled in Chester, Pa., where Louis was born about 1842. At the breaking out of the rebellion he entered the United States navy and served with distinction until the close of the war. About 1867, when the Department of

Charities and Corrections organized the school ship *Mercury*, he accepted the position of paymaster, and the success of this institution was greatly due to his untiring labor and executive abilities. In 1871 he began his journalistic career.

1481   Married at Newburgh, N.Y., Nov. 15th, by Rev. George S. Hare, Mr. William Terwilliger and Miss Mattie J. Fancher, all of Newburgh.

1482   Married at the Reformed Church, New Hackensack, by Rev. Henry Ward, John J. Scofield to Henrietta N., only daughter of John Jones, Esq., all of the above place.

1483   Died at Matteawan, November 9th, Adrian Montfort Waldron, aged 21 years, 7 months and 27 days.

1484   Died at Wappingers Falls, on Monday, November 12th, Mary Jane, wife of George W. Winchell, in the 36th year of her age.

1485   Died, the Rev. Aaron L. Culver, of the New York Conference, son-in-law of the late Rev. J.B. Wakeley, D.D., at Sing Sing, N.Y., November 11, aged 37.

SATURDAY, NOVEMBER 24, 1877

1486   Charles W. Swift, a prominent citizen of Poughkeepsie, died very suddenly of heart disease, on Monday, dropping dead just after stepping out of a wagon. Mr. Swift was a native of the town of Washington, in this county, and his first wife was a daughter of John C. Van Wyck, of this town. Mr. Swift was the second Mayor of Poughkeepsie, and held various responsible positions. He was about 65 years of age.

1487   Mr. Stephen Brinckerhoff, a brother of the late Daniel
      Brinckerhoff, died at the homestead, near Carthage
Landing, on Thursday, in the 68th year of his age. His death
was not unexpected. His life was spent in farming and boat
building. He was engaged in building a new steam yacht at the
time of his death. His funeral will take place on Sunday, from
his late residence.

1488   Married at the Parsonage of the Reformed Church,
      Fishkill Village, on Wednesday, November 14th, by
Rev. Asher Anderson, Walter Dickinson to Dora E. Flood,
both of Carthage Landing.

1489   Died near Low Point, November 22d, Stephen
      Brinckerhoff, aged 67 years and 7 months. Relatives
and friends of the family are invited to attend the funeral on
Sunday, November 25th, at two o'clock, from his late
residence.

1490   Died at Glenham, November 20th, Eugenia, daughter
      of Charles E. and Lydia A. Mackey, aged 15 years.

1491   Died in New York city, October 28th, Margaret, wife
      of Dr. Edward Van Wyck, United States Navy, and
daughter of the late William Frazer, aged 38 years, 8 months
and 7 days.

SATURDAY, DECEMBER 1, 1877

1492   George Buckelew, a man about forty years old, of
      Hightstown, Mercer county, N.J., and employed on the
dredgers of the Atlantic Dredging Company, at Fishkill
Landing, was drowned on Friday night of last week. It is
supposed Buckelew attempted to walk a ten or twelve foot

long plank from the bridge to the mooring of the ferry boat
Union. The deceased leaves a family in New Jersey, whither
the body will be sent by the dredging company.

1493 Rev. A.R. Burroughs, pastor of the M.E. Church at
        Purdy's Station, N.Y., died at his home on last
Wednesday morning. Mr. Burroughs was a cousin of Rev. J.L.
Scott, of Matteawan.

1494 Mrs. Bleecker, wife of Mr. William P. Bleecker, died at
        her residence in this village, on Tuesday, in the sixtieth
year of her age. Her remains were taken to New York for
interment, the funeral exercises taking place at the Church of
the Annunciation, in 14th street, on Friday noon.

1495 Married November 21st, at the residence of the bride's
        father, by the Rev. Henry L. Ziengenfus, of
Poughkeepsie, Isaac D. Hallock, Jr., to Miss Emma L.,
youngest daughter of Joseph East, both of East Mills.

1496 Died at Fishkill-on-the-Hudson, on Tuesday, November
        27th, Maria Holmes, wife of William P. Bleecker, and
daughter of the late William Onderdonk, in the 60th year of her
age.

1497 Died in Matteawan, November 28th, Mary Ivory.

SATURDAY, DECEMBER 8, 1877

1498 Married at the residence of Mr. D.W. Hyatt,
        Matteawan, December 5th, by the Rev. J.L. Scott, Mr.
Anthony Daly, of Fishkill-on-Hudson, and Miss Lu Ella
Warrey, of Matteawan.

1499   Married at Newburgh, November 29th, by Rev. Dr. Carroll, William D. Odell, of Newburgh, to Teresa M., daughter of the late Daniel R. Weed, of Fishkill Landing.

1500   Married at Carthage Landing, N.Y., November 28th, by the Rev. F.W. Shelton, Mr. Abraham S. Doxey to Miss Delia J., only daughter of Mr. John Pinkney, all of Carthage Landing.

1501   Died at Glenham, December 5th, Andrew Biker, in the 78th year of his age.

1502   Died near Ballston Spa, December 1st, William W., son of Elias Phillips, of East Fishkill, in the 55th year of his age.

SATURDAY, DECEMBER 15, 1877

1503   Robert C. Massoneau, a prominent resident of Red Hook, died on Sunday, aged 84 years.

1504   The *Poughkeepsie Eagle* says: The death of Mr. Andrew Biker, which occurred at his residence at Glenham, December 5th, removes another familiar face in this county. Mr. Biker was born in England, and came to this country forty-nine years ago, settling in Glenham, and entering into business with his brother, Mr. Thomas Biker, who came to this country a few years previously. Mr. Biker died full of years, having reached the advanced age of seventy-seven years and six months. He was buried from the M.E. Church at Glenham, and interred in the cemetery at Wappingers Falls.

1505   Died near Fishkill Village, December 10th, John R. Collins, aged 70 years.

SATURDAY, DECEMBER 22, 1877

1506 The Matteawan M.E. Church was the scene of a
     brilliant wedding, on Thursday noon, when Mr. George
C. Humphrey, Jr., and Miss Louie Sypher were joined in bonds
of holy wedlock. The parties reside in Orange county. The
bride was formerly a resident of Matteawan.

1507 Married at Matteawan, December 20th, by Rev. J.J.
     Dean, Mr. George C. Humphrey, Jr., of
Washingtonville, Orange county, and Miss Louie Sypher, of
Newburgh.

1508 Died at Matteawan, December 16th, Charles Frederick,
     son of Eugene and Melissa Smith, aged 1 year, 5
months and 11 days.

1509 Died at Matteawan, December 19th, Wilber Post, aged
     10 years, 6 months and 17 days.

1510 Died at Glenham, December 17th, Mrs. E. Cotton,
     aged 59 years, 6 months and 16 days.

SATURDAY, DECEMBER 29, 1877

1511 Robert P. Parrott, inventor of the celebrated Parrott
     gun, and former proprietor of the West Point Foundry,
died very suddenly, of heart disease, at Cold Spring, last
Monday morning, in the 74th year of his age.
  Robert Parker Parrott was born in Lee, N.H., October 5,
1804. He graduated at the West Point Military Academy in
1824, and became a second lieutenant of artillery. — He was
assistant professor of mathematics and of experimental
philosophy at the Academy from 1824 to 1829. He was

233

afterward with his regiment at Fort Constitution and Fort Independence. Being detailed for ordinance duty in 1834, he acted in the war against the Creeks as a staff officer. In 1836 he was made Captain in the ordinance corps. Resigning shortly after, he became superintendent of the West Point Iron and Cannon Foundry at Cold Spring, Putnam county, N.Y., where he invented and perfected the rifle gun which bears his name. The Parrott guns were first brought into actual use at the battle of Bull Run.

From 1844 to 1847, Mr. Parrott was first Judge of the Court of Common Pleas for Putnam county. *-N.Y. Times.*

1512   Mr. Astor B. Lewis, for many years a prominent livery-stable keeper at Poughkeepsie, died very suddenly on Wednesday morning. He had recently been injured but was getting better, but a sudden contraction of the nerves caused his death. He was in his 76th year.

End of 1877

FISHKILL IN THE REVOLUTION

Articles from a series which appeared between February and July, 1876.

Saturday, May 13, 1876

1513   In celebration of the Centennial year of the United States, we continue our series about Fishkill in the Revolution, by publishing the list of those who signed the Articles of Association, on the 15th of August, 1776, at the house of Jacob Griffin:
     We can scarcely account for the varied spelling.

Theods. Van Wyck	John Brinckerhoff
Zachs. Van Vorhees	Garret Storm
Cornelius Sebring	Dirck G. Brinckerhoff
Daniel Terboss	Richard Van Wyck
William Van Wyck	Joseph Horton
Johannes Wiltse	Gores Storm

1514   Signers of the Articles of Association, cont.

T. Van Wyck, Jr.	Harvey M. Morris
Henry Goodwin	Thomas Storm
John Adriance	Henry Schenck
Jacob Swartwort	Corns. Van Wyck, Jr.
Isaac Sebring	Abm. Brinckerhoff
Roelof Schenck	Abraham Schenck
L.E. Van Benschoten	Isaac Terboss
Jacob Brown	John A. Brinckerhoff
John Wickoff	James Denton
William Tisdale	Joseph Griffin

1515   Signers of the Articles of Association, cont.

William Clanker	George Brinckerhoff

Adrian Brinckerhoff   Abraham Terboss
John H. Sleight   Jacobus DeGraef
John Meyer   John G. Brinckerhoff
John Langdon   George Adriance
George Elsworth   Hendrick Hoerum
Daniel Schenck   Jonathan Langdan

1516   Signers of the Articles of Association, cont.
Daniel Johnsen   John Menems
Abm. Van Voorhis   Hend'k Hardenburg
Moses Bedell   Peter Ter Bush
John Jewell, Jr.   Alexander Turner
James Anning   William Ward
Jacob DuBois, Jr.   Gabriel Hughson
David Barker   Henry Van Tessel

1517   Signers of the Articles of Association, cont.
Claistian DuBois, Jr.   Abms. Risworth
Jacob Brinckerhoff   William Holmes
Thomas Ostrander   Godfrey Heyn
N.E. Gabriel   Abraham Morrell
George J. Brinckerhoff   Christopher Rown
James Weekes   Isaac Van Wyck
Cornelius Smith   Hugh Connor
Andrew J. Lawrence   Nath'l. Fairchild

1518   Signers of the Articles of Association, cont.
Samuel Gosline   John Berray
James Cooper   John Cooper
James Barnes   John Ter Bush
Cornelius Adriance   Abm. De Foreest
Thomas Simonton   Joseph McCord
John Cooper   Richard King
Jacob Van Voorhis, Jr.   Jonathan Haight

1519   Signers of the Articles of Association, cont.

Israel Kniffin [sic]   Daniel Kniffen [sic]
Johnathan Kniffen [sic]   Walter Heyar
Adrian Bogert   Moses Akerly
Luke Ter Boss   James Miller
Cornelius Osborne   Nicholas Brower
Matthias Clark   Nicholas Brower, Jr.
John Wright   Charles Brewer
John Ackerman   John Walters

1520   Signers of the Articles of Association, cont.

James Rathbun   Seth Chase
Adolphus Brower   David Brower
Cornelius Brower   Deriah Hogland
William Haskin   Peter Horton
Jesse Bedell   Martin Schenck
Peter Monfoort   Matthias Horton
Johans De Witt, Jr.   Mad. Van Bunschoten

1521   Signers of the Articles of Association, cont.

Abm. Van Wyck   Steph. Brinckerhoff
George Brinckerhoff   John Scouten
Joseph Balding   J. Scouten, son of Jerry
Jacobus Emans   James Brown
Moses Barber   Abm. L. Losee
Samuel Swartwout   John Swartwout
William Scouten, Jr.   Daniel Rayner
Robert Brett   John Smith

1522   Signers of the Articles of Association, cont.

Jacob Balding   Caleb Cornell
Isaac Storm   Henry Rosekrans [sic]
Benj. Rosenkrans [sic]   Stephen Osborne
Simon S. Scouten   Daniel G. Wright, Jr.

237

Joseph Wiltse   Geo. Van Werkeren
Platt Rogers   Theods. Adriance
Micah Rogers   John Lawrence

1523   Signers of the Articles of Association, cont.
Jeremiah Bedell   Joseph Fowler
Jacob Swartwort   Gideon Way
Merimus V. Vlaikren   Henry Ostrander
John Leyster   Timothy Saikryder
Zachariah Boss   John Bush, Jr.
Josiah Hallstead   Peter Noorstrant
Jeremiah Martin, Jr.   Peter Snyder
John Gray, Jr.   Gershens Martine

1524   Signers of the Articles of Association, cont.
Amos Nettletoe   John Bennitt
Elihu Emmitt   Ab. H. Van Amburgh
Jesse Baker   James Thurston
Joseph Parker   Stephen Thalker
Abraham Gray   John Baker
Jeremiah Ranny   David Mowry
Joseph Lee   Simon Bise

1525   Signers of the Articles of Association, cont.
William Lane   Ezra Mead
James Junes   Isaac Smith
Peter Hulst   David Bennett
David Horton   William Wright
Daniel Canfield   Sabure Main
Johans. Brinckerhoff   And'w Van Hyning
Abm. Van Amburgh   Moses Saikryder
James Rosekrans   Stephen Doxey

238

1526   Signers of the Articles of Association, cont.

Derck Hegerman	Jonathan Talmagee
Solomon Saikryder	Joshua Hicks
Martin Smith	Robert Rogers
Thomas Wright	William Baker
Daniel Wright	John Watts
Johans. DeWitt	Albert Carley
Henry Van Voorhis	Martin Wiltse

1527   Signers of the Articles of Association, cont.

H. Rosekrans, Jr.	James Kilburne
Dirck Brinckerhoff	Zebulon Southard
Evert W. Swart	John Bloodgood
William Moody, Jr.	John Johnson
Simon Ter Bush	Thorn Pudney
Francis Pudney	Henry Carpenter
John Ter Bush	Abraham Schultz
Cornelius Sebring	John Pudney

1528   Signers of the Articles of Association, cont.

Cornelius Ter Bush	David Lyons
Edward McKeesby	Theods. Brett
John McBride	Obadiah W. Cooper
Timothy Mount	Jonas Southard
James Reynolds	George Bump
Tunis DuBois	James Green
Obadiah J. Cooper	Peter Kimp
John Southard	Duncan Graham

1529   Signers of the Articles of Association, cont.

Abm. Van Tine	Jacob Van Voorhis, Jr.
Myndert Cooper	John Runnels
Thomas Bump	Christopher Schultz
Silvinus Pine	Isaac H. Ter Boss

William Somerdike
Nathan Bailey
Austin Fowler

Philip Pine
John Pullick
David Pellet

1530   Signers of the Articles of Association, cont.

Elias DuBois
Caleb Briggs
Isaac Hegemen
E.E. Van Bunschoten
Robert Judd
Bernd. J. Van Kleek
Jacobus Sleight

James Duncan
James Osburn
Jacobus De Groff
John De Groot
Jno. Van Bunschoten
Jacobus De Gruff, Jr
Moses Vanelin

1531   Signers of the Articles of Association, cont.

Adam Dates
William Testsort
Thomas Lewis
Abraham Sleight
Tenries Wilsen
Peter Stienbergh
Moses De Groff
Peter Van Kleeck, Jr.

William Stanton
Isaac Snider
Jacob Cole
Michal Hoffman
Isaac Cole
Gideon Ver Velon
Henry Buys
Jeremiah Mead

1532   Signers of the Articles of Association, cont.

Henry Peltz
Jacob Coopman
Boltes H. Van Kleeck
Henry Bell
Jacob Niffer
Simon Leroy, Jr.
Jacob Lane

Jacob Backer
Barent Dutcher
John Leroy, Jr.
Jurrie Hoffman
P. Vandervoort, Jr
John Leroy
Thomas Youmans

1533   Signers of the Articles of Association, cont.

Constine Gulnack

Johans. Hooghteling

240

Clement Cromwell
Francis Leroy
Jost. Westervelt
Cornelius Griffin
James Vandewater
Garret Beneway
Thomas Pinkney

Peter Deets
Abm. Westervelt
James Howard
William Griffin
Dalf. Swartwout
Jeremiah Var Velan
Henry Marten

1534   Signers of the Articles of Association, cont.

Barthol Hogeboom
David Dutcher
James Rymden
Frederick Rosekrans
Barent B. Van Kleek
Francis Van Dewater
Peter Polmetier

Charreik Van Keuren
Deminicus Monfoort
Andrew Ostram
Peter Van Dewater
Sevaris Van Kleek
John Van Valin
Lawrence Conklin

1535   Signers of the Articles of Association, cont.

Herman Rynder
Thomas Johnson
Joshua Smith
Abraham Ladue
James Swartwout
Ebenezer Clark
Joseph Totten
Johannes Sharrie

John Rosekrans
Francis Way, Jr.
Aaron Brown, Jr.
Cornelius Swartwout
Samuel Roberts
William Lane
Andrew Hill
Jeremiah Jones

1536   Signers of the Articles of Association, cont.

Lawrence Haff
Daniel Outwater
Samson Smith
Abm. Duryea, Jr.
James Culver
James Culver, Jr.

Peter Outwater
T. Van Benschoten
Albert Terhum
John Tirhum [sic]
Dennis Culver
Peter Van Benschoten

241

Jacob Van Benschoten   Henry T. Wiltsey

1537   Signers of the Articles of Association, cont.

John Tappen	James Davison
Henry Burhans	William Hogelandt
Abijah Paterson	Daniel Terhum
Abraham Lent	Tunis Skeet
Cornelius Verwie	Hugh Laughlin
Francis Hegemen	John Culvert
Abraham Cronckheit	John Jewell
Isaac Jewell, Jr.	Cornelius Wiltse

1538   Signers of the Articles of Association, cont.

Hemming Higby	Peter Lent
Isaac Adriance	Johannes Boss
Richard Griffin	Steph. Van Voorhis
Jacob Buys, Jr.	John L. Losee
Jacob Horton	Corns. Ostrander
Richard Comfort	Abraham Shear
William Barnes	Frederick Scutt

1539   Signers of the Articles of Association, cont.

Jerome Van Voorhis	Kane Adriance
Kane J. Adriance	John Devoe
Jac's C. Swartwout	Peter Robinson
Moses Shaw	Jacob Van Dewater
Zach. Van Voorhis, Jr.	William Brock
Jacob King	John Hutchins
John Dorion	James Wildee
William Wildee	Richard Avery

1540   Signers of the Articles of Association, cont.

John Yurkse	Abm. Van Wackere
Jacob Hutchins	Thomas Way

Abm. DeWitt
Elbert Munfort
George Jewell
Peter Schoonhove
Isaiah Wilde

John Phillips
Dan'l Van Voorhis
John Noorstrant
Joshua Griffin
Isaac Southard

1541   Signers of the Articles of Association, cont.

William Winslow
John Vandervoort
Peter Fitz Simmons
John Vermillie
Peter Johnson, Jr.
Jacob Dubois
Peter Meyer
Cosurado Appleye

John Griffin
Daniel Shaw
Nathan Burnes
Richard Osborn
Richard Jewell
Jacob Vandervoort
John Coffin
Joshua Bishop

1542   Signers of the Articles of Association, cont.

William Van Syne
John Van Sulen
William Brooks
Stephen Bates
Isaac Griffin
Isaac Holmes
Richard Jackson

Sylvester Bloom
John Kipp
Jacob Van Tassell
Daniel David
Peter Montross
Aaron Shute
Dirck Hardenburgh

1543   Signers of the Articles of Association, cont.

Peter J. Monfort
Peter Depury
Garret Hardenburgh
John Bogardus
Nathan Somes
Ralph Phillips
George Bloom
Henry Haine

Timothy Talman
William Cushman
Tobias Mabie
Samuel Somes
John Terry
Isaac Jewell
Benjamin Roe
Lawrance Lawrance

243

1544   Signers of the Articles of Association, cont.

Jonas Canniff	Edward Churchill
Samuel Todd	William Roe
James Miller	John Phillips
Daniel Anning	Daniel Ward
William Barker	John Park
Peter Bogardus, Jr.	John Davis
William Earle	Peter Bogart

1545   Signers of the Articles of Association, cont.

Francis Way	William Fowler
Corns. Brinckerhoff	Dennis McSheheey
Isaac Veal	Robert McCutchin
Robert Nichkilson	Elias Concklin
Jesse Purdy	Joseph Odgen
Andrew Renville	William Arden

MAY 20, 1876

1546   A pay roll of Commissioned and Non-Commissioned
            officers and privates of Capt. Abram Schenck's
Company of New Levies in Coll. Jacobus Swartwout's
Regiment and in General Clinton's Brigade, commencing Nov.
1, ending Nov. 31 [sic], including both days, 1776.

Abm. Schenck, Capt. 26 2/3 in dollars,	10£, 13s, 4d	
John Langdon, Lieut. 18	7£, 4	0
Thos. O'Strander, ". 18	7£, 4	0
Peter Norstrant, Serg't. 8	3£, 4	0
Henry Phillips, Serg't. 8	3£, 4	0
Geo. Norstrant, Serg't. 8	3£, 4	0
Thenoth Aridron, Corp'l. 7½	2£ 18	8
Isaac Griffin, " 7½	2£ 18	8

1547   November, 1776 Pay Roll, cont.

Jas. Canfield " 7½	2£	18	8
Jerdon Polhemus, dr'm'r 7½	2£	18	8
Henry Brinckerhoff, fifer 7½	2£	18	8
Andrew Schouten 6 2/3	2£	13	4

[The rest are privates, and receive 6 2/3 dollars, or 2£, 13s, 4d]

Isaac Cromwell	David Berkins
William Barns	Solomon Wood
Robert McCutchin	Paul Nelson
Hugh Laughlin	Peter Rush

1548   November, 1776 Pay Roll, Privates, cont.

Johnah Robinson	[—] Lawrence
[—] Mowre	Benjamin Akerly (Deserted, not paid)
Peter Monfort	Joshua Bishop
Joshua Smith	Benjamin Southard
Coonrad Applee	Timothy Talman
William Halstead	Isaac Lawson
Benjamin Roe	Levi Bishop
[—] Osborne	

N.B. Peter Osborn's pay is deducted for the month of November on the pay roll as he received D.M. pay and also 18 shillings for [—] Shutz, which is also deducted.

1549   On the back of this pay roll are seen the following entries:

_An account of rations due to me and my Commissioned officers in Coll. Jacobus Swartwout's Regiment under the command of Brigadier General Clinton. — Commencing from the first day of October last past untill the last day of December, 1776, both days included. (92 days)

245

	Rations	at s per day	£	s	d
Abm. Schenck, Capt.	276	10	11	10	0
John Langdon, 1st Lieut.	104	10	7	10	0
Thos. Ostrander, 2d Lieut	104	10	7	13	4

1550   Company returns while A. Schenck commanded a
company in the American army:

William Slack deserted August 27th, 1776, and has left a gun
with a leather bag with cartridges [which I] have in my care.

Peter Bush, William Goodfellow, John Lawrence and
William Halstead deserted August 30th, 1776, at night.

Isaac Griffin,Philip Morse, August 31st, 1776, went home on
furlow, sick. I. Griffin left with me 1 gun marked I.G. and
cartridge box marked I.G.,
and tomahawk with a belt marked I.G., and P. Morse left with
me a gun marked P.M. on the brass of the britch [sic] and a
cartridge box marked P., 1777, M.C.; P. Morse dyed [sic]
Sept. 2nd.

1551   October through December, 1776 Pay Roll, cont.

Benjamin Akerly went home sick on furlow August the
31st, 1776, to get his health and return as possible, and has left
his gun marked W.M. and cartridge box marked W.M. and
sword and belt marked B. Akerly.

Peter Bush, John Lawrence, William Halstead returned to
my Company Sep. 2, 1776.

Henry Underwood deserted September the 12th at night.

Andrew Parks, David Mowre, Jonah Robinson, the 27th
Septem. at night, and Jonah Robinson left a musquet [sic].

SATURDAY,MAY 27, 1876

1552   In the small burial ground near the residence of Mr.
Charles Scofield, at Tioronda, just inside of the fence

along the public highway, is a memorial stone that is perhaps scarcely seen: "In / memory of / Major Thomas Pierce / who departed this life / January 9th, 1823 / aged 87 years / 10 months and 15 days."

He was a Major in the revolutionary army. He lived where what is known as the "Wren's Nest" in the limits of our village.

1553 In the Methodist Cemetery, in our village, is a plain stone to the memory of "the Boy Soldier." On it is inscribed: "In / memory of / Henry Brinckerhoff, / who died / Nov. 20, 1834 / aged 75 yrs and 6 months."

He was buried first in the Brinckerhoff family burial ground, near the Elijah Budd place, along the road to Poughkeepsie, and his remains were afterward brought by his son to this village to the Cemetery.

SATURDAY, JUNE 17, 1876

1554 "Pay Abstract of Subsistance Due to the Officers in the Regiment of New York, Associated Exempts in the Service of the United States, Commanded by Collonel Zepheniah Platt" in 1779: Abraham Schenck, Major, Oct. 10 to Nov. 21. Subsistance pr. month £300. No. of Days 43. Amt. of Subsistance, £172.

1555 Return of Bounty, July 1776
"We the Subscribers have Received from the hands of Abraham Schenck Capt. in Coll. Jacobus Swartwout's Regiment the sum of Four Pounds each Continental Currancy [sic] as half of the Bounty money engaged to us by a Resolution of the Convention of the State of New York. Dated July —1776 to serve under him untill [sic] the last Day of December next - unless sooner Discharged.
David Barker   £4: 0: 0   Henry Phillips   £4: 0: 0

John Lawrence	£4: 0: 0	Jonah × Robinson	£4: 0: 0
David Mowry	£4: 0: 0	William × Goodfellow	£4: 0: 0
Elihu Burnet	£4: 0: 0	William × Slack	£4: 0: 0
Andrew × Parkes	$7	Hugh Laughlin	$7

1556   Return of Bounty, cont.

Isaa [sic] Cromwell	$7	William × Barnes	$8
Andrew × Schouten	£4: 0: 0	Hennery Brinckerhoff	$8
Joshua Smith	$7	James Canfield	£4: 0: 0
Henry Underwood	£4: 0: 0	John Carman	£4: 0: 0
Kellys × Moro	£4: 0: 0	Benjamin × Akerly	$9
Solomon × Wood	£4: 0: 0	Peter Noorstrant	£4: 0: 0
Peter Bush	£4: 0: 0	Robert × McCutchin	£4: 0: 0

1557   Return of Bounty, cont.

Jordon × Polhamus	£4: 0: 0	Benjamin Southard	£4: 0: 0
Benjamin Rae	£4: 0: 0	— Applege	£8: 0: 0
Naril Nelson	£4: 0: 0	Thomas Mc Cutchin	£4: 0: 0
Timothy Tallman	£4: 0: 0	Joshua Bishop	£4: 0: 0
Isaac × Lawson	£4: 0: 0	Peter Osborn	£4: 0: 0
Robt. Hill	£4: 0: 0	*— -ishop	£4: 0: 0
*— -ostr-	£4: 0: 0	*— Halstead	£4: 0: 0

*Paper mutilated   × = "his mark"

APPENDIX B

THE BOARDS OF SUPERVISORS OF DUTCHESS COUNTY 1874 - 1877

<u>SATURDAY, NOVEMBER 21, 1874</u>

1558 The following are the members of the Board of Supervisors:

Amenia	George Williams, dem.
Beekman	James E. Dutcher, rep.
Clinton	John H. Otis, dem.
Dover	Cyrus Stark, rep.
East Fishkill	Peter Baldwin, dem.
Fishkill	H.H. Hustis, rep.
Hyde Park	Timothy Herrick, dem.
LaGrange	John D. Howard, rep.
Milan	Edgar Morehouse, rep.
North East	Daniel McElwell [sic], dem.
Pawling	William H. Ross, dem.
Pleasant Valley	John M. [sic] Bowman, dem.

1559 The Board of Supervisors, cont.

Pine Plains	Henry H. Ham, rep.
Poughkeepsie	John C. Pudney, dem.
P. City, 1st Ward	Henry V. Pelton, dem.
" 2d "	Thomas Spross, dem.
" 3d "	Walter B. Sutherland, rep.
" 4th "	Thomas C. Bradbury, rep.
" 5th "	Benjamin H. Trowbridge, rep.
" 6th "	W. Morgan Lee, rep.
Red Hook	Edward Feller, dem.
Rhinebeck	J.H. Baldwin, rep.
Stanford	Silas Germond, dem.
Union Vale	Henry Campbell, rep.
Washington	Timothy W. Preston, rep.

NOVEMBER 13, 1875

1560   The Board of Supervisors

Amenia	George Williams, dem.
Beekman	D. Ludington, dem.
Clinton	John H. Otis, dem.
Dover	Myron Edmonds, dem.
East Fishkill	P.A. Baldwin, dem.
Fishkill	Lyman Robinson, dem.
Hyde Park	J.A. Marshall, dem.
LaGrange	Alexander Sleight, rep.
Milan	William E. Shoemaker, dem.
North East	Daniel McElwee [sic], dem.
Pawling	J.I. Wanzer, dem.
Pine Plains	William Toms, dem.

1561   The Board of Supervisors, cont.

Pleasant Valley	Jno. N. [sic] Bowman, dem.
Poughkeepsie	Clarkson Underhill, dem.
Red Hook	Edward Feller, dem.
Rhinebeck	John H. Baldwin, rep.
Stanford	Silas O. Rogers, rep.
Union Vale	Henry C. Campbell, rep.
Washington	James Dearing, dem.

Poughkeepsie City,

1st Ward	Henry C. Smith, dem.
2d "	Thomas Spross, dem.
3d "	Edward Ellsworth, dem.
4th "	Robert Millard, dem.
5th "	Michael Colleton, dem.
6th "	Andrew King, dem.

NOVEMBER 18, 1876

1562   The Board of Supervisors stands as fourteen
Democrats and twelve Republicans, as follows:
Amenia   Ambrose Mygatt, Democrat
Beekman   John H. Draper, Republican
Clinton   John H. Otis, Democrat
Dover   Myron Edmonds, Democrat
East Fishkill   John S. Emans, Democrat
Fishkill   Charles W. Tompkins, Rep.
Hyde Park   John A. Marshall, Democrat
LaGrange   A. W. Sleight, Republican
Milan   James Herrick, Democrat
North East   Martin Rowe, Republican
Pawling   Jedediah I. Wanzer, Democrat
Pleasant Valley   John M. Bowman, Democrat
Pine Plains   William Toms, Democrat

1563   The Board of Supervisors,cont.
Po'keepsie   Clarkson Underhill, Democrat
City, 1st Ward Thomas Connelly, Democrat
     "   2d   " Otto Faust, Republican
     "   3d   " Aaron Innis,Republican
     "   4th   " John H. Bush, Republican
     "   5th   " F.W. Pugsley, Republican
     "   6th   " Morris G. Loyd, Republican
Red Hook   Edward Feller, Democrat
Rhinebeck   Joseph H. Baldwin, Republican
Stanford   O.H. Smith, Democrat
Union Vale   Henry L. Bostwick, Democrat
Washington   Geo. P. Tompkins, Republican
Wappingers   James H. Seward, Republican

NOVEMBER 17, 1877

1564   The Board of Supervisors consists of the following
members:

Amenia	John D. [sic] Putnam, Dem.
Beekman	John H. Draper, Rep.
Clinton	Mandevile G. Burgher, Dem.
Dover	Andrus [sic] Brandt, Rep.
East Fishkill	Benjamin Hopkins, Dem.
Fishkill	James Mackin, Dem.
Hyde Park	Henry Wilbur [sic], Dem.
LaGrange	John W. Storm, Dem.
Milan	Uriah Teator, Dem.
Northeast	Jeremiah Paine, Rep.
Pawling	William E. Merwin, Rep.
Pine Plains	William Toms, Dem.
Pleasant Valley	J. M. Bowman, Dem.

1565   The Board of Supervisors, cont.

Poughkeepsie	Clarkson Underhill, Dem.
City, 1st Ward	Patrick Kerr, Dem.
" 2d "	R. LaPaugh, Dem.
" 3d "	Joseph G. Frost, Rep.
" 4th "	John H. Bush, Rep.
" 5th "	F.W. Pugsley, Rep.
" 6th "	M.G. Lloyd, [sic] Rep.
Red Hook	E.L. Traver, Dem.
Rhinebeck	James H. Kipp, Rep.
Stanford	Isaac Carpenter, Rep.
Union Vale	John W. [sic] Abel, Rep.
Washington	George P. Tompkins, Dem.
Wappingers	James W. Lawson, Rep.

NOVEMBER 24, 1877

The Status of the Board of Supervisors

1566   The *Poughkeepsie Eagle* gives the following table, to which we have added a D or R to each name, to distinguish their political complexion:

Town	Representative	Occupat'n	Age
Amenia	John W. Putnam, D	Farmer	50
Beekman	John H. Draper, R	Merchant	29
Clinton	M.G. Burgher, D	Farmer	32
Dover	Andreas Brandt, R	R.R. Supt.	52
East Fishkill	Benjamin Hopkins, D	Farmer	37
Fishkill	James Mackin, D	Banker	54
Hyde Park	H.K. Wilber, D	Farmer	35
LaGrange	John W. Storm, D	Farmer	67
Milan	Uriah Teator, D	Farmer	53
North East	J.W. Paine, R	Farmer	63
Pawling	William E. Merwin, R	Merchant	44
Pine Plains	William Toms, D	Gentleman	53
PleasantValley	John M. Bowman, D	Farmer	45

1567   The Board of Supervisors, cont.

Town	Representative	Occupat'n	Age
Poughkeepsie	Clarkson Underhill, D	Undertaker	36
City, 1st Ward	Patrick Kerr, D	News Store	62
" 2d	R. LaPaugh, D	Livery	49
" 3d	J.G. Frost, R	Undertaker	36
" 4th	John H. Bush, R	Printer	53
" 5th	F.W. Pugsley, R	Lawyer	34
" 6th	M.G. Lloyd, R	Livery	65
Red Hook	E.L. Traver, D	Farmer	50
Rhinebeck	James H. Kipp, R	Farmer	48
Stanford	I.S. Carpenter, R	Farmer	49

Union Vale	John U. [sic] Abel, R	Farmer	55
Washington	G.P. Tompkins, D	Merchant	47
Wappingers	J.W.P. Lawson, R	Merchant	34

James Mackin, William Toms, John H. Bush, F.W. Pugsley and Henry K Wilber constitute the single men on the board. M.G. Lloyd is the oldest, and John H. Draper the youngest — both Republicans.

APPENDIX C

Issue of March 3, 1877
[Found on Microfilm pasted in 1878 Section]

1568   Judge Barnard has granted Dr. Charles K. Barlow, dentist, of this village, a divorce from his wife, nee Jennie A. Owen. Charge, adultery. The case has excited a great deal of gossip in this village and vicinity.

1569   Benjamin Havens, familiarly known as "Benny Havens O," is reputed dangerously sick. He is nearly ninety years of age, and lives at Highland Falls.

1570   Married at Pittsburg, Pa., February 21st, in Trinity Church, by the pastor, Rev. William A. Hitchcock, Richard Morrison Gulick, of New York city, and Margaret Romaine, daughter of Dr. John Scott, of Pittsburg.

1571   Died at Matteawan, February 26th, Benjamin H. Beach, aged 70 years, 9 months and 7 days.

1572   Died in Fishkill Village, February 27th, Mrs. Margaret Brown, aged 68 years.

1573   Died at Matteawan, February 23d, Rebecca Hurd, widow of the late Sylvester H. Boice, aged 68 years.

257

BACKER Jacob 1532
BACON Oscar F. 0141
BADEAU J.N. 0183
BADGLEY George 1204 George, wife
of 1204
BAILEY Catharine Ann 0898 Clare
Mead 0321 Elisha 0898 Nathan 1529
Nathan J. 0321 Sarah A. 0851
BAKER Dora 0538 Jesse 1524 John
1524 John W. 0342 Stephen 0549
William 1526
BALDING Jacob 1522 Joseph 1521
BALDWIN J.H. 1559 John H. 1561
Joseph H. 1563 Mary Elizabeth 0151
P.A. 1560 Peter 1558 Rev. Mr. 0262
Rev. Mr., daughter of 0262 William
0151
BALL Albert 0634 E. 0520, 0531 E.,
Mrs. 0520
BALLARD Ophelia J. 1210
BANCROFT C.F.P. 1242
BANKS Edgar J. 0302
BARBER Moses 1521 William 0488
BARDEN E.H.W. 0057, 0069, 0301,
0302, 0339, 0496 E.W. 0381
BARKER Absalom 0947 David 1516,
1555 George 1281 Sarah 0947
William 1544
BARKLEY Ann 1293
BARLOW C.K. 0435 Charles K. 1568
infant son 0435 Jennie 0435 Jennie
A. Owen 1568 Mary A. 0357
BARNARD George G. 0264 George
G., wife of 0264 Joseph H. 1260
Judge 0844, 1074, 1568
BARNES Howard 1198 James 1518
O.S. 1198 William 1538, 1547, 1556
BARNUM P.T. 0817
BARRET Jonathan 0988
BARRETT Emma 1426 Martha 0833
Samuel J. 0561 Theodore 0322
BARRON Patrick 0924
BARROWS Nathan 0564
BARTLETT E.T. 1160 Edward T.
0589, 0644, 0650, 0718 Joseph 1040,
1272

BARTLEY Anna H. 1171 Catharine
1171 Edgar 1171 Mary F. 0969, 0972
BARTON John 1027 Morton 1209
Willard I. 0546
BARTOW Augustus 0203 Charles E.
1147 Charles E., Mrs. 1147 Jane E.
0203 Mary Sherwood 0203
BARTRUM Charles W. 0400
BATES Josie E. 0681 Stephen 1542
William 0113
BAXTER George W. 0031 Mary 0026
Norris 0026 William 0593
BAYLEY Daniel Y. 1115 Dr. 0156
Guy 0102
BEACH Benjamin H. 1571
BEARDSLEY H.S. 0926
BEATTIE Charles 0785 E.H. 0785
BEATTY Eliz. N. 0926
BECK Isaac B. 0781
BEDELL Jeremiah 1523 Jesse 1520
Moses 1516
BEEBE George W. 1362
BEECHER Betsey 0127 Erastus 0127
John 0189 Mr. 1373
BEEDE N.B. 1265 Sarah L. 1265
BELCHER Henry W. 0981
BELKNAP Lynde 1372
BELL Charles 0237 Henry 1532
William E. 0232
BEMAN J.L. 0842
BENEDICT James 0217
BENEWAY Garret 1533
BENJAMIN Eli 1279
BENNETT Charles T. 1382 David
1525 Mary L. 0341 Walter S. 1370
BENNITT John 1524
BENSELL Albert A. 0783
BENSON May E. Wood 1136
BENTLY E.W. 0030
BERGEN Edgar 1410
BERGER M.L., wife of 1036 Martin L.
1435
BERKINS
David 1547
BERRY Egbert L. 1320 Henry T. 1078
John 1518

BICKEL W.P., Mrs. 0903 William P., Mrs. 0895
BIKER Andrew 1501, 1504 Thomas 1504
BIRDSALL Mary E. 0546
BISBEE Otis, wife of 1272
BISE Simon 1524
BISHOP E.S. 0159, 1264, 1381, 1425, 1453 Joshua 1541, 1548, 1557 Levi 1548
BLACK Chauncey B. 0313, 0320
BLAIR Lizzie 0443
BLEECKER Maria Holmes (Onderdonk) 1496 William P. 1494, 1496 William P., Mrs. 1494
BLIGHT Charles 0089
BLOODGOOD John 1527
BLOOM George 1543 Sylvester 1542
BLOOMER Edgar C. 0652 John 0134, 0165, 0167 Lewis 0652 Sarah 0134 Sarah E. 0652
BOARDMAN Dr. 0435
BOARDS of SUPERVISORS 1558 -1567
BOEHM Henry 0242
BOGARDUS Catharine 0042 Charles W. 0042 Dewitt 0349 Elizabeth M. 0927 H.D. 0060 James 0497 John 1543 John S. 0927, 0988 Lavinia 0060 Lewis D. 0734 Peter, Jr. 1544 Samuel, Jr. 0053, 0059
BOGART Adrian 1519 Peter 1544
BOICE Rebecca Hurd 1573, Sylvester 1573
BOLDING John A. 0939
BOLSON D. Secor 0369
BONTECON George H. 0492
BOORAEM A.C.1304 Anna H. 1304 C.V.B., Mrs. 1304
BOOTH George 1296 John 0926
BOSS Johannes 1538 Zachariah 1523
BOSTWICK Henry L. 1563
BOSWELL Judge, daughter of 0970
BOUNTY Returns of 1555 - 1557
BOWMAN Henry 0362 J.M. 1564 Jno. N. 1561 John M. 1558, 1562, 1566 Thomas 1435

BOWNE George 0568 Marietta 0378
BOYCE Ellen 0829 George A. 0076 George A., Jr. 0076 John 0454, 0461 Kate Rankin 0076
BRADBURY Thomas C. 1559
BRADLEY Maurice 0149
BRADY James 0926
BRANDT Andreas 1566 Andrus 1564
BRETT Aletta 0097 Augustus 0406 Caroline A.W. 0926 Charles 1407 Charles F. 0510 Cornelia 0926 E. Augustus 0623 Edgar 1407 Harvey 1407 James W. 1254 Lucy 0510 M.A. 0614 Mary C. 0623 Mary Louisa 0623 Peter 0024 Rachel 0024 Robert 1521 Sarah M. 0137 Theodore 0097 Theodorus 0406 Theods. 1528 Virginia 0614 Virginia A. 0614 Walter 0926, 0988 Walter, Mrs. 0988 Walter W. 0927 William 0137, 1407 William, widow of 1407 Winnie 0510
BREWER Charles 1519 William 0962
BREWSTER Dr. 1026
BRIADY Edward S. 1068
BRIDGE Jeptha 0240
BRIGGS Caleb 1530 Edw. 0926 Elijah A. 0214 Jerome 0526 John 0197
BRINCKERHOFF Abm. 1514 Abraham 0021 Adrian 1515 Corns. 1545 Daniel 1487 Derrick 1394, 1419, 1421.Dirck G. 1513 Dubois 0970, 0973 1276 Garret B. 0773 George 1515, 1521 George J. 1517 Gertrude 0345 Hannah 0859 Hennery 1556 Henry 1547, 1553 Jacob 1517 Johans. 1525 John 1513 John A. 1514 John G. 1515 John Henry 0773 Kate 0854 Matthew V.B. 0854 P. Remson 0515 P.R. 0512, 0518 Peter R. 0515 Sarah 1394 Steph. 1521 Stephen 1487, 1489
BRINKERHOFF Dirck 1527
BROAD family 1353 George 1235, 1334 Mary Anne 1235
BROCK William 1539
BROMFIELD Louisa 1423

BROOKS Spencer C. 1111, William 1542
BROOM Rev. Mr. 1104
BROWER Adolphus 1520 Cornelius 1520 David 1520 James H. 1451 John M. 1458 Nicholas 1519 Nicholas, Jr. 1519
BROWN A.M. 0738 Aaron, Jr. 1535 Benjamin 1223 C.F. 0083 Charles 0254 George H. 1472 Jacob 1514 James 1440, 1472, 1521 Jennie E. 0914 John 0805, 0837 John W. 0655 Margaret 1572 Margaret Scott 1219 Maria 0837 R.M. 1365 Rev. Mr. 0493 Robert 0908 Samuel 0832 Stephen D. 0438 T.B., Mrs. 0425 Truman B. 0425 Walter 0254 William 1000
BROWNE Adeline 0420 Calvin 0420
BROWNELL George H. 0122 Sarah A. 0339
BROWNING Emilie 0314 W.G. 0013, 0314
BROWNSON Anne Elbertina 0922 H. 0922 Hector 1290
BRUNDAGE C.W. 0268, 0275 Charles W. 0926, 1371, 1375 Mary 0268, 0275
BRUSH Annie May 1108 Augustus A. 0116, 0128 Augustus A., wife of 0116 Gertie (Gesner) 1300 Jennie A. 1108 Susan E. 0128 W.F. 0609, 0665, 0671, 0834, 1090, 1108 1166, 1209, 1263
BRYANT Chloe 0673 Samuel H. 0673
BUCK Libbie 0381 Stephen 0143
BUCKELEW George 1492
BUCKHOUT Isaac C. 0296
BUDD Elijah 1553 Josiah S. 1314 Martha 0517
BULL Daniel 0541
BULLIS Peter G. 0529
BULLOCK Charles 0519 ex-Governor 1448 John J. 1448
BUMP George 1528 Thomas 1529
BUNNELL A.O. 0115 A.O., Mrs. 0115 A.O., son of 0115 Mark Holden 0216

BURGHER M.G. 1566 Mandeville G. 1564
BURHANS Henry 1537 James E. 1179 James E., wife of 1179 Mr. 1188 Peter 1179
BURNES Nathan 1541
BURNET Elihu 1555
BURNETT Isabella R. 0489 Lavinia 0135 Rachel A. 0563
BURNS Catharine 0667 M.W. 0348 Mary Ann 1161 Patrick 0667 Thomas 1161
BURRITT Josiah 0456
BURROUGHS A.R. 1493 Clinton 0758
BURROWS Sarah A. 1209
BURTON Ann 1031 Richard 1031 Richard [Sr.] 1031
BUSH Gilbert T. 0456 John H. 0456, 1563, 1565, 1567 John, Jr. 1523 Peter 1550, 1551, 1556 W.F. 0704
BUTLER Dora 0536
BUTTERFIELD Frederick 0840
BUTTS Isaac 0337
BUYS Henry 1531 Jacob, Jr. 1538
BYRON Joseph 1158
CABLE Harriet A. 0855
CADY P.K. 0249
CAE Mary R. 0057 R.L. 0057
CALKIN William 0341
CALLAN George 0117, 0129
CAMACK Mrs. 1136
CAMELON D. 0572
CAMERON Hannah C. 0475 William F. 0475 Willie F., Jr. 0475
CAMPBELL Allan S. 0904, 0906 Henry 1559 Henry C. 1561
CANDEE Wales A. 0243
CANFIELD Daniel 1525 James 1556 Jas. 1547
CANNIFF Jonas 1544
CARLEY Albert 1526
CARLIGAN Patrick 1134
CARMAN Charles 1267 John 1556
CARMICHAEL Ann 1138 William 1138

CARPENTER B. Platt 0091, 0102, 0864, 1379 Henry 1527 I.S. 1567 Isaac 1565 Leonard 0845
CARROLL Rev. Dr. 1499
CARSON Emma E. 1229 John C. 1229
CARSWELL G.H. 0481, 0483, 0507
CARY Alida 1099 Elizabeth 0695 infant son 0695 John 0695 Thomas 1099 William F. 0849
CASSIDY Philip 0011
CAULDWELL Alex 0272
CAVENAUGH John 0504
CHAMBERLAIN William 0532
CHAPMAN John 0499 Minnie J.V. 0719 William Rogers 0719
CHARLOCK Charlotte A. 1157 Charlotte B. 1157 Henry A. 1157 Lebbeus S. 1220
CHARLOUIS John L. 0228 Prof. 0225
CHASE Seth 1520 William B. 1021 Zachariah 1116
CHATARD F.S. 0580
CHATTERTON Bennett 0204 Sarah E. 0953 Wesley 0204
CHERRY Ephriam 0616 John, Mrs. 0054
CHICKERING William H. 1126
CHILDS Millie S. 1321
CHRIST Carrie M. 1302 Herman 1302
CHRISTIE Christina 0401 Henry H. 0401 William H. 0401
CHURCH William R. 1010
CHURCHILL Edward 1544 Helen 0464 Henry 0464
CLANKER William 1515
CLAPP Caroline A. 1126 George M. 1126
CLARK Bernard 0927 Ebenezer 1535 G. 0393 Matthias 1519 William R. 0672
CLARKE George 1376 W.E., 0103 William E. 0220, 1283 Wm. E. 0146
CLARKSON Henry 0103
CLAUSON Yoner 1277
CLAY Henry 0099
CLEARY Bridget 1329 Charles 1329 Thomas 1329

CLEMENT Emily L. 1145
CLEMENTS H.B. 0303
CLINTON Brigidier General 1549 General 1546
COBB O.E. 0316
COE Lewis 0003
COFFIN Johnn 1541
COGSWELL William 0927
COLE Benjamin I. 0562 Isaac 1531 Jacob 1531 Sarah (Owen) 1055 Townsend M. 0681
COLEMAN William 0089
COLLETON Michael 1561
COLLIAR Ella F. 0302
COLLINGWOOD James 0174
COLLINS Abby 0309 Ella G. 0882 John R. 1505 Minnie 1176 Morris 0309 Samuel G. 0314
COLLYER John L. 0411 Lottie 0411
COLWELL Archibald 1182 C.P. 0914 Frank S. 0927 R.E., Mrs. 0927 Samuel 0260 W. Scott 0927 W.S. 0982
COMFORT Richard 1538
CONCKLIN Elias 1545
CONKLIN Angie 0236 Egbert 0163 Eliza 0163 Emma A. 1128 Jennie 1425 Joseph 0236 Julia 0236 Lawrence 1534 Mary 0369 Mr. 0781 William J. 0537
CONNELL A.O. 1319
CONNELLY Thomas 1563
CONNOR Hugh 1517
CONNOVER Dewitt C. 0613 Nettie 0613
CONOVER Benjamin 1369, 1380 DeWitt Clinton 0384 Hannah Virginia 0535 Jane 1369
CONSTANTINE Charles 0882
COOK Allie 0326 Carrie Smith 0651 J. Hervey 0927, 1241 J. Hervey, Mrs. 0649 James Hervey 0651 Louisa W. 0927
COOKE Watts 1085
COOLEY J. Henry 1079
COONS A. 0995, 0996, 1136, 1159, 1208, 1239,1283, 1340

COOPER Addie D. 1392 Bertie 1467
Charles D. 0676, 1392 Eliza (Day)
0155 Fannie 1180 James 1518 Jane
0017 John 1518 John [2d] 1518
Maria 0055, 0065 Maria F. 1467
Mortimer 1467 Myndert 1529
Obadiah J. 1528 Obadiah W. 1528
Sarah 1392 Stephen 1249 Steve 1249
Tunis 0055
COOPMAN Jacob 1532
CORBIT W.P. 1122
CORCORAN Tommy 0254
CORNELL Caleb 1522 Susan E. 1456
William A. 1037
CORWIN Catharine 0554 Daniel
Wells 0554
COSTELLO Patrick 0462
COTHEAL Henry L. 0318 Laura
Hoppock 0318
COTTON E., Mrs. 1510
COUTANT Gabriel D. 0138, 0342
COWLES David S. 0171
COXE Rev. Mr. 0326
CRAIG Hector 0785
CRAMER Peter S. 1007
CRAWFORD M. D'C. 0379
CRIMMINS Dennis 0580
Elizabeth 0580
CRINDLAND Jennie 0010 Maggie
0010 Shadrack H. 0010
CROFFIRD David 0741
CROFT Caroline Augusta 1143 Emma
0668 Emma Place 0670 Joel 0670
CROMMELIN Judith 0675 Mrs., nee
Johnson 0675
CROMWELL Clement 1533 Eliza
0948 Isaa 1556 Isaac 1547 J. Sebring
1160 Jennie A. Northrop 0991 John
W. 1423 Louisa Bromfield 1423
Lucy B. 0798 Oliver 0991, 1277
Peter 0948 Rebecca 0991 Squire
1423 Walter 0798
CRONCKHEIT Abraham 1537
CROSS George E. 0522
CROUSE A.R. 0678 Lottie E. 0678
CULL James A. 1319
CULLEN George E. 0995

CULVER A.L. 0257, 0856 Aaron L.
1477, 1485 Dennis 1536 James 1536
James, Jr. 1536 Josie R. 0257 Lilie
Martin 0257
CULVERT John 1537
CUNNINGHAM John H. 0521
Matthew 0152, 0927 Susan 0152
CUSTISS M.E. 0927
CUSHMAN William 1543
CUSTER General 1364
DAINS H. Lizzie 1376
DAKIN James H. 1210
DALY Anthony 1498 Daniel M. 0046
Daniel M., Mrs. 0046
DANFORTH Mr., widow of 1407
DANIEL G. 0808, 0936 George 0382,
0383, 0384, 0385, 0894
DANIELL Philip B. 0013
DANIELS George 0525 Lina 0842
DARLING George E. 0460
DARRACH James 0785 Mary W. 0785
W.B. 0785
DARRAGH James S. 0927 Mr. 0608
Robert 0927
DARROCH Forrest 0107
DART James 0742 Russel 0742
DATES Adam 1531 Mary A. 0422
Peter 0422 Willet 0089
DAVENPORT Esther 0974 Isaac B.
0142 Morris 0974
DAVID Daniel 1542
DAVIDS Henry 0420
DAVIDSON George 1355 M.K. 1259
Mary 1355 Morrison M. 0694 Moss
Kent 0694
DAVIES Alice M. 1396, 1401 C.E.
0200 Charles 1060, 1063 Helen
0718, 1401 Henry E. 0200, 0468,
0477, 0718 Julien T. 1396, 1401 Lt.
Col. 0965 Rebecca W. 0477
Theodore 0468, 0477 Thomas Alfred
1396
DAVIS David 0137 Jessie 0648 John
1544 Mary L. 0720 Wm. 1328
DAVISON James 1537
DAY Eliza 0155 John 0155 Peter F.
0234

DEACON George 0171 William, Mrs.
0523
DEAN A.M., Miss 0940 J.J. 1297,
1434, 1507 Julia 0940 M., Miss 0940
Rev. Mr. 1309
DEARING James 1561 Thomas S.
0711, 0713
DECKER R. 1103
DEETS Peter 1533
DeFOREEST Adm. 1518
DeGRAEF Jacobus 1515
DeGROFF Jacobus 1530 Moses 1531
DeGROOT John 1530
DeGRUFF Jacobus, Jr. 1530
deGUINON See Fountainville
DeHART William 0028
DELAHAY Andrew 1176
DELAMATER Sarah E. 0786
DELANEY Daniel 0070
DeLONG Charles 1114
DENIKE Ella A. 0013 Hattie D. 0561
DENNING GUARD — 0089
DENNIS Major 0089
DENNISTON J.O. 1312
DENTON Alexander 1473 James 1514
DePEW Sarah F. 0218
dePEYSTER J. Watts 1238
DEPURY Peter 1543
DEVINE Harriet 0032
DEVOE John 1539
DeWINT Arthur 0927 E.A., Mrs. 0940
J.P. 0294 John A. 0291, 0294, 0295
John P. 0291, 0295
DeWITT Abm. 1540 Johannes, Jr.
1520 Johans. 1526 Thomas 0176,
0180
DEWYRE Patrick, Mrs. 0241
DICKINSON Charles 0434 Mrs. 0939
Walter 1488
DIETRICH M.E. 0927
DOANE Right Rev. Bishop 0228
DODGE Henrietta 0525
DODRIDGE John 0858
DOLSEN Dewitt 0994
DOLSON Ira J. 1376
DONALD Effie 0618 John W. 0618
Sarah M. 0618

DORION John 1539
DORLAND Adrian 0478 Annie 0495
Catharine E. 0753 Jane 0689 John G.
0878 Jonathan 0494, 0495 Libbie
0494 Mary 0690 Myron H. 0753 P.H.
0014 Pauline 0478 Peter 0753 Philip
G. 0612, 0687 Samuel P. 0688
Samuel T. 0689 Surrogate 1408
Susan E. 0478
DORR Anna W. 0577
DOUGHERTY Daniel S. 0210 James
1158 Sarah 0871
DOUGHTY Dr. 0183 Ellathan G. 0301
DOWNING Richard 0959
DOXEY Abraham S. 1500 Stephen
1525
DOYLE Bartley 0109 Mary 0109
DRAPER John H. 1562, 1564, 1566
DREW Daniel 0831 Kate 0359 Maggie
0359 Roxanna M. 0831 William H.
0359
DRUHAN John 0605 Mary 0605
DRUM Elizabeth 1412
DuBOIS / DUBOIS Adelia 1324
Charles 0816, 0824, 1047, 1150
Claistian, Jr. 1517 Cornelia 1324
Dewitt 1150, 1151 Elias 1530
Elizabeth 1333 Helena 0195 Jacob
1541 Jacob, Jr. 1516 John 0958 Mary
Ida 1047 Peter C. 1150 Tunis 1528
DUDLEY William S. 0256
DUFF Thos. 0348
DUFFY Annie 0927
DUMOND Abram M. 0370
DUNCAN Catharine B. 0479 Edith
0479 H.E. 0467 H.E., daughter of
0467 Henry E. 0479 Ida E. 0069
James 1530 James S. 0706
DUNHAM Bevenla 0722 Caroline
0722 William 0927 William W. 0722
DUNNICAN James 0191
DURLAND Stewart L. 1184
DURYEA Abm., Jr. 1536 J.H. 0967
Rev. Dr. 1465 Rev. Mr. 0971
DUTCHER Barent 1532 David 1534
James E. 1558 Josie 0759
DWAN Daniel 1243 Elizabeth 1243

DWAN, cont.
    Joseph 1243
DWIGHT A.C. 0977
DYKEMAN Esther 0110
EAGAN Andrew 0089
EARL Carrie 0207 N.W. 0207
EARLE William 1544
EAST Emma L. 1495 Joseph 1495
EASTWOOD John J. 0138
EDGAR Amelia 1450
EDMOND William Romain 1360
    William Romain, Mrs. 1360
EDMONDS Myron 1560, 1562
    Thomas A. 0036
EIGHMIE Albert 0339 Elias 0495
    Harvey 0496 Libbie 0496
ELLIOTT T. 0078, 0131
ELLIS Mary Ann 0150
ELLSWORTH Edward 1561
ELSDEN Benjamin 1009 R.F. 1017,
    1143 Robert F. 1009
ELSWORTH George 1515
ELTING Dubois 1374
ELY Anna Eliza 1457 Henry A. 1457
    Thomas C. 1457
EMANS Abby 0826 Francis 0496
    George W. 0494 Jacobus 1521 John
    F. 1426 John S. 1399, 1403, 1562
    John Seymour 1399 Mr. 1397
EMIGH Frederick D. 1119 Hubert
    0583
EMMITT Elihu 1524
ENO William 0335
ERNEST John 0842
ERWIN James 0491 John 0491
EVANS Buel 0800, 1337 Peter 0800,
    0804, 1337
EVERETT George E. 1453 Thomas T.
    0307
FAHERTY Catherine 1170 John 1170
FAIRCHILD Nath'l. 1517 Stanley 0231
FALCONER John 0840
FALLON John 1374
FANCHER Mattie J. 1481
FARLEY Margaret 0276
FARRELL Christopher A. 0847

FARRINGTON Ezra 0436, 0551 T.T.
    0375 Thomas T. 0551
FARROR Thomas 1165
FAULKNER Josiah 0902
FAUST Otti 1563
FAWCETT Louisa 0362
FEDDEN Dora 0126
FELLER Edward 1559, 1561, 1563
    Peter I. 0354
FELTER Antoinette 1162 George H.
    1162, 1177 Henry H. 1162 Nettie
    1177 Nettie May 1177
FELVUS J.W. 1411
FERDON Belle 1091
FERGUSON Antha J. 0739 Burtis D.
    1003 Joseph Bertie Perry 0739 Lewis
    B. 0739
FERRIS D.C. 1452 Lavina 0579
FERVIS Walter 0914
FIELDING Aaron 0325 Mrs. 0325
FIELDS Mary Ann 0005
FINK Austin T. 0457
FISH Secretary 1113 Secretary of State
    1023
FISHER Charles 1049 Isaac 1049
FISK James, Jr. 0999
FITZGERALD Mary 1251 Mrs. 0560
FITZPATRICK Mary Annie 0927
Fitz SIMMONS Peter 1541
FLAGLER Ella 0705 Philip D. 0705
    Sarah J. 0442
FLAHERTY Laurence 0928
FLANEGAN Thomas 0125
FLEET Ida 0838 John B. 0838 John J.
    0838
FLETCHER I.D. 0111, 0123 Mr. 0121
    Mrs., nee Pickering 0121
FLOOD Dora E. 1488
FOGG Alfretta 0782
FOLEY George 0208 George M. 0208
    Kate 0208
FORBES Isabella R. Burnett 0489
    Walter 0489, 1133 Walter E. 1133
FORBUS Martha 1200
FORMAN Elizabeth H. 0779, 0791
    L.S. 0779, 0791

FORRESTAL Anastasia 1273 Captain, cousin of 1270
FOSDICK W.A. 0315
FOSHAY John 0925 John T. 0378
FOSTER Emma 0403 James 0403
FOUNTAINVILLE de GUINON Richard V. 1136
FOUQUET J.D. 0548 Louis M. 0548
FOWLER Austin 1529 Ella J. 0307 Ella L. 0190 Joseph 1523 Milton A. 0190 William 1545
FOX Dr. 0090
FRALEIGH John 0666 Phebe 0666 Susan A. 0666
FRAST Emma 0178
FRAZER Margaret 1491 William 1491
FREAR Elizabeth A. 0154 Simon 0154
FREELAND Annie E. 0967, 0971 D.N. 0967, 0971
FREEMAN Ellen 0819 Hannah 1076
FRIESE John 0927
FRITTS C.W. 0757, 1047, 1324 Charles W. 0315, 0544, 0545, 0734, 0833, 0969, 0972, 0994 Chas. W. 0130 Rev. Mr. 1239, 1309
FROST Charles 1143 Elizabeth 1144 Gertrude 0392 J.G. 1567 Joseph G. 1565 Laura Ann 1165
FULLER John 0536, 0538 Josiah 0272, 0998, 1002 M.A. 1424 Martin 0272 Rudolph 0089
FURGUSON Dorothy (Owen) 0631
FURMAN Susie B. 0644
GABRIEL N.E. 1517
GALLAGHER Henry 0350
GALLIGAN Bartholomew 1158
GALLUDET Rev. Dr. 0318
GARDINER Cicero A. 0447
GARNER Thomas 1008 William T. 1008
GARRETTSON Freeborn 0862 Richard J. 0862
GARRISON Almond H. 0645 Evelena 0737 George 0928 Phœbe 0709 William H. 0737, 0928
GATES Peter B. 0992

GAYLORD Charles J. 0961 George R. 0961
GEE Deborah 1232 John 1232 Sarah A. 1142
GEORGE Moses 0550
GERMAN Hannah 0624 Nicholas 0624 Pamelia 0624
GERMOND Emma (Croft) 0668 Philip 0178, 0213, 0217, 0231, 0232, 0237, 0273, 0367, 0369, 0380, 0391, 0576, 0668, 0670, 0828, 0829 Philip A. 0214 Rev. Mr. 0230 Silas 1559 William 1416
GEROW Alfred 0431 Angeline 1201 Charles 1363 Charles N. 1201 Ellen 0431 Mary 1363 Mary E. 0104 Willie 1363
GESNER Gertie 1300 J.H. 1300
GIBBS Alfred T. 0772
GIDDINGS Charles H. 0834
GIFFORD Mary F. 0473 William H. 0473
GILBERT Melissa B. 0383
GILBERTS Peter 1191
GILDERSLEVE Ai 1246 Mary Smith 1028 William H. 1208 William H., wife of 1025 William, Mrs. 1015
GILGAN James 0033 James H. 0033 Margaret 0033
GILL Allie M. 1402 Carry 1402 Jonathan I. 1402
GILMOR John S. 0849
GILMORE John S. 1078
GILMOUR John S. 1456
GIVEN James 0364
GLEASON Ellen A. 0611 Frank 0842 William H. 0611, 0771
GLOVER Darius 0254, 0915 Darius Thorne 0915 Darius, son of 0254 Deborah A. 0915 Mrs. 0254
GOELTZ Louis 1480
GOLLOW George F. 0227
GOODFELLOW William 1550, 1555
GOODRICH F.B. 0928
GOODWIN Henry 1513
GORDON Adelia Emans 1286 Allen W. 0380 Annie 0222 R.W., Sr. 1286

GORDON, cont.
Robert 0222 Theressa 0222 Violet 1449
GORHAM Melissa 1103
GORING John M., Jr. 0198 Thomson E. 1332
GOSLINE Samuel 1518
GOSS William 1061, 1066 William, wife of 1278
GOULD Jeannette, 0469 John Stanton 0255 Matilda 1014
GRACEY Rebecca L. 0697
GRADY Mary Ann 0338 Owen 0519 Philip 0338
GRAHAM Dr. 1121 Duncan 1528 Pompey 1121 Rev. Mr. 0151 Sarah E. 0772 William 0557
GRANT Aminda C. 0132 Rev. Mr. 0274
GRAY Abraham 1524 John 0823, 0941 John, Jr. 1523 Lizzie 0823
GREEN Abram W. 0182 Ada C. 0266 Anna Virginia 1260 Barlow 1256 Edgar 0450 F.R.M. 0202 Harriet F. 0202 Henry A. 0450 James 1528 Joseph I. 0928, 0935 Joseph R. 1225 Mary 0182 Mary Frances 0202 Rachel 1256
GREENFIELD Henry 1154 Lizzie Hiser 1154
GREENWOOD J.R., Mrs. 0928 John, Jr. 0880
GREGORY Albert 1139 Gilbert E. 0867, 1139 Hattie 1139 Hetty 0867 James 0189 Libbie 0680 Lucy 0867
GREY William 0776
GRIDLEY Junius 1465 Mary S. 1465
GRIER Andrew M. 0942
GRIFFIN C.M 0314 Cornelius 1533 I. 1550 Isaac 1542, 1546, 1550 John 1541 Joseph 1514 Joshua 1540 Laney 0004 Richard 1538 Susan 0091 William 1533
GRIMES J. 1283
GUERNSEY Eleanor 0404 Stephen A. 0118 Stephen G. 0404
GUINON See Fountainville

GULICH Ellen P. 0343 James C. 0343 Richard Morrison 1570
GULNACK Constine 1533
GUTGESELL Alvira 0503 Conrad 0503 Liby 0503
HADDEN infant son 0007 James 1475 Julia 0007 Theodore 0007 William J. 0752
HADFIELD John 0987 Levi 0987
HAFF Lawrence 1536
HAGAR Abijah 0219
HAIGH Ann 1342 Susie 1342 Thomas 1342
HAIGHT Andrew 1417 Charles 1159 Eugene 0677 Gertrude L. 0679 Henry 0012 Jennie E. 0340 John C. 1452 Jonathan 1518 Reuben S. 0679 Silas 0045
HAINE Henry 1543
HALL Charles Cuthbert 1093 Elizabeth 0432 Gertie 1320 J.B. 0269, 0285 James 1027 James A. 0432 John B. 0432 W.K. 0534 William 1312 William K. 0714
HALLIWELL George W. 0524
HALLOCK Cornelia 1048 Isaac D., Jr. 1495 Lemuel 1048 William 1048
HALLSTEAD Josiah 1523
HALSEY Stephen B. 1129
HALSTEAD — 1557 Charles L. 0540 Sheriff 1120 William 1548, 1550, 1551
HALSTED David 0863 John G. 0863
HAM George 0353 Henry H. 1559
HAMER Mary E. 0092
HAMILL James 0821
HAMLIN Annie 1434 Belle 1016 Henry E. 0008
HAMSHER Edward 1181
HANSON Christiana 0787 Emma 0787 Frank H. 0787 Noah 1214, 1218
HARDENBURG Hend'k 1516
HARDENBURGH Dirck 1542 Garret 1543
HARE George S. 1481
HARP Rose L. 0349

HARRINGTON Annie 1296 Emily 0393
HARRIS Adeline 0808 Annie 0391 Edna 1173 Eliza 1393 Grace 1391 H.W. 1129 Howard H. 1393 Isaac 1391 John 1173 Justice 1325 Mary 1173 Minnie 1391 Susan 0372 W.B. 1426 William 1067 William C. 0806
HARRISON Walter 0077
HART Benjamin H. 0756 Walter N. 0316
HASBROOK Frances I., Mr. 1116 Hattie M. 1365 William 0936
HASBROUCK Ira 0963
HASKIN William 1520
HATCH E.R. 0103 Emma 0103
HATFIELD Rev. Dr. 0970
HAVENS Benjamin 1569 Bennie 1317 Benny 1569
HAVER Alveretta 0367 James W. 0928 Mr. 0163
HAVILAND Alfred Treadway 0279 Barclay 0279 Horace J. 1237 Justus C. 1079 Mary 1079 O. 1237 Susan T. 0279 Thomas T. 0249
HAWES Charles S. 1275
HAWKES Anna 0866
HAWKS Anna 0194 Caleb 0194 Courtland 0704 Ellen Jane 0194 Filmore 0665 Hattie 1116
HAWXHURST J.H. 0188, 0210, 1071, 1137 P.R. 0350, 0786
HAYT Ada F. 0389 James H. 1001 Lucius N. 0389 William B. 0491
HAZARD O.H. 0040, 0563, 0680, 0705
HAZZARD Capt. 0366 H.H. 0368 Harry 0366 Henry H. 0366 O.H. 0056
HEADY Alexander 0372 Jesse 0371 William R. 0441
HEATON Charles 0812 Edwin Elmer 0812 Ruth W. 0812
HEDGES James H. 0833
HEGEMEN Francis 1537 Isaac 1530
HEGERMAN Derck 1526
HEIGHT Amelia Wanzer 0096

HEIGHT, cont.
Caroline 0096 William H. 0096
HELLERICH Anton Frederick 0392
HEMBT Jacob 0022
HENDERSON A. Butler 0702 George 0745
HENDRICKS John 1032
HENIAN Charles Henry 0855
HENRY Eliza 0516 Samuel 0405 William 0516
HEROY John B. 0089, 0780, 0788 M. 0780 Mary F. 0048 Wilbur 0048
HERRICK James 1562 Timothy 1558
HESTON Ephraim 0928
HEWLETT Samuel D. 0682
HEYAR Walter 1519
HEYN Godfrey 1517
HIBBARD Rev. Dr. 0230
HICKS Annette (Wilkens) 0121 Coroner 0090, 0156 Henry W. 0121 Joshua 1526 Samuel 0121
HIGBY Caswell L. 1304 Hemming 1538
HIGGINS Annie 0751 James 0608, 0615 Kate 0068 Mary Ann 0396
HIGGS Andrew J. 0698, 0710, 0712 John 1325 Laura Ida 0078 Lydia J. 0562 Samuel 1117
HILL A. 0790 Abraham 0163 Andrew 1535 Hezekiah D. 0790 John M. 1228 Robt. 1557 William B. 0163
HILLMAN W.G. 0422, 0782
HILLS Sarah 0928
HITCHCOCK Albert 1264 Albert D. 1053 Anna C. 1454 Charles 1454 P.W. 1310 P.W., Mrs., nee Monell 1310 Phebe A. 1053 William A.1570
HOARD Anna 0073 Cora May 0073 John 0073, 0344 Julia A. 0227
HOERUM Hendrick 1515
HOFFMAN Jurrie 1532 Michal 1531
HOGEBOOM Varthol 1534
HOGELANDT William 1537
HOGLAND Deriah 1520
HOLDEN J.G.P. 0100, 0224, 0265 Sarah A. 0224 Sarah Parker 0100, 0112

HOLLAND Michael P. 1208
HOLMAN S.L. 0393
HOLMES Isaac 1542 William 1517
HOOGHTELING Johans. 1533
HOOKEY Edward L. 0020 Ophelia G. 0020 Willie 0020
HOPKINS Benjamin 1564, 1566
HOPPER Alida 0617 Carrie 1102 Harriet 0334 James A. 0617 Nicholas 0333, 0334, 0928, 1347 Nicholas, wifeof 0333 Richard 1347, 1350 Wilber 0617 Wilbur F. 0940
HORN Annette 1236
HORTON David 1525 Elizabeth 0319 Hattie N. 0828 Isaac 0188 Jacob 0719, 1538 James 0319 Joseph 1513 Mary 1211 Matthias 1520 Peter 1520 Richard J. 0146 Vincent 1166
HOUGHTALING Minnie 0232
HOWARD James 1533 John D. 1558
HOWE Edwin 0671
HOWELL Eugene N. 1455
HOWLAND Gardner G. 1039 Joseph 0988 Joseph (Sr.) 0988 Joseph, Mrs. 0329, 0988 Rebecca 1039 Rev. Dr. 0329 Una Felicia 0329
HOYT Franklin Skidmore 1442 S. 0721
HUBBELL Benjamin 1088 Joseph L. 0104 Mary 1088 Mary Ella 1088
HUFF Eglebert 0448
HUGGINS Emma F. 1430 James 1430
HUGHES Alice 0650 Brooks 1398 D.C. 0521
HUGHSON Gabriel 1516 Henry 0595 Julia F. 1208 Thomas D. 1099
HULBERT Edward A. 0533
HULSE Alfred 1340 James B. 0643
HULST Peter 1525
HULTZ Charlotte 0983
HUMPHREY George C., Jr. 1506, 1507 Susie L. 0721
HUNT A.S. 0314 Charles F. 0717, 0723 George 0379 Jane 0792 Robert 0835
HURD Rebecca 1573
HURLBURD Merritt 1314

HURST Rev. Dr. 0321
HUSTED Caroline 1024 James W. 1024
HUSTIS Elizabeth Ann 1335 H.H. 0928, 1558 Henry 1101 Josiah 0876, 1335 N.B. 1067
HUTCHINS Jacob 1540 John 1539
HUTCHINSEN Eva 0835
HYATT D.W. 1498 Harriet 0565 Harry 0565 Nelson F. 0280 Nelson F., Mrs. 0280 Salathiel 0565 Salathiel O. 1434
HYDE P.J., Mrs. 1424
HYDEN J.C. 0766
HYSER Angeline 0040
HYSON Edith 0459 Edward 0459 Emma 0459
HYZER Abm. D. 1104
INGRAHAM Ella M. 0458
INNIS Aaron 1563
IRELAND Benjamin 0106 Cornelius 0556 Freddie 0556 Frederick 0726, 0733 Hannah 0573 Jacob 0609 Levi 0140 Mary J. 0665 Nancy 0556 Sarah C. 0704 Teressa 0140
IRVING Gabriel F., daughter of 1146
IVES Frederick 0577
IVORY Mary 1497
JACKSON D.W. 1098 Elizabeth Mary 0813 John 0259 John F. 0607 Judge 0463 Katie L. 0146 Lizzie P. 0070 Margaretta 0607 Mary Ann 0463 Richard 1542 Robert 0131 William F. 0813
JAMES William, daughter of 1146
JANDEN F. Duncan 1375
JAYCOCKS Harvey A. 0213
JAYCOX David 1433 Gussie 1433 Mary Augusta 1433, 1438 Mrs. 0272,1433 Thomas W., Jr. 0422 William O. 0250
JENKS Julius 0411
JERLS Rachel 0598
JEWELL Edgar D. 0399 Edwin 1377 George 1540 Isaac 1543 Isaac, Jr. 1537 John 1537 John, Jr. 1516 Phœbe Townsend 1377 Richard 1541

JEWETT Jacob B. 0830
JOHNSEN Daniel 1516
JOHNSON Amelia B. 0979 David
0283 Dr., daughter of 0675 Francis
0072 General 1121 Harvey 0072
John 1527 Louisa 0072 Mary 0283
Peter, Jr. 1541 Thomas 1535 Robert
0943
JONES Albert 0639 Amos 0553
George 0639 Henrietta N. 1482
Henry G. 1427 Jeremiah 1535 John
1482 Sarah J. Pollster 1427 William
0928
JUDD Robert 1530
JUNES James 1525
KAIN Bernard 0873 boy 0873 Richard
0873
KAINE George 0089
KALAKANA King 0420
KANE Mary E. 1000
KARR R. 0767
KASTENDIECKH. 1128
KAY R. 0032
KEATING Thomas 1280
KEELER F.M., Mrs. 1010
KEENE Annie M. 0917
KELLER Mary Anna 1435
KELLEY Joshua B. 0040
KELLOGG Clara Louise 0799
KELLY Anna 0402 Edward 0402
Reuben H. 0402
KEMBLE Gouv. 0428 Gouverneur
0669 Peter 0669
KENDALL Anna H. Bartley 1171
Jerome F. 1171
KENDRICK J.R. 1314, 1412
KENWORTHY ex-Sheriff 0455
Geraldine 0952 John 0455 Sheriff
0863 Thomas 0952
KERNAN Thomas 0049
KERNEY Celia 0848
KERR Patrick 1565, 1567
KETCHAM Charles A. 0985 J.H. 0052
KETCHUM Franklin D. 0721
KEYS Charles C. 1056
KILBURNE James 1527
KIMBALL Joseph 0187, 0356

KIMBARK John, Mrs. 1381, 1384
KIMP Peter 1528
KING Andrew 1561 Jacob 1539 L.H.
0801, 1313 Richard 1518
KINNAN Mary F. (Heroy) 0048
KIP P.M. 0537
KIPP Estella 1071 James H. 1565,
1567 John 1542 P.E. 0218
KITTREDGE C.M. 0186, 0245, 0674,
0928, 1224, 1242 Eddie W. 0245
Fanny (Marsh) 1242 George B. 0674
George D. 0928, 1224, 1234 George
Dimick 1242 Marcia E. 0928
Timothy 1242
KLANKA Mary Ann 0041
KLENKE Ellen 1255 Lewis 1255
Lewis Francis 1255
KNAPP Abbe 1022 Addie 0486
Charles B. 0238 Chauncey 0564
Elias J. 1474 Emeline F. 0584 Etta
0564 G.W. 0190 Geneva B. 1330
Gilbert 0693 H. DuBois 1194 Hubert
C. 0661 Isaac 0351 Israel 1022 James
0584 James H. 0661 Jane 0661
Joseph W. 1137 Julia B. 0238 Maria
0894 Mary Hester 0584 Mary S.
0301 Melissa B. 1330 Philena 0586
Robert L. 0383 Robert T. 1330
Theodore 1097 William 0586, 0890
William H. 0890
KNEVELS A.V. 0810 Adrian V. 0928
Isaac A. 0810 Isaac Adrian 0810
KNICKERBOCKER Perry 1188, 1190,
1197
KNIFFEN Daniel 1519 David 0360
George 0360 Gracie May 0692 John
L. 0692, 0853 Jonathan 1519 Josie
0853 Maria 0692, 0853 Mary E.
0360
KNIFFIN David 0352 Israel 1519 Mary
E. 0352 Phebe E. 0352
KNOWLES Anna J. 1064 Annie E.
0997 Annie J. 0997 Eleazer J. 1314
George L. 1064 Henry M. 0997, 1064
KNOX Starr B. 0928
KRATZ F. 0662, 0737, 0781
KRIEBIEL H.E. 1361

LaCOSTE Charles 0842
LADUE Abraham 1453, 1535 Andrew
   H. 0747 Ann 0899 Carrie A. 1202
   Charity 0951 Charles 1358 Charles
   W. 0298 Edward 0910 Elizabeth
   0298 George H. 1358 George R.
   0951 Hannah 1254 James 0899
   Jennie H. 1453 John O. 0662 Lavina
   0910 Lewis H. 1202 Lizzie 1297
   Mary E. 1202 Mary Jane 1358
   Nathaniel 0910 Oliver 0153 Walter
   0298 William 0736, 0735, 0743
LaFORGE/LAFORGE Elias 0856
   Elizabeth Bowne 1388 Francis, Miss
   0856 John 0211, 1163 Misses, the
   0378 Peter 1388 Phebe 1163 Susan
   0250
LAHRBUSCH Captain 1238
LAKE Edward P. 1425
LAMOREE Sheriff 0863
LAMOX Mary C. 0213
LANE Anna J. 0891 Jacob 1532 John
   G. 0891 Minnie 0082 William 1439,
   1525, 1535
LANGDAN Jonathan 1515
LANGDON John 1515, 1546, 1549
LANSING Dr. 0156
LaPAUGH R. 1565, 1567
LASHER Mr. 0409 Philip 1026
LATHRAP Lizzie 0228
LAUGHLIN Hugh 1537, 1547, 1555
LAWLER Timothy 0104
LAWRANCE Lawrance 1544
LAWRENCE— 1548 Andrew J. 1517
   Jane A. (Schenck) 0490 John 1522,
   1550, 1551, 1555 Robert 0490
LAWSON Isaac 1548, 1557 J.W.P.
   1567 James W. 1565 John 1420
   William A. 1142
LEACH Charles 0133, 0860, 1292
   Daniel 0133, 1034 Lucy A. 1033
   Sarah 0860
LEE Ann E. 0809 Emma 1098 George
   H. 0809 George McGawley 0062
   Joseph 1524 Rebecca 0062 Rinda J.
   1474 Simeon 1474 W. Morgan 1559
   William 0062

LEED Charles 0644
LeFEVRE Mattie 1349
LELEVER Josephine 0196
LENT Abraham 1537 Peter 1538
   T.S. 1097, 1098, 1099
LEONARD Chauncey M. 0347
   Mayor 0365
LEROY Francis 1533 John 1532 John,
   Jr. 1532 Simon, Jr. 1532
LESLIE James 1011
LESTER Anna R. 0928 Frank 0597
   Henry S. 0597 Rebecca 0940 Thomas
   S. 0597
LEVERICH J.B., Mrs. 0929
LEWIS Astor B. 1512 B.N. 1320 B.W.
   1254 E. 0712 Thomas 1531
LEYSTER John 1523
LIGHT Emma 0771 Mary Ellen 0385
LIVINGSTON A.M. 0587 David 0186
   J.R. 0011, 0578, 0664, 1291,1338,
   1352 John R. 0191, 0308, 0392,
   0504, 0627, 0807, 0822, 0848, 0855,
   0983, 1144, 1165, 1191, 1228 Mary
   C. 0587
LIVINGSTONE Jane 0627
LLOYD See also Loyd
   M.G. 1565, 1567 William 0823
LOBDELL William Henry 0983
LOCKE Urania 0988
LOCKWOOD George 1437 John 0610
   Josie 1437 William H. 1415
LOMAS Amelia 1341 Joseph 0928,
   1341 Josephine W. 0783
LONGACRE Andrew 0266
LONGBOTTOM Mrs. 1339
LONGLEY M.M. 0672
LONSBERRY Kate 0544 M.D. 0544
LOOMIS J.H. 1102
LORD Jennie 1314
LOSEE Abm. L. 1521 Clara E. 0488
   Freddie 1386 John 1386 John
   Cornelius 0078 John L. 1538 Laura
   1386
LOTTIMER William 1075, 1081
LOUNSBERRY Albert 0089 Nelson
   0064 Phebe 0064
LOUNSBURY Eugene 0701

LOVETT Susie 0590
LOWERY Robert 0627
LOYD See also Lloyd
  Morris G. 1563
LOZIER Charles 1103
LUCAS Mary Eliza 0663
LUDDINGTON Lorena 1193
LUDINGTON D. 1560
LUDLOW James M. 0321
LUYSTER Charles 1188, 1207, 1213,
  1227 Edmund 1227 John 1323
  Peter 1275 Sarah A. 1275
LYON Charles L. 0727 Clara M.
  Sullivan 0635 Ella Louise 0635 Mr.
  1175 W.H. 0635
LYONS David 1528
MABIE Alonzo 0844 Catharine A.
  0844 Tobias 1543
MACDONALD George 0509
MACK Thomas 0303
MACKAY Alexander Rufus 0930
MACKEY Charles E. 1490 Eugenia
  1490 Lydia A. 1490 Marcus 0590
MACKIN James 0158, 0864, 1564,
  1566 Sarah E. Wiltsie 0158
MacNEIL Crawford C. 0376, 1153
  Harry 0376 Jennie 0376 Jennie M.
  Yates 1153
MADAUGH Sarah E. 1411
MAGAR Maggie 1274
MAIN Sabure 1525
MANES Stephen 0929
MANN Elmore 0905 George 0474
  Jane A. 0474
MANNING B. 1383 Edgar 1172 Mary
  1383 Mary J. 0098
MANWEE Eunice 1253
MANY Sarah E. 0941
MAPES Dr. 0571 S. 0750, 1470, 1479
MARA Hannora 0192 Nicholas 0192
MARQUART Peter 0409
MARQUET Frank 1144
MARSH Zacheus 0909, 1408
MARSHALL A.A. 0114 Albert A.
  0124 Augusta 0682 J.A. 1560 Jabez.
  0004, 0077, 0227 John A. 1562
MARTEN Henry 1533

MARTIN Charles E. 0929, 0969
  Jeremiah, Jr. 1523 Julia A. 0414
  Michael 0306 Sanford 1411 Thomas
  S. 0414 Thomas S. [2d] 0414
MARTINE Gershams 1523
MASE Adaline 0044 Emma 0492 J.E.
  0394, 0395 Jennie 0390, 0394 Kittie
  0390, 0395 Lyman P. 0888 W.H.
  0394, 0395, 0554 Willard E. 0852
  Willard H. 0390, 0726
MASON Anna 0942 David 0896 Jane
  0896
MASSONEAU Robert C. 1503
MASTERS F.R. 0193 Francis R. 0183,
  0184, 0185 Thomas 0184 William H.
  0184, 1303
MATHEWS Alvaretta 1231 Laura A.
  1231, 1436 Samuel 1231 Samuel J.
  1231 Samuel S. 1436
MATHEWSON Gertie E. 1410
MATTHEWS John 0815
McALPINE James 0770 Jane 0770
McARDLE Ann 1308 Eugene 0629
  James 1308
McBRIDE John 1528
McCABE — 1074 Michael 1070
McCAFFERY Thomas 0338
McCARNAC Charles 1450
McCLELLAND J.R. 0536, 0538, 0866,
  1142
McCLOSKEY Augusta L. 0252
McCOLLUM Selah T. 0415
McCORD James 0221 Joseph 1518
  Letitia 0373 Robert 0373 William F.
  1443
McCORMICK Rose Ann 0451
McCOURT P. 0068, 0338, 1062 Peter
  0148, 0776, 1158, 1447 Rev. Father
  0751,1273
McCREADY Rev. Father 1273
McCREARY Almira 0476 George
  0476, 0619
McCUTCHINRobert 1545, 1547, 1556
  Thomas 1557
McDOUGALL Mary 0374 William
  0374

McELWEE See also McElwell
Daniel 1560
McELWELL See also McElwee
Daniel 1558
McEVOY Ann 1400 William 1400
McFARLANE Grace 1160 Robert 0089
McFARLIN Lafayette 0487 Mary E.
0487 Norris E. 0487
McGARRAH Mr. 0971
McGIBBON James 0714
McGINNIS Mary 1428
McGREGOR John 0239
McKEE Samuel 1370
McKEESBY Edward 1528
McKINLEY John 0509 Mr. 0530
McKINNON John B. 0879
McLAUGHLIN Mary 0760 Samuel
1261
McMANUS Catharine C. 0930 Edw.
0930 James 0930 John 0930 Mary
0930 Mary A. 0930
McMILLIN Daniel 0050, 0051
McNALLY See Nally
McNEALAN William 0498
McNEIL Charles D. 0708 Hannah E.
0708 John C. 0708
McSHEHEEY Dennis 1545
McVEY Mary Ella 0131
MEAD Charles E. 0085 Emma A. 0297
Ezra 1525 Frank 0086 Hattie S. 0303
Jeremiah 1531 Jeremiah P. 1293
MEARNS Catharine 0507
MEEK T.H. 1321
MEEKS Albert 1385 Carrie E. 1385
Edward 1071 Eliza L. 1385
MELLOR Harriet (Pierce) 1476
Thomas 1476
MEMBER Edward J. 0603, 0929,
1268, 1389 George A. 0442, 0929
Hattie E. 1268 (infant) 0642 James
E. 0001, 0929 James Edward 0603
Mary F. 0603 Mary Frances 1268.
1389 May 1389 Ralph 0930
MENEMS John 1516
MERRITT A.W. 0955 Alfred T. 0249
Andrew 0685 Benjamin 0016 Fanny
0016 Isaac 1124 John D. 0015

MERRITT, cont.
Lillie 0842 Lillie S. 0249 Sarah 0015
Stephen H. 0685 Willie W. 0015
MERWIN William E. 1564, 1566
MESIER Peter A. 0108
MESSITER Uriah 1240
METCALF Joseph 0470, 0905
MEYER Carrie 0929 James 0929 John
1515 Lizzie 1186 Lottie 1106 Louie
1186 Louis 1186 Mary 0929 Minnie
0929 Peter 1541 Phenie 0929
William N. 0929 Willie 0929
MEYERS Delancy L. 0340
MICHAELS M.B. 1262
MILLARD Annie E. 0724 C.W. 0262,
0209, 0281, 0357, 0399, 0492, 0533,
0546, 0577, 0656, 0663, 0699, 0701
0955, 0960, 0977, 1010, 1016, 1309
Charles W. 0349 Hattie L. 0977 J.
0699 0977, 1010 J., daughter of 1010
J.E. 0724 Rev. Mr. 0267 Robert 1561
Walter 0724
MILLER A. 0974 Amand 0926 Aminda
C. (Grant) 0132 Charlotte 0658
Charlotte Emily Louisa 0412
Emeline 1258 J. 0412 James 1519,
1544 James H. 0199 M. Frank 0281
Margaret J. 1228 Mary A. 0658 Mary
Ann Ellis 0150 Mary C. 0714 Peyton
F. 0589 Theodore 0893 William H.
0150, 0658 Wm. 0132
MILLIKEN Robert 0091
MILNER James E., Jr. 0308
MILSPAUGH Sarah M. 0701
MITCHELL Annie 1035
M'KINLEY S.A. 0398 S.A., Mrs. 0398
MOHURTER Fanny 0802 Mark 0802,
0930
MOITH A.T. 0929 J.E. 0929
MONELL Caroline E. 0929 Gilbert C.
1310 Gilbert C., daughter of 1310
John J. 0929, 1310 Mary G. 0929
MONFOORT Deminicus 1534 Peter
1520
MONFORT Charles D.B. 1365 Charles
Irving 1422 James E. 0786 John P.
1100 Lizzie H. 0214 Mary 1422

MONFORT, cont.
Mr. 0214 Peter 1548 Peter J. 1543
William 1422
MONTAGNIE Dr. 1354
MONTFORT Charles 1418 Eddie 0173
Mary 1418 Mary A. 0173 Rachel E.
0502 William 0173 William E. 1418
MONTROSS Evelina 0223 Peter 1542
MOODY William, Jr. 1527
MOORE David 1406 Elizabeth 0375
George 0273 George, Jr. 1112, 1118
James, Jr. 0321 Kate 1093
MORAN Thomas 1083
MOREHOUSE Edgar 1558
MOREY J., Miss 0014
MORGAN Emma A. 0572 John 0572
MORISON Elizabeth 0371
MORO Kelly 1556
MORRELL Abraham 1517
MORRIS Edmund 0284, 0456 Harvey
M. 1513
MORRISON Emma 9726, 0733 John
0930 William 0930
MORSE Abram 0019 James 0621
James H. 0019 Josephine 0019 P.
1550 Philip 1550 Sarah 0621
MORSEMAN Jacob 0011
MOSHER Henry 0163, 0957 Henry M.
0828 Kate (Lounsberry) 0544 Lavina
0957 Mary 0161 Mary E. 1319 Mary
F. 0822 Nellie 0161 Platt 0161
Salemma 1092 W.H. 1319 William
A. 0866
MOSHIER Angeline 1073 John 1073
Coles 0825
MOUNT Matilda E. 1413 Timothy
1528
MOWATT James W. 1223, 1230, 1239
MOWRE — 1548 David 1551
MOWRY David 1524, 1555
MULCAHEY — 0287
MULLEN John 0074 Louisa Strong
0074 Rebecca 0074
MUNFORT Elbert 1540
MURPHY Ella E. 1371, 1375 Patrick
1352 Prof. 1371
MURRAY Elizabeth 1169

MUSTERMAN Henry 1156 Mary 1156
MYATT James 0198, 1332 Jane E.
0198 Mary J. 1332 Maud E. 0198
MYERS Gertrude 1100 Harriet 0892
MYGATT Ambrose 1562
MYRICK Lucia 0949 Samuel S. 0949
NALLY Jas. J.M. 0087 Phebe Adeline
0087
NARIUS Fred 1125
NASH Charles B. 0513
NAYLOR Arthur 1092
NEEDHAM Henry D. 0407
NELSON Charlotte 0930 John 1287
John P. 0954 Naril 1557 Paul 1547
NESBITT Louise 0842
NETTLETOE Amos 1524
NEWCOMB R.P. 0660 Robert P.1354,
1357 Samuel 0654, 0660
NEWTON Oscar H. 0159
NICHKILSON Robert 1545
NICHOL Elizabeth 1017
NICHOLSON Clark A. 0090
NIFFER Jacob 1532
NOBLE John A. 0449, 0453
NOBLES Henry 0302
NOORSTRANT John 1540 Peter 1523,
1556
NORMANTON Owen 0848
NORRIS Charles 0588 Isaac O. 0758
Joanna 0588 Minnie 0758 William J.
1199 William J., Mrs. 1199 William
S. 0029
NORSTRANT Geo. 1546 Peter 1546
NORTHROP Edwin I. 0482 Jennie A.
0991 Joseph H. 0482 Mary 0887
Mary E. 0308 Sarah I. 0482
NOSTRAND George F. 0703
NUGENT Thomas 0572
NUNNICK Katie 0645
NYE Valentine C. 0437
OAKLEY Louise 0172 Lulu 0172
William C. 0172
O'BRIEN Annie 1082
ODELL Abbie 1469 Charles 0622
Daniel W. 0485 Edward 0782
William D. 1499 William H. 0562,
1325

O'FARREL M.C. 1158
OGDEN Henry 0346, 0355 Joseph 1545
O'HARA Peter 0930
O'LEARY Anna 1130
OLIVER Daisey May 1367 J.T. 1367 Kate 1367
O'MARA John, Jr. 1089
OMRAD Richard 0177
ONDERDONK Maria Holmes 1496 William 1496
ORANGE Prince of 0448
ORGAN Lizzie 0293
ORMSBEE A.G. 0955 Justice 0590 Nathaniel 0562 Oscar A. 0653
OSBORN John 0101 Peter 1548, 1557 Richard 1541
OSBORNE — 1548 Cornelius 1519 Helen V. 1361 Stephen 1522
OSBURN James 1530
OSTRAM Andrew 1534
OSTRANDER Corns. 1538 Fannie L. 0030 Henry 1523 Thomas 1517 Thos. 1549
O'STRANDER Thos. 1546
O'SULLIVAN Agnes 1366 Bernard 0930 Eugene 0930 Eugene B. 1366 James J. 0930 Margaret 1366 Mary 0930 Mary Agnes 0930
OTIS John H. 1558, 1560, 1562
OUTWATER Daniel 1536 Peter 1536
OWEN Charles R. 0797, 0803, 1459 Dorothea 0631 J.W. 0229 Jennie A. 1568 Joseph W. 0226 Joseph W., Mrs., nee Valentine 0226 Levi 0631, 1054, 1055 Phebe 1054 Robert J. 0163 Samuel J. 0774, 1459, 1462 Sarah 1055
OWENS James H. 0751
PADDOCK Rev. Dr. 0458
PAGE John 0918 Martha 0995
PAINE J.W. 1566 Jeremiah 1564
PARK John 1544 Mary 1115
PARKER Dr. 0091 E.H. 0090 Joseph 1524
PARKES Andrew 1555
PARKS Andrew 1551 Chauncey 1126

PARMENTIER Emile 0829
PARRIS Edward Lowden 1047
PARROTT Robert P. 1511 Robert Parker 1511
PARTRIDGE Charlotte (Van Buren) 0956 Frederick 0956
PASSMORE Harry 0823
PATERSON Abijah 1537
PATTERSON Albert W. 0990 Ann Augusta 0990
PATTLETON Richard 0764 0766
PATTON Cyrus 0544
PAXTON Mary L. 0455
PAYE Esther 0684
PAYNE J.C. 1379
PEARCE Susie A. 0493
PEARSALL Robert 0151
PEATIE John 1346 John, Mrs. 1346
PEATTIE George, Mrs. 0451 James 1273 Sargeant 1270
PECK Edgar F. 0607 Jane A. 0102 Margaretta (Jackson) 0607
PECKHAM Anna May 1432 Egbert S. 1432
PEIRCE J. Everett 1441 Jane Dow 1441 Rebecca A. 1441
PELLETT David 1529
PELLS Carrie 0849
PELTON Henry V. 1559
PELTZ Henry 1532
PENDLETON Elizabeth 0147
PENNY Ophelia 0342
PERRINE C.E. 1187, 1196 C.H. 1187, 1196 Cattie Jane 1187, 1189 Charles H. 1185, 1189 Charles H., Mrs. 1185, 1189 Emma 1189 Emma M. 1196 Ralph 1189 Ralph Lefever 1196 Sarah Bell 1189, 1196
PERRY Joseph Bertie 0739 Thomas N. 0456
PETER Catharine E. 0936
PETERSON Harriet Ann 0079
PETTIT James S. 0705 William 1018
PFISTER Elizabeth 0380
PHALEN M. 1158
PHESAY C.E., Miss 0578 John 0930
PHILLIPS Ann 0937 Cornelius 1222

PHILLIPS, cont.
Elias 1502 Ella L. 0793 Ellen 1233
Euphana T. 0027 Euphemia D. 0136
Euphemia T. 0090, 0091 Henry
1546, 1555 James D. 0090, 0091,
102, 0136 John 0793, 1183, 1233,
1540, 1544 John D. 0156 John D.,
wife 0156 John R. 0937 Mary, 0217
Mrs. 0102 Poisoning Case 0090,
0091, 0102, 0136, 0156 Ralph 1322,
1543 William 1222 William F. 0069,
0079 William W. 1502
PICKERING Adeline 0111, 0123
Adeline (Schenck) Wilkens 0120,
0121 Timothy 0121 William L. 0123
William Langdon 0121 Wm. L. 0111
PIERCE See also Peirce
Caleb 1476 George T. 0463 Harriet
1476 Hettie 0384 Mary Ann
(Jackson) 0463 Sarah Louise 0807
Thomas 1552 William A. 0843
PINE Ann 0889 Jane 0038 Philip 1529
Silvanus 1529
PINKNEY Cynthia 0149 Delia J. 1500
John 1500 Thomas 1533
PITCHER Sheriff 0863, 1120
PITTS John D. 0964
PLACE John 0930, 0969
PLATT Ebenezer 0162 Jennie Pells
0162 Zapheniah 1554
POLHAMUS Jordan 1557
POLHEMUS Jerdon 1547
POLICK Sarah 0312
POLLARD Ann 0034 John 0034
Julia 0034
POLLOCK Augusta 0323 Cynthia
0323 Fred. 0931 George H. 0323
Gracie A. 0323 Helen M. 1044 Jacob
1044 John C. 1463 Mary A. 0931
Watson T. 0323
POLMETIER Peter 1534
PORTER Catherine E. 1269 Edward
S. 0745 William 1269, 1269
POST James E. 1217 Wilber 1509
POTTER Bishop 0244 Horatio, Jr.
0244 Joseph 1460 Lucinda 0504

POWELL Joseph W. 1226 Nathaniel
0397
PRAGUE S. 0322
PRALATOWSKI Leon 0596, 0986
Leon, wife of 0596 Mary E. 0931
W.J. 0089, 0988 Wladyslaf J. 0931
PRATT E.H. 1321 Justice 0083
PRAY Hamilton 0680
PRESTON Timothy W. 1559
PRIME W. 0469 Wendell 0122, 0734
PUDNEY Francis 1527 John 1527
John C. 0457, 1559 Libbie E. 0457
Thorn 1527
PUGSLEY Charles B. 1311 F.W.
1563, 1565, 1567 Frederick 1311,
1315, 1318 Oakley 0757 Samuel C.
0144
PULLICK John 1529
PURDY Catherine A. 1191 Francis
1277 Isaac 0363 James E. 0920
Jesse 1545 Margaret 0907 Sarah M.
0322 Susan 0418
PUTNAM D.I. 0014 D.L. 0505 John D.
1564 John W. 1566 Washington 1205
PUTNEY R.C. 0706
QUICK Eva W. 0897 Jennie Maud
0539 Joseph 0539, 0897 Sarah M.
0539, 0897
RAE Benjamin 1557
RALPH Justus E. 0535, 1086 Virginia
C. 1086 William Edward 1086
RANKIN Charles Chauncey 0731
Laura W. 0731 Nellie 0969 Robert
G. 0731
RANNY Jeremiah 1524
RAPELJE Aletta 0885 John 0528
RATHBUN James 1520
RATIGAN Elizabeth 1123
RAYNER Daniel 1521
RAYNOR Julia 1452 William 1452
REA Maud A. 0767
READ Charles S. 0569 Charlie 0569
Hannah E. 0569
REEVE Hiram E. 1102
REICK Emma 0201 Frederick 0201
Hattie 0201

REID L.W. 0686 Lena 0686
REINHART Louisa 1159
REMSEN Bartow W. 0931 Edward
0865, 0931 Livingston 0931 Martha
0377 Matilda W. 0931 Sarah 0931
RENVILLE Andrew 1545
REVOLUTIONARY Articles of
Association Signers 1513 - 1545
Pay Roll 1546 - 1551
REYNOLDS Aunt Katy 0602
Catharine 0964, 0993 Cornelius H.
1120 Flora 0522 James 1528 William
S. 1095
RHONE James 0317
RICHARDS Anna A. 0500 Fanny 1252
John S. 1252 Lucy Matilda 1252
William 0170
RICHARDSON Marvin 0975 N.S.
1332
RICHMOND Charles H. 1349
RIDER Alfred P. 0738 David 0601
John A. 0458
RIGGS Horace M. 0215
RILEY Ann 0789 Mary 1444 Silas F.
0315
RISWORTH Abms. 1517
ROBBINS Wm. H. 1413
ROBERTS Elder 1076 Ella 0707
Harriet 0707 R. 0720 Samuel 1535
William 0707
ROBERTSON Carrie 0883 Charles
0883 Elizabeth 0883
ROBINSON Esther 0219 Frank M.
0525 Governor 1405 Ida 0553
John 0620 Johnah 1548 Jonah 1551,
1551, 1555 Kate 1429 Lyman 1560
Lyman A. 1429 Lyman, Jr. 0093
Mary E. 0553, 1127 Milo 1429
Nettie B. 0505 Peter 1539
ROCHE John J. 1387
RODGERS Jane E. 0857 John 1107
Peter 0857, 1107
ROE Benjamin 1543, 1548 Mary A.
0424 William 1544
ROGERS Anna M. 0940 B.A. 0368
Catharine 1316 Charles H. 0921,
1195 Daniel D. 0592 Dewitt C. 0931

ROGERS, cont.
Edward, Jr. 0068 James 0931 Joseph
J. 0931 Laban 0393 Lizzie C. 0940
Maggie 1195 Maria S. 0444 Micah
1522 Platt 1522 Rev. Mr. 0366
Robert 1526 Samuel B. 0931
Samuel, Sr. 1316 Samuel, Sr., Mrs.
1309 Sarah 1038 Silas O. 1561
ROOSEVELT James 1039
Rebecca H. (Howland) 1039
ROOT George 0771
ROSCOE Emerett, Miss 1473
ROSEKRANS Frederick 1534 H., Jr.
1527 Henry 1522 James 1525 John
1535
ROSENKRANS Benj. 1522
ROSS John H. 0370 Mary DuBois
0370 William H. 1558
ROTHERY Albert 0326 George 1461
John 0552 John (Sr.) 0552 John (Sr.),
Mrs. 0552 William 0552
ROTHLIN — 1205
ROWE Martin 1562
ROWN Christopher 1517
ROYS E.H. 1283
ROZELL Adrianna 0630 Alson 0080,
0088, 0744 Harvey 0630, 0676
Helena 0080, 0088 Helena A. 1378
Jane A. 0630 Mabel Helena 1378
Robert 0744 Sarah 0676 W.H., Mrs.
0931 William H. 0080, 0088, 0931,
1378
RUDE E. 0442
RUMSEY Charlotte A. 0657 J.S. 0657
RUNNELS John 1529
RUSH Peter 1547
RUSSELL Austin P. 1263
RYAN James 0931 Timothy 0966,
0968
RYMDEN James 1534
RYNDER Herman 1535
SACKETT Rachel 0796 Stephen 0796
SAGE Milo 0932 William F. 0932,
0969
SAGER C. 1450,1451 Chas. 1413
SAIKRYDER Moses 1525 Solomon
1526 Timothy 1523

SALES Diana 0047
SAMPSEN Samuel 1390
SAMPSON Ulysses S.G. 0638
SANDERS Annie 0210
SANDFORD Christiner 0659
SANDFORD, cont.
  John W. 0659
SANDS Moses C. 1069
SARGENT H.W. 0234, 1373
SARTWELL Rev. Mr. 0983
SATTERLEE H.Y. 1333
SAXTON Alfred 0938
SAYRE W.N. 0682
SCHAGHTICOOK Indians — 1253
SCHENCK A. 1550 Abm. 1546, 1546,
  1549 Abraham 1514, 1554, 1555
  Abraham H. 0120, 0490, 1046 Annie
  0633 Carrie A. 0836 Charles 1046
  Cornelia A. 0836 Daniel 1515 Dr.
  0067 Frederick B. 1465 Henry 1514
  Henry B. 0969, 0972 J.P. 1027 Jane
  A. 0490 Jefferson B. 0940 John B.
  1094 John P. 1046 Martin 1520
  Oscar 0836, 1046, 1050 Roelof 1514
  Samuel B. 1094 T.J.B. 1094, 1105
  Wilkens 0633 Wilkens, Jr. 0633
  William T.Y. 0969
SCHLOSSER J.F. 0932 John F. 0969
SCHOLEFIELD Enos 1368
SCHOONHOVE Peter 1540
SCHOUTEN See also Scouten
  Andrew 1547, 1556 Coroner 0050,
  0067 Isabella F. 1466 Jeromus 1466
  John 1521 Stephen 1311
SCHRAM William 1271
SCHULTZ Abraham 1527 Christopher
  1529
SCHUTT Mary 1344
SCOFIELD Charles 1552 Edward 0594
  Eliza V. 0932 Emily 0159 Ezekial
  0023, 0585 Frank G. 0932 J.L. 0932
  Jacob L. 0865, 0970, 1147, 1216
  John J. 1482 John S. 1147 Mary C.
  0932 Olivia A. 0585 Sidney 0058,
  0932, 0988 William R. 0970, 0973
  William R., Mrs., nee Boswell 0970

SCOTT J.L. 0147, 0348, 0430, 0434,
  0470, 0522, 0561, 0733, 0905, 0942,
  1000, 1493 1498 John 1570 Margaret
  Romaine 1570 Rev. Dr. 0715 Rev.
  Mr. 1309
SCOUTEN See also Schouten
  J., son of Jerry 1521 Simon S. 1522
  William, Jr. 1521
SCUDDER John 1135 Joseph 1135
  Rev. Dr. 0029
SCUTT Frederick 1538
SEAMAN George A. 0932 George B.
  1122 George M. 0767 John B. 1077,
  1080 Mary C. 0932
SEAMANS James E., Mrs. 0429
SEBRING Cornelius 1513, 1527 Isaac
  1514
SEDGWICK Charles H., Mrs. 1460
  Hettie A. 1460
SEDORE Mary L. 0189
SEELEY William 1412
SELDEN J.E. 0884 John E. 0729 Laura
  0729 Louisa 0729 Lucy E. 0884
SERRINE Ada 0299 Martha 0794
  William 0299 William S. 0794
SEVER W.W. 1229
SEWARD James H. 1563 William H.
  1288
SEWELL Jennie 0932 John 1298
  Katie D. 1298 Mary E. 1298
SHANN Oscar 0190
SHARP Henry E. 0266
SHARRIE Johannes 1535
SHAW Catharine 0501 Daniel 1541
  Elizabeth 0877 Enoch 0501 H.
  Berrien 0534 Moses 1539 Thomas
  1203 Zebedee 0332
SHEAR Abraham 1538
SHEARMAN Ann Maria 0075 Garrett
  0075
SHEEHAN Denis 0070, 0732 Father
  0725
SHEERER Sarah E. 1292
SHELDON Allie M. 0206 Wilson B.
  0206
SHELTON F.W. 0411, 0854, 1500
  Rev. Mr. 0882

SHEPPARD Harvey 1180
SHERMANFannie T. 0122 Leonard B.
0839 Phebe Jane 0839
SHERWOOD B.F. 0754, 1470, 1479
D.W. 0031, 0219 Emma 0750 Emma
J. 0754 Isaac 0543 Kate Townsend
0754 Mr. 0571 Mrs. 0571 Stephen H.
0095 Thomas D. 0543
SHOEMAKER William E. 1560
SHOONMAKER William H. 0220
SHOVE Ellen 0054, 0066 Seth 0054
SHRADER Almira 0304
SHRAYER Albert 1005 C. Herman
1012 H. Albert 1012 Hermann 1005
Louisa 1012
SHURTER
Felix 0626, 0628 Isaac 0626 Isaac H.
0775, 0777 James E. 0626, 0775,
0932 R.L. 0221 Sarah A. 0221
SHUTE Aaron 1542
SHUTTLEWORTH William 0989,
1020, 1356
SHULTZ — 1548
SIMONTON Thomas 1518
SIMPSON Amelia Lomas 1341
Elizabeth 1149 Joseph 1341
SINCERBAUGH Mrs. 0025
SINCLAIR George 0814 George (Sr.)
0814 Mary 0814
SISSON Jacob 0099 Mary A. 0368
Molly 0366
SKEET Tunis 1537
SLACK Frances H. 0084 Frances M.
0084 H. 0084 Helen M. 0084
William 1550, 1555
SLAUSON Joseph A. 0672 Julia A.
0672 Seely 0672
SLEIGHT A.W. 1562 Abraham 1531
Alexander 1560 Benjamin A. 1395
Frank 1395 Jacobus 1530 John H.
1515
SLIDDERS Ida 0604
SMALLEY Daniel 1475 Mary F. 1475
SMITH Alexander 0808 Andrew W.
1297 Anning 0886 Benjamin V. 0251
Bradish Johnson 0799 Cadet 1149

SMITH, cont.
Carrie 0651, 1414 Charles Frederick
1508 Cornelius 1517 Daniel 0534
Dewitt Clinton 0656, 0663 E. 0425
Edward 0391 Elizabeth Simpson
1149 Ellen 0566 Emma 1166 Eugene
0591, 1508 Everet A. 1449 Everett
B. 1301 George C. 0674, 0940
Guernsey 0425, 0827 H. Isabel 0534
Hannah 0235 Harry 0005 Hattie A.
0077 Hattie E. 0703 Henry 0179
Henry C. 1561 Henry T. 0599 infant
child 1414 Isaac 1525 J.G. 1337
James 0940 John 0875, 1521 John
Jay 1113 John S. 0869, 0875 John T.
0932, 1414 Joshua 1535, 1548, 1556
Kate S. 1301 Lafayette G. 0297
Lillian 0591 Madison 0322 Maggie
M. 1263 Maggie T. 0148 Martin
1526 Mary A. 0875 Mary Eliza 0656
Mary G. 0711, 0713 Melissa 0591,
1508 Morris S. 0811 O.K. 1563
Patrick 1373 Peter 0651, 1241
Phebe Jane 1097 Philip 0148, 1373
Samson 1536 Sarah M. 1110 Silas G.
0932 T.B. 0506 Theda 0610 Thomas
0263 W. Wallace 0274 William
0566, 0759
SMULLER H.W. 0719
SNIDER Isaac 1531
SNODEN Rev. Mr. 0645
SNODGRASS Rev. Dr. 1006
SNOOK Carrie W. 0576 Griffin N.
0452 Matthew I. 0736, 0743, 0748
SODEN Thomas 0579
SOMERDIKE William 1529
SOMES Nathan 1543 Samuel 1543
SOUTHARD Benjamin 1548, 1557
Isaac 1540 John 1529 Jonas 1528
Sylvester 0976 Zebulon 1527
SOWDAN James 0835
SPAIGHT Eliza J. 0931 J.W. 0931
John W. 0001
SPEARS Rev. Mr. 0616
SPOONER Isaac 0328 Patience 0328
SPRAGUE F.J. 1210 Fanny 0387
Joseph 0387 Nathaniel 0978, 0984

SPRAGUE, cont.
Samuel 1473, 1474, 1475
SPROSS Thomas 1559, 1561
St. JOHN D.B., daughter of 1405
Frank 0206
STANFORD Gertrude E. 1314
STANTON William 1531
STARK Cyrus 1558
STEARNS President 0186 William F.
0186
STEBBINS Jessie W. 0932 Joseph
0932 Samuel C. 0030
STEINER John 0677 Millie R. 0677
STEPHENSON Grace 0130
STERLING Antoinette 0509, 0530
STEVENS L., Jr. 0727 Samuel M.
0944
STEVENSON Frankie 1305 Griffin
Snook, Mrs. 1348 J.W. 1305 Jennie
1101 Jennie M. 0806 Jeremiah 0089
John W. 1299 Martha 1305 Martha
A. 1299 Susan Elizabeth 1299
Thomas 1348
STEWART R. 0783
STIENBERGH Peter 1531
STITT David 0209 Nellie 0209
STOCKHOLM Abram B. 0388 Abram
E. 0386 Charles 1178, 1443 Dora
1178 Elsey D. 0386, 0388 Harriet A.
1443 Sarah 1178
STOKES Edward S. 0999
STORM Cornelia 0316 Garret 1513
Gores 1513 Isaac 1522 J.T. 0316
John V. 0976 John W. 1564, 1566
Sarah Frances 0976 Thomas 1514
STOTESBURY Charlotte F. 0931
Helen 0931 Lottie Meyer 1106
William 0523 William, Jr. 1106
William, Mrs. 0523
STOUTENBURGH Richard D.C. 0542
STREETER Annie M. 0399 Eliza J.
0247
STRINGHAM Silas Horton 0846
STRONG Benjamin 0166, 0932
Charles L. 1057, 1058 Mattie 1122
Oliver S. 0166
STURGES C. 0370 John 0932

STURGES, cont.
Rev. Dr. 0758, 1116
SULLIVAN Benjamin 0169 Bernard
0290 Clara M. 0635 Delia Frances
0766 George M. 1175 Mary 0169
Terrence J. 0290
SUNDERLAND Emma 0740 Emma
Elizabeth 0740 Joseph 0740, 1067
SURRINE Ellen 0905 William H. 0470
SUTCLIFFE Henry 1017 William 1291
SUTHERLAND Walter B. 1559
SUTHERLIN Sarah E. 0430
SUTTON Elias, Mrs. 0484 G.L. 0091
G.S. 0090 Mary E. 0745
SUYDAM J. Howard 0923 J. Howard,
wife of 0912 Sarah Augusta 0923
SWART Evert W. 1527
SWARTWORT Cornelius 1535 Dalf.
1533 Jacob 1514, 1523 Jacobus
1546, 1549, 1555 Jac's C. 1539
James 1535 John 1521 Samuel 1521
SWIFT Albert F. 0679 Charles W.
1486 Charles W., Mrs., nee Van
Wyck 1486 E.L., Mrs. 0932 Esther L.
1059 H.N. 0932, 0982 James D.
1229 Nathan G. 1059
SNYDER Peter 1523
SYPHER Louie 1507 Louie, Miss 1506
TAGGART George 0209
TAINTER Charles E. 0718
TALBOT Benj. M. 0113 Benjamin M.
0933 Emily 0237
TALLMAN John F. 0636 Timothy
1557
TALMAGEE Jonathan 1526
TALMAN Timothy 1543, 1548
TANNER Carrie A. 1104
TAPLIN John A. 1445 Sophronia R.
1445
TAPPEN John 1537
TAYLOR Charlotte H. 0289 Charlotte
H. (Telford) 0288 Edmund G. 0650
Edward 0955 George W. 0880
Graham 0297, 0316, 0340, 0341,
0444, 0494, 1275, 1349, 1443, 1454
James 0288, 0289 Judge 0681
W.J.R. 0809

TEATOR Uriah 1564, 1566
TELFORD Charlotte H. 0288
TELLER Caroline M. 1029 Catharine
  Storm 0919 Charles W. 1029 Henry
  S. 0919 James C. 0488 Oliver 1164
  William 1164, 1167, 1174
TerBOSS / TERBOSS Abraham 1515
  Daniel 1513 Isaac 1514 Isaac H.
  1529 Luke 1519
TerBUSH / TERBUSH Charles 0801
  Cornelius 1528 John 1518, 1527
  Peter 1516 Simon 1527
TERHUM See also Tirhum
  Albert 536 Daniel 1537
TERRY Frederick 0440 John 1543
TERWILLIGER Anna 1340 Sarah A.
  1312 Silas 0430 William 1481
TESCHKE F. William 1013 William
  1005
TESTSORT William 1531
THALKER Stephen 1524
THEAL Gilbert D. 0327 Sarah 0327
  Walter L. 0327
THEALL Frank 0933 Gilbert D. 0421,
  0423, 1065 Gilbert D., Mrs. 1065
  Mrs. 0421 Sarah Jane 0423
THIELHAUSEN 1009
THOMAS Milton H. 0218 William P.
  1096
THOMPSON James E. 0945 John 1379
  Mary J. 0738 Walter L. 0967, 0971
  Welcome A. 0738 William 1190
THORNE Georgianna 1001
  Lettie 1336 William P. 1336
THURSTON James 1524 Rebecca
  0841
TIBBALS Sarah P. 1266
TICE Isaac 0331
TICEHURST David 1327 David J.
  1327 Ebenezer 0547 Emmet 0547
  Tamer 0547
TILDEN Governor 0774
TILLMAN Ernest 0640 H.A. 0640
  S.H. 0640
TILLOTT Caleb M. 1042 Deborah
  0223, 1042, 1043
TIPPLE Hattie 1283

TIRHUM See also Terhum
  John 1536
TISDALE William 1515
TODD Eliza 0043 John A. 0400
  Samuel 1544
TOLMIE Colin, Jr. 0934
TOMLINS Elizabeth 0292 William
  0292
TOMLINSON Abraham 0625 Evans R.
  0160
TOMPKINS Bissel 0955, 0960 C.W.
  0872 Charles W. 1562 G.P. 1567
  Geo. P. 1563 George P. 1565 J.M.
  0372, 0579 Jane A. 0868 John M.
  0441, 0610 Laurie P. 0031 Lewis
  0933 Nelson 0004 Rachel I. 0778
  Sarah J. 0778, 1433 Solomon 0872,
  1404 Webster A. 0778, 1433
TOMS William 1560, 1562, 1564,
  1566
TOOHEY William A. 0148
TORREY Charles 0178
TOSER Edward 0678
TOTTEN Joseph 1535
TOWNSEND Albert 0955, 1313
  Alonzo 0330 George 1155 George W.
  0818 George W., Mrs. 0818 Hannah
  0191 Mary Eliza 1291 Sarah Jane
  0330 Susan A. 1155
TRACY Elizabeth 0768 John 0375,
  0768, 0933 May 0768
TRAVER Annie F. 0893 E.L. 1565,
  1567 Edward E. 0893 Egbert 0057
  Frederick H. 0901 George Godfrey
  0205 H.E. 0205 M.A. 0205 Robert
  H. 0105 Van Ness 0105
TRAVIS Jeremiah E. 0822
TREADWELL Mary E. 1451
TRIPP Howard T. 1109
TROW Lillie A. 0317
TROWBRIDGE Benjamin H. 1559
TRUMPER Georgianna 1409
TURNER Alexander 1516
TURRELL C. Wesley 0037 Mary E.
  0037 Willie W. 0037
TUTHILL Albert B. 0856 Dr. 0091
  R.K. 0090

TYSON Eddie R. 0145 Ira C. 0146
UHL A.M. 0678
UNDERHILL Clarkson 1561, 1563, 1565, 1567 Samuel 0933
UNDERWOOD Henry 1551, 1556
UPTON John 0749
VAIL Benjam 0105 Clara Virginia 0029 Elias 1295 George W. 1295 Jacob 0720 Joseph 1431 Julia C. 0105 M.E., Mrs. 0933 Wellington 0056
VALENTINE D.T. 0226 daughter of 0226 Lucy A. Leach 1034 W. 1033 W.J. 0719 William 1034
VALK Margaret A. 0220
VAN AMBURGH Ab. H. 1524 Abm. 1525 Adaline 1168 David H. 0874 Martha 0874 Walter 1444
VAN ANDEN Joseph 1141
VAN BENSCHOTEN Jacob 1536 L.E. 1514 Peter 1536 T. 1536
VAN BUNSCHOTEN E.E. 1530 Jno. 1530 Mad. 1520
VAN BUREN Anna Virginia Green 1260 Catharine H. 0589 Charlotte 0139, 0956 John 1146 Lorenzo 0933, 0956 Martin 1146 Mr. 0602 S.T. 0589 Smith T. 1146, 1152 Smith, T., Mrs., nee James 1146 Smith T., Mrs., nee Irving 1146 Virginia 0139 Willis 0139, 0933, 1260
VAN BUSKIRK Rebecca 1052 W.G. 1041 W.G., sister of 1045
VAN CLEEF Rev. Dr. 0558
VAN COTT Mary A. 0545 W.H. 0545
VAN DEVENTER J.C. 0784, 1442
VAN DEWATER Francis 1534 Jacob 1539 Peter 1534
VAN DUSER Milton S. 0696
VAN DYNE Katie 0350
VAN ETTEN Henry S. 0861
VAN GIESEN Rev. Dr. 0564, 1460 Rev. Mr. 0149
VAN HOUTEN Maggie A. 0434
VAN HYNING And'w 1525
VAN KEUREN Charreik 1534
VAN KLEECK Abigail A. 0632

VAN KLEECK, cont.
Andrew J. 0632 Boltes H. 1532 F.B. 0488 Katie Ethel 0632 Monfort 1078 Peter, Jr. 1531 R.B., Jr. 1409 Sarah A. 1078
VAN KLEEK Barent B. 1534 Bernd. J. 1530 Sevaris 1534
VAN NOSDALL Francena 0671 Mary L. 1264
VAN NOSTRAND Caroline 0465 DeWitt H. 0466 Hasbrook B. 0018 Hasbrouck B. 0011 Helen J. 0466 James A. 0465
VAN PELT Harriet 1276 Washington 1276
VAN RENNSELAER E., Mrs. 0933 Mrs. 0988
VAN RENSSELAER D.S. 0755 Harriet Bayard 0600 Hendrick, Mrs. General 0755 Stephen 0600
VAN SICKLIN Augusta 0061 George 0061 Nettie 0061
VAN SLIKE Baron 0253
VAN STEENBURGH Abram T. 0286 "Boots" 0286
VAN SULEN John 1542
VAN SYNE William 1542
VAN TASSEL Anna 0996
VAN TASSELL Jacob 1542
VAN TESSEL Henry 1516
VAN TINE Abm. 1529 Arabella 0933 John 0933, 1440 Lela 1245 M. Louise 1245 Orren T. 0563 Robert T. 0933 Willis 1245
VAN VALIN John 1534
VAN VECHTEN Louisa (Van Wyck) 0408 Samuel 0408, 0637
VAN VELAN Jeremiah 1533
VAN VLIET Amelia 1248, 1250 Benson 0024 Henrietta Wiltsie 0746 John 0746, 1248 Sarah A. 0946 Stewart 1046 Sylvanus 0933 William H. 0946
VAN VOORHEES Zachs. 1513
VAN VOORHIS Abm. 1516 Alice A. 0056 Carrie 0246 Charles A. 0996 Coert A. 0728, 0730 Dan'l 1540

VAN VOORHIS, cont.
Elizabeth 0426 Eva 0757 F. 0757
Frank (Lester) 0597 Frederick 0933
Henry 1526 Jacob, Jr. 1518, 1529
Jerome 1539 Sarah 0762 Steph. 1538
Stephen T. 1454 W.H. 0419 William
C. 0762 William H. 0246, 0933
William Henry 0597 Zach, Jr. 1539
VAN VORT Charles W. 0258 Eva
0258 Sarah E. 0258 William W.
0358
VAN WACKERE Abm. 1540
VAN WAGNER Isaac H. 0941
Sylvester 0130
VAN WERKEREN Geo. 1522
VAN WYCK Abm. 1521 Abraham
0408 Abr'm 0417 Caroline 0641
Cornelia Polhemus 0769 Corns., Jr.
1514 Edward 1491 Elizabeth 1285
Henry 0702 Herbert 0809 Isaac 1517
John C. 1129 John C., daughter of
1486 Joseph G. 0769 Louisa 0408,
0647 Margaret (Frazer) 1491 Martha
(Van Wyck) 0417 Peter 0691
Peter S. 0715 Phebe E. 1285 R.S.
1285 Richard 1513 Richard T. 0647
Sarah E. 0647 Susan 0702 Susan
(Andrews) 0364 T., Jr. 1513
Theodorus 0417 Theods. 1513
William 1513
VANDERBILT Commodore 0654
VANDERBURGH George 1128
VANDERVOORT Addie 1129 J.B.
1129 Jacob 1541 John 1541 P., Jr.
1532
VANDERWERKER Minnie Lane 0082
Mrs., No. 1 0083 Rebecca 0082,
0801 William N. 0082, 0083
VANDEWATER Aurelia 0305 Bartow
1359 Bartow, Mrs. 1359 I.R. 0160
James 1533
VANELIN Moses 1530
VANSONY Addie M. 0273
VARICK Henry D. 1326 Richard A.
0480
VEAL Isaac 1545
VELIE George A. 0582 James L. 1456

VELIE, cont.
Maggie E. 0582 Melissa J. 0849
VER PLANCK Samuel 0448
VER VELON Gideon 1531
VERMILLIE John 1541
VERMILYEA Eliza 0527 Gideon T.
0527 Peter I. 0911 Rosanna 0911
VERNOL Joseph 0894
VERPLANCK Daniel Crommelin 0675
Gulian 0675 Judith (Crommelin)
0675 Mary Hobart 0940 Robert N.
0854 Samuel 0675, 0933 William S.
0933
VER VALIS David 0039
VERWIE Cornelius 1537
VICKERY C.A., Mrs. 1147
VICTORIA Queen 0530
VINCENT Edgar 0175 Henri Mathias
0580 L.M. 0975 Leonard J. 0339
VINES S.R. 0429
VLAIKREN Merimus V. 1523
VOSBURG David H. 0307
WADE James 0439, 0445 James, Mrs.
0439 Ralph 0439
WAKELEY J.B. 0514, 1477, 1485
WALCOTT Etta B. 0537 H.F. 0371
WALDRON Adrian Montfort 1483
Deborah Ann 0472 George 0181,
0472 Monfort 1274, 1471 Mrs. 0119
WALKER S.L. 0157
WALL William J. 0248
WALLACE Hugh 1289, 1294
Mandeville 0737 Mary (Northrop)
0887
WALSH Jane 1247 Mary 0776
WALTERS John 1519
WANZER J.I. 1560 Jane 1084
Jedediah I. 1562
WARD D.B. 0102 Daniel 1544 Dr.
0156 Ellis 0881 Gill 0881 H. 0759
Henry 0457, 0881, 1100, 1448 1482
Henry, wife of 1448 Isaac 0881 John
0881 Joshua 0881 O. 0206 William
1516 Winifred 0881
WARDLE J.K. 1180
WARNER John F. 0913 Miss, father of
0508

WARREN Mary L. 0609
WARREY Lu Ella 1498
WARWICK David G. 1087
WASHBURN Cordelia 0261 Jacob
0261
WASHINGTON — 0765 Amos 0933
WATSON Mrs. 1067 William 1067,
1072
WATTS John 1526
WAY Ann 0361 Charles I. 0385
Francis 1545 Francis, Jr. 1535
Gideon 1523 James W. 0367 Jas. T.
0361 Jennie E. 0933 Katie E. 0834
Thomas 1540 Walter W. 0763, 0784,
0795
WEBB Henry 0094
WEED Daniel R. 1499 Elizabeth 1137
Ermon R. 0147 Teresa M. 1499
WEEKES James 1517
WEEKS Albert 0784 Charles Herbert
1446 child 0300 Electa Jane 0311 G.
Washington 0311 Hattie 0311
Henrietta 0784 Jas. H. 0149 Melissa
A. 0416 William 1446 William H.
0416
WELCH Francis A., Miss 0781
WELLER Mary 1351 William 0270,
1351
WELLING Frank 0606 John 0032
Lillian F. 0606 Mary 0606
WELLMAN Celia M. 0281
WELLS Jesse 0870
WESTERVELT Abm. 1533 Jost. 1533
WESTLAKE Charles 0511
WESTON E. Anna 0274
WHEELER Francis B. 1455 Rev. Dr.
0703 William A. 0981
WHITCOME E.L. 1304
WHITE Alfred 1215, 1221 Bartow
0785 Eliza 1221 Harriet 0282 Henry
0509 William H. 1215, 1221
WHITED William J. 1093
WHITEHOUSE James O. 0450 John
O. 0052, 1455 Mary Josephine 1455
William 1345
WHITING Joseph B. 1343

WHITNEY Levi 0138 Phebe (Owen)
1054
WHITSOUR Thomas 0493
WHITTEMORE J. DeWint 0933
WHITTLE Mr. 1191
WHRITNER William M. 1015, 1019
WICKHAM Joseph 1282 wife of 1282
WICKOFF John 1514
WICKSON See also Wixon
Adelia 1074 Herbert 1244 Lemuel
1245 Mr. 1074
WIEDNER Frank 1333
WIGHT Mary Lomas 0706
WILBER H.K. 1566
WILBUR Henry 1564
WILCOX E.M. 0933
WILDE Isaiah 1540 Susie 0160
WILDEE James 1539 William 1539
WILE R.F. 1132
WILEY J.W. 1148
WILKENS Adeline (Schenck) 0120
Annette 0121 Hendrick 0120 Wilco
Peter 0120, 0121
WILLIAM III King 0448
WILLIAMS Agnes 0955, 0960 Amy
0761 Emalinda 0441 F.T. 1092, 1101
George 1558, 1560 George B. 0933
Josephine 0662 William H. 0410,
0413
WILLIAMSON Francis Edward 0664
Jennie 0231
WILLSEA D.D. 0400 Hannah E. 0400
WILMAN George P. 1016
WILSEN Tenries 1531
WILSEY Samuel M. 0212
WILSON Charles W. 1127 Dr. 0183
Emma 0994 Mary 0664 Robert 0271,
0277
WILTSE Alonzo S. 0940 Cornelius
1538 Johannes 1513 Joseph 1522
Martin 1526 Martin, Sen. 0988
WILTSEY Henry T. 1536
WILTSIE Elsie M. 0315 James 0158
John 1307 Loretta R. 0734 Sarah E.
0158 W.H. 0625
WINANS Seth K. 0505

WINCHELL George W. 1478, 1484
Mary Jane 1478, 1484
WINFIELD Lester 0980
WING R. Wiley 1140
WINSLOW Margaret 0900 William
1541
WIXON See also Wickson
Adelia 1070 Lemuel 0567 Mr. 1070
WIXSON Elemuel 0716
WODELL Walter, Mrs. 1004
WOLCOTT Charles M. 0933
WOLVEN Godfrey 0381
WOOD Anna A. 1442 Barton 1090
Emma Jane 1284 Fernando 0164
Gilbert 1117 I.C. 0570 Isaac Secor
0572 Isaac, Jr. 1190 John J. 1284
Joseph 0427 Lavina 1284 Lillie 1313
Maria 0081 Mary A. 1090 Mary Ann,
0616 Mary E. 0188 S.S. 0820 S.S.,
sons of 0820 Sarah 0427, 1331
Solomon 1547, 1556 W. Anson 0081

WOODHULL Erastus Henry 1409
Vincent 1409
WOODIN R.M. 0357
WOOLHISER Mary E. 0533 Sylvester
H. 0850
WRIGHT Daniel 1526 Daniel G., Jr.
1522 George 0433 John 1519
Thomas 1526 William 1525
WYCKOFF A.N. 0522
WYGANT Edgar 0446
WYNNE Helen M. 1303 Williamson
1303
YALE Guydon 0945
YATES A.H. 0578 Jennie M. 1153
YOUMANS P.D. 0933 Stephen D.
0310 Thomas 1532
YOUNG Frank Wood 0555 Gulumas
0988 J. 0555 John 0988 Mary J. 0555
YURKSE John 1540
ZAHN Lawrence 1125, 1131
ZIENGENFUS Henry L. 1495

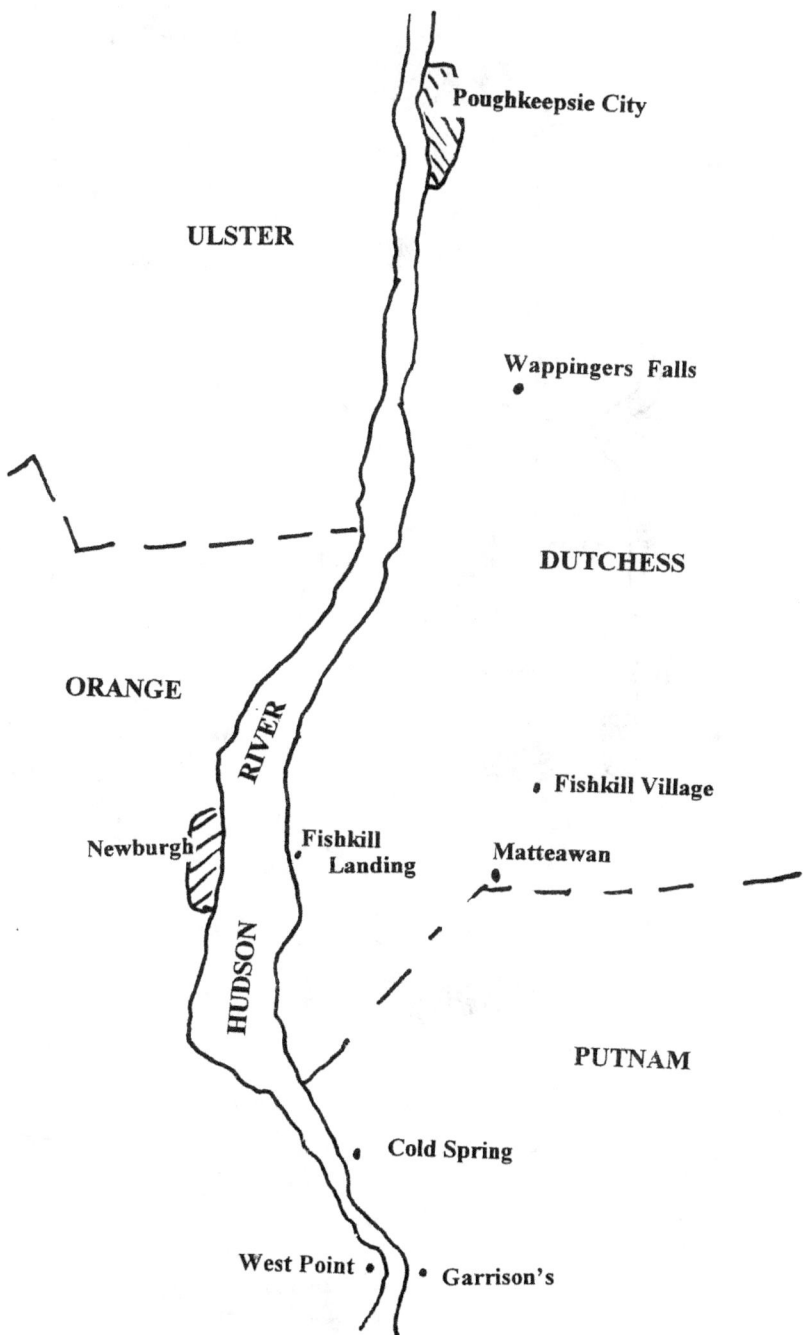

Poughkeepsie City

ULSTER

Wappingers Falls

DUTCHESS

ORANGE

RIVER

Fishkill Village

Newburgh

Fishkill
Landing

Matteawan

HUDSON

PUTNAM

Cold Spring

West Point •

• Garrison's

285

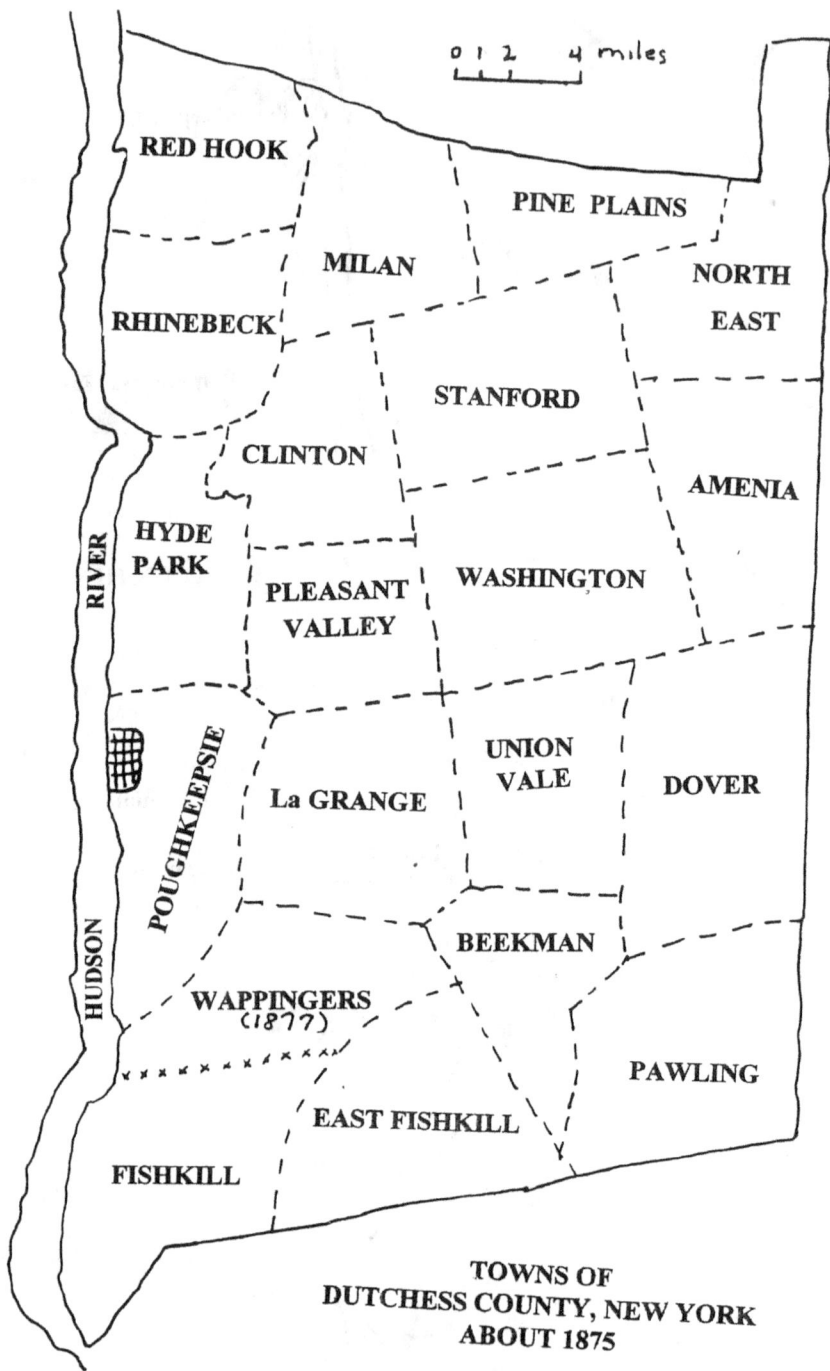

RED HOOK

PINE PLAINS

MILAN

NORTH
EAST

RHINEBECK

STANFORD

CLINTON

AMENIA

HYDE
PARK

RIVER

PLEASANT
VALLEY

WASHINGTON

UNION
VALE

DOVER

La GRANGE

POUGHKEEPSIE

BEEKMAN

HUDSON

WAPPINGERS
(1877)

PAWLING

EAST FISHKILL

FISHKILL

0 1 2   4 miles

TOWNS OF
DUTCHESS COUNTY, NEW YORK
ABOUT 1875

www.ingramcontent.com/pod-product-compliance
Lightning Source LLC
Chambersburg PA
CBHW061718270326
41928CB00011B/2027